D1580670

grow your own house

grow your own house

simón vélez und die bambusarchitektur
simón vélez and bamboo architecture

Vitra Design Museum / ZERI / C.I.R.E.C.A.

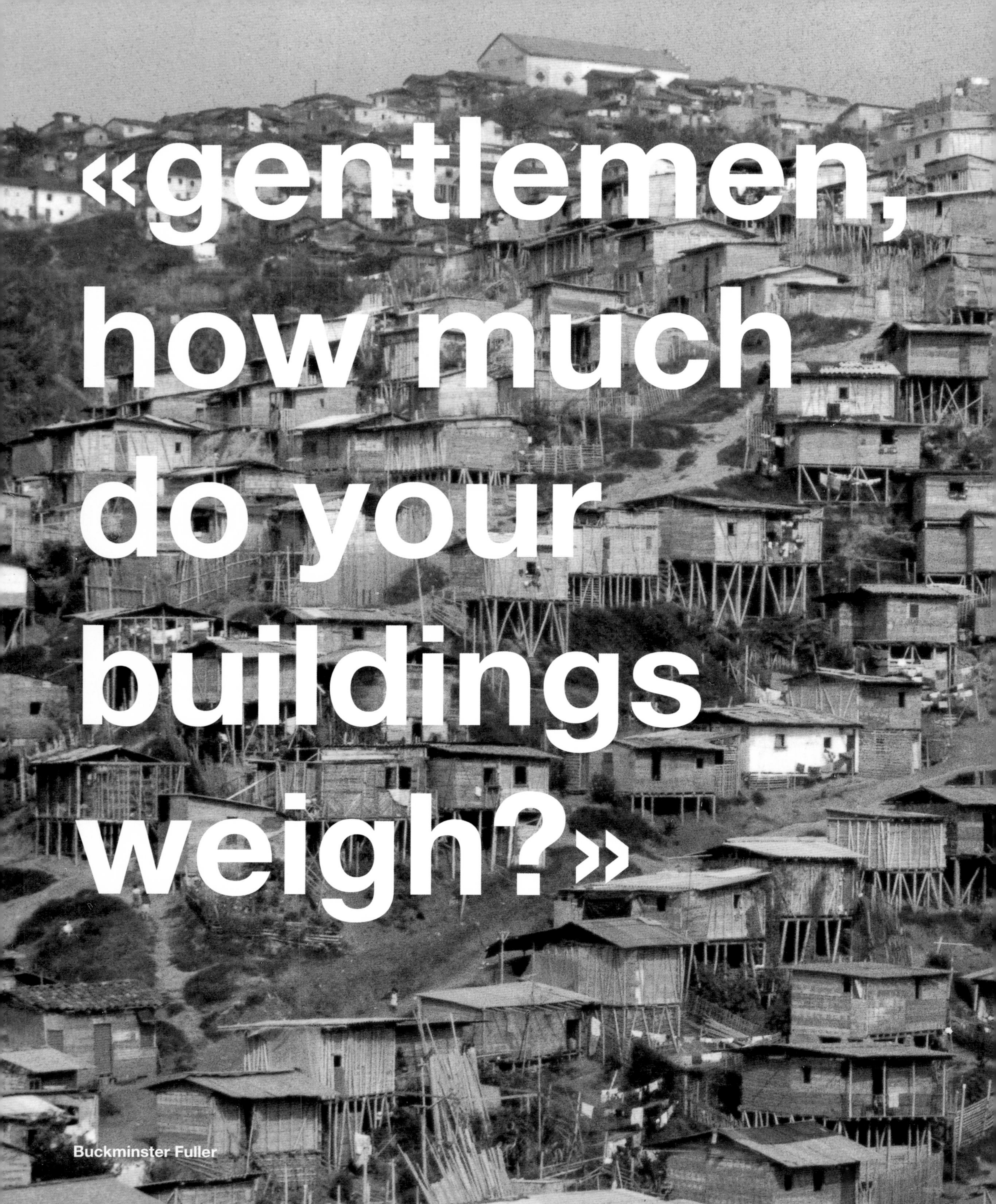
«gentlemen,
how much
do your
buildings
weigh?»
Buckminster Fuller

inhaltsverzeichnis / contents

einleitung / introduction

einleitung / introduction

mateo kries

Bambus spielt in vielen Ländern Asiens, Lateinamerikas und Afrikas eine zentrale Rolle im täglichen Leben vieler Menschen. Aus ihm werden Häuser, Brücken und andere Konstruktionen gebaut, er wird zu Gebrauchsgegenständen verarbeitet, gegessen, verfüttert, exportiert und vielen anderen Verwendungen zugeführt. An vielen Orten haben Stahl, Beton und Glas das Material Bambus aus der Architektur verdrängt oder ihm den Ruf als «Holz des armen Mannes» eingebracht. Doch von diesem Stigma befreit sich Bambus, seitdem die Schattenseiten der westlichen Kultur zu Tage treten und verstärkt nach regionalen und nachhaltigen Technologien gesucht wird. Dabei werden die Vorteile von Bambus als Baustoff neu entdeckt: sein innerer Aufbau, der das Prinzip vieler High-Tech-Werkstoffe vorwegnimmt, seine Nachhaltigkeit, sein gutes Preis/Leistungsverhältnis und seine Ästhetik.

Dieses Buch handelt von der historischen Bedeutung, der heutigen Renaissance und den vielfältigen Perspektiven der Bambus-Architektur. Im Zentrum steht der kolumbianische Architekt Simón Vélez, der wohl bekannteste Architekt, der heute mit Bambus baut. Er hat wesentlich zur neuen Reputation von Bambus beigetragen und steht für einen konstruktionsbetonten Umgang mit diesem Werkstoff. Die beeindruckende Ingenieurleistung von Vélez manifestiert sich in weit auskragenden Dächern, raffinierten Stützkonstruktionen, ausgefeilten Verbindungen und innovativen Materialkombinationen. Vélez praktiziert eine erfolgreiche Synthese traditioneller kolumbianischer Bauformen mit ökologischen Verfahren und avantgardistischer Technologie. Erstmals liefert dieses Buch einen Überblick über sein Schaffen und endet mit dessen vorläufigem Höhepunkt, dem Bambuspavillon für die ZERI-Stiftung auf der Weltausstellung Expo 2000 in Hannover.

Neben der Architektur von Simón Vélez bezieht dieses Buch zahlreiche andere Tendenzen des gestalterischen Umgangs mit Bambus sowie Vergleiche zu anderen Architekturbeispielen ein. Wer wußte schließlich, daß auch Buckminster Fuller, Frei Otto, Renzo Piano oder Arata Isozaki mit Bambus experimentierten? Oder daß Charlotte Perriand faszinierende Möbel und der Japaner Hiroshi Teshigahara beeindruckende Bühnenbilder daraus schufen? Auch die Verwendung von Bambus für Konstruktionen aus Gitter-

Bamboo plays a key role in the daily lives of countless people in many countries in Asia, Latin America, and Africa. It is used to make houses, bridges, and other buildings, is processed to form consumer goods, eaten, fed, exported, and is added to many other applications. In many places steel, concrete, and glass have replaced bamboo as a building material or given it the reputation of being the «poor man's wood». However, bamboo has liberated itself from this stigma as the downsides to Western culture have emerged and people are increasingly turning toward regional, sustainable technologies. In this context, the advantages of bamboo are being rediscovered: its intrinsic structure anticipates the principle of many high-tech materials, it is excellent value for money, and it boasts an attractive appearance.

This book examines the historical significance, present renaissance, and the variety of prospects offered by bamboo architecture. It focuses on Colombian architect Simón Vélez, arguably the most renowned architect using bamboo today. He has contributed considerably to bamboo's enhanced reputation and his approach emphasizes structural considerations. Vélez's impressive engineering achievements are manifested in generously overhanging roofs, ingenious load-bearing structures, sophisticated joints, and an innovative combination of materials. In his oeuvre, Vélez brings to bear a successful synthesis of traditional Colombian structural designs, ecological processes, and avant-garde technology. This book provides a first overview of his work, concluding with its highlight to date, the bamboo pavilion for the ZERI foundation at Expo 2000 in Hanover.

In addition to examining Simón Vélez's architecture, this book also includes numerous other design trends for bamboo, as well as comparisons with other architectural works. Who was aware that Buckminster Fuller, Frei Otto, Renzo Piano, or Arata Isozaki also experimented with bamboo? Or that Charlotte Perriand used it to produce fascinating furniture, and Hiroshi Teshigahara created impressive stage sets from it? Moreover, the utilization of bamboo for grid matrix structures or in high-tech composite materials is a trend which completely eclipses the radical-critical attitudes of the do-it-yourself movement of the 1960s and 1970s when bamboo was primarily discovered as a cheap material for home building.

schalen oder in High-Tech-Verbundwerkstoffen sind Tendenzen, die weit über die radikal-kritischen Positionen der Do-it-yourself-Bewegung der sechziger und siebziger Jahre hinausweisen, als in Bambus primär ein billiges Material für den Eigenbau entdeckt wurde.

Bambus ist, ebenso wie Holz, recyceltes Papier oder Lehm, der Baustoff einer neuen Bewegung in der Architektur – dies ist die Grundaussage des Beitrags von Jean Dethier zu diesem Buch. Nachhaltigkeit und integratives Denken sind zwei wichtige Charakteristika dieser neuen Bauweise, bei der Vertreter aus Ländern der sogenannten Dritten Welt in einem fruchtbaren Ideenaustausch gleichberechtigt neben etablierten Architekten der Industrieländer agieren. Und ebenso wie diese Architektur setzt auch das vorliegende Buch auf nicht-lineares, assoziatives Denken. Wichtiger als eine abgeschlossene und akademische Bilanzierung ist es, eine entstehende Vielfalt zu begleiten und die Bedeutung des Materials Bambus im Kontext einer noch jungen Bewegung aufzuzeigen. Im Layout verdeutlichen visuelle Analogien von Bambus-Architektur zu anderen Architekturbeispielen die Unterschiede und Gemeinsamkeiten. Hier wird deutlich, daß Bambus selten als einziges Baumaterial auftritt – wie jedes andere Material entfaltet es erst in Kombination mit anderen Materialien seine Stärken.

Integratives Denken in Synergien, Kreisläufen ist gleichsam das Leitmotiv dieses Buchs, denn es kennzeichnet nicht nur Inhalt, Konzept und Gestaltung, sondern führte auch zu seiner Entstehung. Dieses Buch ist das Ergebnis der experimentellen Arbeit und Forschung des Vitra Design Museums, deren Hauptelement die jährlich stattfindenden Sommerworkshops in Kooperation mit dem Centre Georges Pompidou sind. Diese Workshops ergänzen unser Programm hochkarätiger Wanderausstellung um praktische Dimensionen, hands-on-Erfahrungen und aktuelle Themen wie das der Nachhaltigkeit. Die Verlagerung dieser Workshops auf das Gelände der C.I.R.E.C.A. in Boisbuchet (Frankreich) bietet seit 1996 die Möglichkeit, auch architektonische Experimente durchzuführen. Auf diesem Landgut errichtete Simón Vélez 1998 seinen ersten Bau in Europa, einen Gartenpavillon, dem 1999 ein komplettes Low-Cost-Haus aus Bambus folgte. 2000 wird Vélez dort ein wei-

Like wood, recycled paper or clay, bamboo is a premier building material in a new architectural movement, or at least this is the main claim made in Jean Dethier's essay. Sustainability and an integrative approach are two important characteristics of this new building trend. It is bamboo which brings together representatives of the so-called third world countries as equal partners in a fruitful exchange of ideas with architects from the industrialized countries. And like the architecture, the present book is also based on non-linear, associative thought. Accordingly, preference has been given to documenting bamboo's emerging diversity and significance in the context of what is still a fledgling movement, instead of attempting to provide a conclusive, academic survey. The layout makes use of visual analogies to point up differences and similarities between bamboo architecture and other types of architecture. What also becomes clear is that bamboo seldom occurs on its own as a building material; here it is not alone in revealing its true strengths only in conjunction with other materials.

A further leitmotif of this book is an integrative approach embracing synergies, cycles, and cooperation, since such a stance not only characterizes the book's content, concept, and design, but has equally engendered its very history. The book is the result of experimental work and research by Vitra Design Museum centering mainly on its annual summer workshops, organized together with the Centre Georges Pompidou. These workshops complement the program of high-quality traveling exhibitions by adding a practical side, hands-on experience, and current topics such as that of sustainability. Since 1996 the workshops have been held in the C.I.R.E.C.A. grounds in Boisbuchet, France – an excellent location fully conducive to conducting architectural experimentation. It was on this estate in 1998 that Simón Vélez constructed his first building in Europe, a garden pavilion, followed in 1999 by a complete low-cost house made of bamboo. In 2000, Vélez will erect another bamboo building. These buildings are the product of cooperation with the French CRAterre foundation for clay architecture. Incidentally, contact with Simón Vélez was first established by the exhibitions section of Vitra Design Museum, whose shows have been presented in Latin America since 1997 (Asia and Australia are planned future locations).

teres Bambusgebäude errichten. Fertiggestellt werden diese Bauten in Zusammenarbeit mit der französischen CRATerre-Stiftung für Lehmarchitektur. Der Kontakt zu Simón Vélez kam wiederum durch den Ausstellungsbereich des Vitra Design Museums zustande, denn bereits seit 1997 sind Ausstellungen des Vitra Design Museums in Lateinamerika zu sehen (mittlerweile stehen auch Asien und Australien auf den Tourneeplänen).

Bei aller Vielfalt der Ansätze, die in diesem Buch zusammenfinden, bleibt es Aufgabe einer Publikation mit wissenschaftlichem Anspruch, einen Fokus zu definieren und daraus eine griffige These zu entwickeln. Für unser Fachgebiet der Architektur- und Designgeschichte lautet sie: Bambus kann als Beitrag der Länder des Südens die Architektur der westlichen Länder bereichern – ähnlich wie die japanischen oder afrikanischen Ästhetik die moderne Kunst zu Beginn des 20. Jahrhunderts oder Zeltkonstruktionen die Architektur seit etwa 1960. Denn Bambus verkörpert in der Architektur eine zukunftsweisende Tendenz, ohne die ein Überleben im 21. Jahrhundert kaum möglich sein wird: die Rückbesinnung auf lokale Traditionen und ihr enormes Potential an intelligenten, nachhaltigen und lang erprobten Lösungen. Im «global village» sind viele Häuser aus Bambus.

Given this complex context it remains the task of a publication which aspires to be scholarly to define a focus and subsequently develop a tangible theory. As regards the areas in which we are specialized – namely the history of design and architecture – the theory is: Bamboo is probably an enriching contribution that countries in the Southern hemisphere can make to the architecture of the Western world, just as Japanese or African aesthetics complemented modern art at the start of the 20th century, or tent constructions have done for architecture since about 1960. Bamboo will continue to form part of a trend in architecture and it will be one without which man will hardly be able to survive in the 21st century: the return to local traditions with their enormous wealth of intelligent, sustainable solutions which have stood the test of time. In the global village, the bamboo houses will be many.

simón vélez und die
bambusarchitektur
simón vélez and
bamboo architecture

ZERI-pavillon / ZERI pavilion

Der Prototyp für den ZERI-Pavillon in Manizales (Kolumbien), Simón Vélez, 1999
Prototype for the ZERI pavilion in Manizales (Colombia), Simón Vélez, 1999

der ZERI-pavillon von simón vélez – ikone einer neuen nachhaltigen architektur aus bambus, lehm und papier /
the ZERI pavilion – a symbol of a new sustainable architecture with bamboo, raw earth, and recycled paper

jean dethier

Das Jahr 2000 bietet mancherlei Anlaß sich damit auseinanderzusetzen, wie Regierungen, Entscheidungsträger und andere gestaltende Kräfte der Zivilgesellschaft zu Beginn des neuen Jahrtausends die Sorgen und Erwartungen zum Ausdruck bringen, die sie und ihre Zeitgenossen im Hinblick darauf hegen, wie die gemeinsame Zukunft des Planeten am besten zu gestalten ist. Zu den wichtigen Fragen für die Gesellschaft wird auch in Form anspruchsvoller Großveranstaltungen Stellung genommen, für die in bisher nicht dagewesenem Maß Mittel aufgebracht werden, um zum Teil nur vorübergehend für einige Monate Treffpunkte für Millionen von Besuchern dem Anlaß entsprechend auszugestalten. Errichtet werden dabei auch kurzlebige Bauwerke – als äußere Behältnisse – in denen in unterschiedlicher Form Inhalte vermittelt werden. Zum Vergleich bieten sich hier zwei Mega-Ereignisse in zwei europäischen Großstädten an – London und Hannover.

der millennium dome in london

In Großbritannien wurde zum Jahrtausendwechsel am Rand der Hauptstadt, in Greenwich, nach den Plänen des Architekten Richard Rogers der Millennium Dome gebaut, die größte Kuppel der Welt, eine gigantische Metallkonstruktion von ca. 400 Metern Durchmessern mit einer durchsichtigen Synthetikhaut über 80.000 m2 Nutzfläche. Ein Kraftakt, mit dem die britische Regierung – erst die rechte, der dann die neue Labour–Regierung unter Tony Blair in nichts nachstand – der Welt eine vorgebliche technische Überlegenheit vorführen will. Dabei läßt die klassische Hightech-Architektur ihre überzüchteten Muskeln spielen, um das einfache Volk mit ihren immer unglaublicheren Kunststückchen zu beeindrucken. Aber abgesehen von der Materialschlacht und der Superleistung, den Weltrekord der mit einer solchen Konstruktion überdachten Fläche gebrochen zu haben, treten die Grenzen und Mängel des grandiosen Wurfs recht bald zutage. Der Millennium Dome ist ein Muskelmann mit Spatzenhirn. Die aus dem Altertum überlieferte Vorstellung vom «Mens sana in corpore sano» wird hier in spektakulärer Weise karikiert, weil der Inhalt des architektonischen Mega-Behältnisses lächerlich ist. Das fragwürdige Planungs- und Finanzierungssystem für ein solches Unterfangen und das offenkundige Desinteresse der britischen

Millennium Dome in London (Großbritannien), Richard Rogers, 1998–2000
Millennium Dome in London (Great Britain), Richard Rogers, 1998–2000

The year 2000 provides various opportunities to contrast the way in which certain governments, decision-makers, or civil society stakeholders intend, at the dawn of a new millennium, to express the hopes and fears of their contemporaries as they confront their responsibility for a best possible common future. In some places, this has proved a major inspiration, this great debate within our society taking the form of a particularly ambitious exhibition, draining sometimes unprecedented resources to attract tens of millions of visitors to vast sites specially arranged to this end for a matter of months. This implies building ephemeral structures – the container – and deploying within them in various forms appropriate messages – the content. Two of these mega-manifestations in Europe bear comparison in the way in which they are being interpreted in two metropolises: London and Hanover.

great britain's millennium dome

Great Britain has chosen to build in Greenwich, in the outer reaches of its capital city, a Millennium Dome, the largest dome in the world in fact, a gigantic metallic structure, 400 meters in diameter. Designed by the architect Richard Rogers, its translucent synthetic film covers a useable surface area of 80,000 m^2. Initially a right-wing government project subsequently ratified by Tony Blair's New Labour, one of the tours de force by which the government hopes to demonstrate to the world a purported technological supremacy is its so-called «high tech» architecture. As in a body-building sports show, the aim is to display an overdeveloped musculature, with sensational posturings intended to impress hoi polloi. Setting aside the materialistic and neo-Olympic offering of the world record for a surface area covered by such a structure, however, the limitations and deficiencies of this «grand design» are immediately apparent. The ancient concept of «mens sana in corpore sano» is here absurdly ignored: the architectural mega-container displays a derisory content. The Millennium Dome is a Mr Universe with a pea-sized brain. The distortion of design and funding systems for such an enterprise, and the notorious indifference of this country's government (even a left-wing one) to culture has led the organizers to strike a deal – unprecedented on this scale – with all-pervading business sponsors

[1] **Auszug aus Gro Harlem Brundtlands Vorwort zum Bericht der Weltkommission für Umwelt und Entwicklung: Our common future: Report of the World Commission on Environment and Development, Oxford University Press, 1987.**

[1] Extract from Gro Harlem Bruntland's introduction to the book, Our common future: Report of the World Commission on Environment and Development, Oxford University Press, 1987.

Regierung (auch der linken) an kulturellen Entwicklungen hat dazu geführt, daß die Organisatoren in einem in diesem Umfang bisher nicht dagewesenen Maß zu Zugeständnissen an die allgegenwärtigen kommerziellen Sponsoren bereit waren und diesen das Feld überlassen haben – eine größenwahnsinnige und aus der Sicht des Staatsbürgers höchst fragwürdige Vorgehensweise, durch die das ganze der Mittelmäßigkeit anheimfällt. Das Desaster – für den Mißerfolg stehen die Reaktion der Medien und die weit hinter den Erwartungen zurückbleibenden Besucherzahlen, zumindest in den ersten Monaten – verschlingt ein immenses Budget (in Höhe von über 700 Millionen englischen Pfund). Gleichzeitig wird offenbar in voller Absicht vermieden zu thematisieren, was in Großbritannien, Europa und global die Welt bewegt, und man ist unfähig, die entscheidenden Fragestellungen unserer Zeit herauszustellen und zu erörtern. Eine Mißachtung der Besucher, die auf Konsumenten kindischer Spielereien, Illusionen und Flitter reduziert werden.

who are «cannibalizing» the event. This kind of megalo-maniac and – from a civic point of view – questionable choice tips the whole manifestation into mediocrity. The budget of over 700 million pounds sterling sunk into this disaster (a failure decried by the media and manifested by a significantly lower number of visitors than predicted, at least in its early months) also reflects a deliberate intention to avoid addressing the major challenges facing global society today (in Britain, in Europe, indeed throughout the world), an inability to pinpoint and tackle the genuine big issues of our time in terms of decent creativity, and thus a contempt for the public, who are reduced to consumers of infantile games, illusions, and bright lights. What we have here is the caricature of a mind-boggling waste of talent and energy.

nachhaltige entwicklung – warum und wie?

Die Vergeudung ist auch eine Mißachtung des ethischen, politischen und praktischen Konzepts des «sustainable development», der nachhaltigen Entwicklung, eines neuen grundlegenden Begriffs für die Zukunft der Menschheit, der auf dem Erdgipfel der Vereinten Nationen 1992 in Rio de Janeiro von über hundert Nationen festgelegt und gemeinsam beschlossen wurde. Die kürzeste und vielleicht beste Definition des Konzepts der nachhaltigen Entwicklung hat die ehemalige norwegische Premierministerin Gro Harlem Brundtland bereits 1987 formuliert, als sie für die Vereinten Nationen den Vorsitz des Weltausschusses für Umwelt und Entwicklung führte: «Entwicklung ist nachhaltig, wenn sie den Bedarf in der Gegenwart deckt, ohne zukünftigen Generationen die Möglichkeiten zu beschneiden, ihren Bedarf zu decken».[1]
Der kanadische Wirtschaftswissenschaftler Maurice Strong, der als Generalsekretär der Konferenz der Vereinten Nationen für Umwelt und Entwicklung (UNCED) in Rio de Janeiro tätig war, führte den Begriff 1997 wie folgt weiter aus: Man wisse ja nun, daß unsere Zivilisation und sogar sämtliches Leben auf unserem Planeten dem Untergang geweiht sei, wenn man nicht einen gemeinsamen, für Arm und Reich glei-

sustainable development – why and how?

This wastefulness also reflects decision-makers' contempt for the ethical, political, and operational concept of sustainable development. This notion, of recent date but fundamental for the future of humanity, was defined and adopted by over a hundred nations in 1992 at the «Earth Summit» held by the United Nations in Rio de Janeiro. The shortest and perhaps the best definition of this concept was put forward in 1987 by Gro Harlem Brundtland (the then Prime Minister of Norway) when she was chairing the World Commission on Environment and Development: «Development that meets the needs of the current generation without undermining the ability of future generations to meet their own needs».[1]
In 1997, Maurice Strong, a Canadian economist and Secretary General at the Rio de Janeiro United Nations Conference on Environment and Development (UNCED) added the following observations (here paraphrased): we now know that our civilization, indeed the whole of life on our planet, is doomed, unless we place ourselves on the only path which is valid for both the poor and the rich. For this to happen, the North must moderate its consumption of resources and the South escape from poverty. Development and environment are inextricably linked and must be

[2] **Übersetzt aus Maurice Strongs Einleitung zu Ignacy Sachs' Buch: L'Eco-développement: stratégies pour le XXème siècle.**

[2] Translated extract from Maurice Strong's introduction to Ignacy Sachs: L'Eco-développement: stratégies pour le XXème siècle.

chermaßen gangbaren Weg beschreite. Hierfür müsse der Norden seinen Ressourcenverbrauch einschränken und der Süden sich aus der Armut befreien. Entwicklung und Umwelt seien unlösbar miteinander verknüpft und müßten aus geänderten Wachstumsmodalitäten, Inhalten und Gepflogenheiten gespeist werden. Dazu seien als grundlegende Kriterien soziale Gerechtigkeit, ökologische Umsicht und ökonomische Effizienz miteinander zu vereinbaren. Das Grundkonzept sei auf der UNO–Konferenz 1972 in Stockholm unter der Bezeichnung «Öko-Entwicklung» erarbeitet und später in «nachhaltige Entwicklung» umbenannt worden. (...) Heute seien die Voraussetzungen günstiger, von der Planung zur Tat zu schreiten und den Beweis dafür anzutreten, daß ökologische Entwicklung erstrebenswert und gleichzeitig machbar ist. Man stehe nun vor der Herausforderung, einen umfassenden Prozeß auf allen Ebenen – regional, national und global – zu fördern und die 27 Grundsätze der Erklärung von Rio (siehe unten) und die Empfehlungen der Agenda 21 umzusetzen (...)[2]. In diesem Sinne wurden unter anderem folgende Beschlüsse in der «Erklärung von Rio» gefaßt:

«Die Staaten müssen systematisch nach dem Grundsatz der Prävention verfahren, um die Umwelt zu schützen. (...) Wissenschaftliche Zweifel dürfen nicht geltend gemacht werden, um von lohnenden Grundsätzen abzuweichen.»

«Die Ausrottung der Armut und die Verringerung der Ungleichheiten zwischen den Völkern sind grundlegende Voraussetzungen für eine Entwicklung, durch die der Bedarf der Mehrheit der Bewohner des Planeten gedeckt wird.»

«Die entwickelten Länder erkennen in Anbetracht der von ihren Gesellschaften auf die Umwelt des gesamten Planeten ausgehenden Belastung und der ihnen zur Verfügung stehenden technologischen und finanziellen Ressourcen die ihnen obliegende Verantwortung bei der internationalen Förderung nachhaltiger Entwicklung an.»

«Die Staaten müssen ökologisch widersinnige Produktions- und Konsumabläufe einschränken bzw. abschaffen.»

«Verbessertes wissenschaftliches Verständnis für Probleme ist eine grundlegende Voraussetzung für jede nachhaltige Entwicklung, deshalb ist eine enge Zusammenarbeit der Nationen beim Austausch von Wissen und Technologie anzustreben».

nourished by a change in the means, the contents, and the uses of growth. The three key criteria to be retained are social justice, ecological prudence, and economic efficiency. The United Nations Conference held in Stockholm in 1973 identified the key idea known then as «eco-development», later renamed «sustainable development».... Today, conditions are far more favourable for moving from ideas to action and for demonstrating that eco-development is both desirable and feasible. The challenge facing us now is therefore promoting a worldwide process at all levels – local, regional, national, and global – in order to translate into concrete proposals the 27 principles laid down in the «Rio Declaration» (see below) and the recommendations of its «Agenda 21».[2] The Rio Declaration solemnly proclaims that, «Recognizing the integral and interdependent nature of the Earth, our home, ... the assembled nations have adopted a series of principles which will dictate future approaches to development.

«These principles for action enshrine, amongst others, the following decisions: «In order to protect the environment, the precautionary approach shall be widely applied by States. Where there are threats of serious or irreversible damage, lack of full scientific certainty shall not be used as a reason for postponing cost-effective measures.

«All States and all people shall cooperate in the essential task of eradicating poverty as an indispensable requirement for sustainable development, in order to decrease the disparities in standards of living and better meet the needs of the majority of the people of the world.

«The developed countries acknowledge the responsibility that they bear in the international pursuit of sustainable development in view of the pressures their societies place on the global environment and of the technologies and financial resources they command.

«To achieve sustainable development and a higher quality of life for all people, States should reduce and eliminate unsustainable patterns of production and consumption.

«States should cooperate to strengthen endogenous capacity-building for sustainable development by improving scientific understanding through exchanging of scientific and technological knowledge.

«Indigenous people and their communities ... have a vital role in environmental management and development because of their knowledge and traditional practices. States should recognize and

[3] Auszüge aus der Erklärung von Rio zu Umwelt und Entwicklung, verabschiedet von der United Nations Conference on Environment and Development (UNCED), auch bekannt als Klimagipfel von Rio de Janeiro, 1992.

[3] Extracts from the Rio Declaration on Environment and Development approved at the United Nations Conference on Environment and Development (UNCED), otherwise known as the Earth Summit, in Rio de Janeiro in 1992.

«Kreativität, Ideale und Wissen indigener Gemeinschaften stellen einen wertvollen Reichtum dar. Die Staaten müssen deren Identität, Kultur und Interessen berücksichtigen und fördern.»
«In all diesen Bereichen müssen die Staaten die Bewußtseinsbildung und die Beteiligung der Öffentlichkeit fördern, indem sie ihr alle nützlichen Informationen zugänglich machen.»[3]

«modernität um jeden preis»

Die Grundsatzbeschlüsse aus der Erklärung von Rio sollten nun eigentlich seit Jahren bekannt sein und umgesetzt werden. Trotzdem ist gerade auch in diesem Zusammenhang selten die Rede davon, wie wichtig und unumgänglich neue designerische Gepflogenheiten in Industrie, Architektur, Wohnungsbau, Städtebau, Ingenieurwesen, Tiefbau und zahlreichen anderen Bereichen sind, in denen unter Materialeinsatz in der Stadt und auf dem Land unsere «bauliche Umgebung» gestaltet wird. Die Industrie im allgemeinen und der Automobilbereich im besonderen werden häufig als die größten Energieverbraucher, Ressourcenverschwender und Umweltverschmutzer bezeichnet, all die Bereiche jedoch, die unter den Oberbegriff «bauliche Umgebung» fallen, werden kaum dazugerechnet. Dabei trugen die gängigen Verfahren im Baubereich nachhaltig dazu bei, daß in unterschiedlicher Hinsicht das überlebenswichtige Gleichgewicht unseres Planeten geschädigt, daß Ressourcen aller Art unmäßig verbraucht und verschwendet werden, daß Schadstoffe und Industrieabfälle ausgestoßen werden, die oft giftig sind oder keiner Wiederverwertung zugeführt werden oder schlimmer noch gar nicht wiederverwertbar sind. Dadurch wird dem Treibhauseffekt Vorschub geleistet, das klimatische Gleichgewicht und das Gleichgewicht unserer Ökosysteme sind bedroht. Hier wird im Namen eines überzogenen Kults der «Modernität um jeden Preis» zu einer ungeheuren Verschwendung beigetragen.

duly support their identity, culture, and interests.»
«States shall facilitate and encourage public awareness and participation by making information widely available.»[3]

«modernity whatever the cost»

These principles are supposed to have been known – and applied – for the last few years. And yet there is rarely any reference in this context, and in regard to these same objectives, to the relevance of a new, and now vital, way of practicing industrial design, architecture, housing, urban development, engineering, public works, and all the innumerable activities which, in terms of material infrastructure, contribute to the actual construction of our built environment. Industry in general, and automobiles in particular, are frequently cited as principle sources of energy waste, of over-consumption of natural resources and of the worst forms of pollution. By contrast little attention is paid to all the activities encompassed by the built environment. And yet this too is one of the major sources of these damaging effects in the world.
At one end of the chain is the misuse of non-renewable resources (mineral, energy, and others) by processing them into building materials and marketable products, and then assembling them into built structures; at the other, the rates of energy consumption which these kinds of buildings and infrastructure require for their use and maintenance.
Current building sector practices thus play a very active part in the various activities which threaten the planet's vital balances. They also produce polluting emissions and industrial waste which is all too often toxic or not recycled, if not actually impossible to recycle. All these processes clearly contribute to the greenhouse effect, threatening our climate and our global eco-system. Thus they are part of the immense wastage maintained by an extreme cult of «modernity whatever the cost».

[4] **Victor Papanek: The Green Imperative: natural design for the real world, Thames and Hudson, London, 1995.**

[4] Victor Papanek, The Green Imperative: natural design for the real world, Thames and Hudson, London, 1995.

soziale anforderungen und berufsethos im wandel

Das System lebt insbesondere deshalb weiter und nimmt immer mehr Raum ein, weil die Abnehmer bisher praktisch völlige Gleichgültigkeit – und damit als Staatsbürger und Fachleute eine gewisse Verantwortungslosigkeit – gegenüber den Folgen ihres Handelns an den Tag legen, das heißt sie machen sich keinerlei Gedanken darüber, wie negativ sich ihre technologischen und baulichen Entscheidungen auf die Umwelt auswirken. Auch im Industriedesign war ökologische Blindheit bei der Berufsausübung bisher gang und gäbe. Allerdings sind hier nun auch die ersten Symptome eines neuen fachlichen Bewußtseins und einer neuen postindustriellen Ethik zu erkennen, als deren Vorläufer Andrea Branzi in Italien und Victor Papanek[4] sowie William Mc Donough in den Vereinigten Staaten zu sehen sind. Sie alle haben ihre Kollegen darauf aufmerksam gemacht und ihre Studenten darüber aufgeklärt, wie schwerwiegend die Folgen ihrer Blindheit sind. Andere Berufszweige werden ebenfalls von diesem Bewußtseinswandel erfaßt, so auch Architekten und Ingenieure. Das neue Berufsethos der solchermaßen in einem Wandlungsprozeß begriffenen Branchen wird zunehmend von Effizienz und Integrität der Arbeit nicht mehr zu trennen sein. Spürbar werden auch erste Auswirkungen des Verbraucherdrucks. In ähnlicher Weise entsteht Druck in Richtung eines korrekten, verantwortungsbewußten Umgangs mit Finanzanlagen an der Börse. Es ist deshalb damit zu rechnen, daß dieselbe Entwicklung bald auch die Bauindustrie erfassen wird und diese dann ihre Umweltverträglichkeit auf globaler Ebene unter Beweis stellen muß. Wenn die Staaten keine geeigneten Regulative für die Bauindustrie vorgeben, um Auswüchsen in diesem Bereich Einhalt zu gebieten, könnte eine entsprechende Bewegung entweder von den Verbrauchern oder von besonnenen Kunden (Architekten usw.) ausgehen, die ihre neue Rolle als Träger verantwortungsbewußter Entscheidungen wahrnehmen. Sie könnten sich für andere Baustoffarten entscheiden, die weniger schädlich sind bzw. ganz ohne industrielle Herstellungs- oder Verarbeitungsprozesse auskommen (oder in geringerem Maß davon abhängig sind), und zwar im Zuge einer systematischen Umsetzung der Erklärung von Rio mit dem Ziel, ökologisch widersinnige Produktions- und Konsumabläufe abzuschaffen

changing social demand and professional ethics

If this system continues to survive, and even to grow, it is notably because the clients of these industrial giants have so far manifested a virtually total indifference to the consequences of their choices, an indifference amounting to a kind of civic and professional irresponsibility. They pay no heed to the negative impact on the environment of the technological and building choices they make. This ecologically blinkered practice was still recently common amongst industrial design professionals. And yet the first hints of a new lucidity and of a post-industrial morality have emerged, stimulated by a handful of pioneers: Andrea Branzi in Italy and Victor Papanek[4] as well as William Mc Donough in the United States. They have alerted their colleagues and drawn the attention of their students to the grave implications of this blinkered approach. This awareness is now gaining ground in other milieus, including that of architects and engineers, where a new ethical approach is also emerging. The latter is even becoming inseparable from the notions of efficiency and of integrity embraced by these changing professions. Moreover, the effects of pressure being applied by consumer groups keen to check that the products they are buying have not resulted in any negative, illegal, or perverse effects in the course of their production are beginning to be felt (starting with combating the exploitation of children kept in a form of industrial slavery). Similar forms of pressure are already emerging to introduce ways of monitoring financial investments on the stock market in a way which reflects greater civic responsibility. It is therefore reasonable to assume that this significant change will soon affect the building industries sector, and it will then be possible to assess their global impact on the environment. If States fail to introduce adequate regulation of these industries to redress the excesses observed, this move could then come either from end-users, or from well-informed clients (architects, etc.) who are more and more aware of their new intermediary role. They could then adopt other families of materials, which are less compromising in their requirements for industrial or manufacturing processing (or rely much less on these). This could be achieved by systematically applying the Rio Declaration, in order to «reduce and eliminate unsustainable patterns of production and consumption». These positions will soon be taken up in turn by new emerging

Erste Skizze für den ZERI-Pavillon, Simón Vélez, 1997
First sketch for the ZERI pavilion, Simón Vélez, 1997

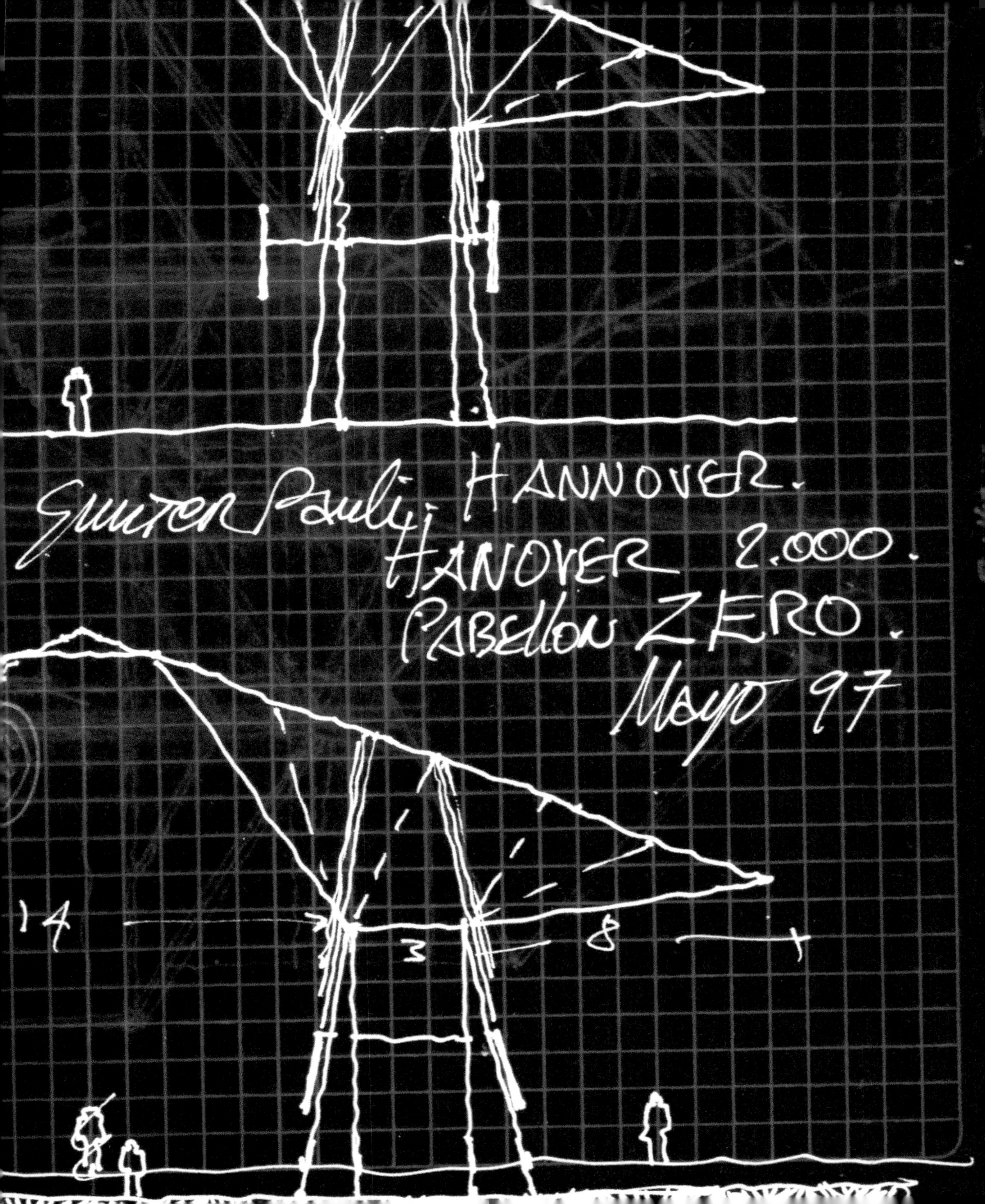
Gunter Pauli
HANNOVER.
HANOVER 2.000.
PABELLON ZERO.
Mayo 97
14
3
8

oder einzudämmen. Diese werden bald von neuen Anforderungen abgelöst werden. Dann werden neue Architekten dringend benötigt, damit angesichts der unterschiedlichen Anforderungen an die nachhaltige Entwicklung Konzepte, Techniken und Verfahren in realistischer Weise neugeordnet werden. Kein besonnener Beobachter ist so naiv, daß er meint, jetzt müsse eine vollkommene Kehrtwendung weg von den vorherrschenden Praktiken im Bausekter erfolgen; laufende Veränderungen können jedoch mit der Zeit ernstzunehmende Neugewichtungen auf dem Markt einleiten, insbesondere zugunsten von Erzeuger- und Abnahmeketten, die durch Routineabläufe und die Interessenlage bisher an den Rand gedrängt wurden. Aus diesem Grund ist es so wichtig, genau zu beobachten, welche Experimente gemacht werden, selbst in Randbereichen. Es gibt sie bereits, die neuen Baumeister, und manche von ihnen handeln seit zehn oder zwanzig Jahren konsequent nach den neuen Grundsät-zen. Wer sind die Architekten der nachhaltigen Entwicklung? Zu nennen sind Shigeru Ban in Japan, Simón Vélez in Kolumbien, Elie Mouyal in Marokko, und in Frankreich Patrice Doat, Hubert Guillaud oder John Norton (aus Kanada) und viele andere mehr. Auch andere Berufszweige wurden von einem neuen Berufsethos erfaßt, Ingenieure, Wirtschaftsfachleute, Entscheidungsträger, wie zum Beispiel Hugo Houben oder Gunter Pauli. Was haben sie gemeinsam, zumal wenn die einen aus reichen Ländern und die anderen aus sogenannten Schwellenländern kommen? Sie haben gelernt, Ethik, Klarsicht, Kreativität, Realismus, Glauben und neue Kompetenzen selbst zu entwickeln, um auf die zum Teil dogmatischen Konventionen zu reagieren, die in der Architektur und im Baubereich, in der Industrie und in den Ingenieurbüros vorherrschend sind. Die genannten Personen haben den Willen gemeinsam, Alternativen zu fördern. Wohnumgebung und gemeinschaftliche Ausrüstungen für ärmere Bevölkerungsschichten sind ihnen ein Anliegen. Sie bauen alle mit alternativen Baustoffen, durch die der Verbrauch von Stahl und Zement, von Aluminium, Kunststofferzeugnissen oder Stahlbeton erheblich gesenkt wird. Die Erzeuger– und Verbraucherketten, die sie sich erschlossen haben und für ihre Zwecke nutzen, beinhalten in unterschiedlicher Weise den Trend zur Befreiung von den Zwängen der Moderne und der Industrie. Die verschiedenen

demands in our society, increasingly aware that it has to protect itself from the excesses committed in its name to enable it to consume the orthodox «modernity whatever the cost». In addition, «New Architects» or «New Builders» will prove vital in taking on – in the light of the various requirements of sustainable development – a realistic realignment of design, technological, and operational choices. Clearly, no informed observer would be naive enough to believe that there will be a sudden shift in predominant building sector practices. However, changes currently taking place may ultimately lead to sensitive readjustments in the market, notably in favour of building alternatives that existing habits and interests have until now reduced to a «marginal seat». Hence the importance of carefully observing the experimental activities which are coming to light. Such new builders already exist, some of them having fully embraced these options a decade or two ago. So who are these architects of the age of sustainable development? In Japan, Shigeru Ban is his name. In Colombia, meet Simón Vélez. In Morroco, there's Elie Mouyal. In France, Patrice Doat, Hubert Guillaud or John Norton (once based in Canada). There are many more. Their ranks are already swelling to embrace other professions: engineers, economists, decision-makers, including Hugo Houben and Gunter Pauli, to name but a few. And what do they have in common, particularly those from wealthy countries with those from so-called emerging countries? An ethical approach, clarity in their ideas, a civic sense of responsibility, a form of creativity combined with pragmatism, a faith, and new skills which they have learnt to explore themselves in reaction to the sometimes dogmatic practice of architecture, construction, or industry. They share a common determination to promote alternatives to the excesses outlined above. They are also involved in design and assistance for housing and community facilities for the most underprivileged of our world. All build using materials and processes which eliminate or considerably reduce the use of steel and cement, aluminum, synthetic products, or reinforced concrete. In sum, all are eco-builders. The building design and logistic processes they have explored and ultimately mastered all tend, in various ways, to bypass certain heavy constraints of the orthodoxy of the Modernist and Industrial cult. Within these various approaches, at least two families of different practices can be differentiated. One is based on the principle of recycling and the other

Ansätze lassen sich zumindest in zwei Hauptgruppen unterschiedlicher Verfahren unterteilen. Die eine basiert auf Recycling, die andere auf dem Einsatz von Naturbaustoffen, die ohne industrielle Verarbeitung verwendet werden können. Dazu gehören insbesondere Lehm und Bambus.

on the use of natural materials capable of being used without requiring industrial processing. Amongst the latter, raw earth and bamboo figure notably.

Der Prototyp des ZERI-Pavillons in Manizales (Kolumbien), Simón Vélez, 1999
Prototype for the ZERI pavilion in Manizales (Colombia), Simón Vélez, 1999

[5] Übersetzter Auszug aus der englischen Pressemitteilung: Expo 2000 Hanover: The World Exposition, vom Jahresbeginn 2000, Herausgeber: Expo 2000 Hannover GmbH, Deutschland.

[5] Extract from the press release: Expo 2000 Hanover: The World Exhibition, published early in 2000 by Expo 2000, Hannover GmbH, Germany.

die weltausstellung in hannover

Deutschland setzt seine Absicht, im Jahr 2000 ein Zeichen zu setzen, anders um als Großbritannien mit dem Millennium Dome. Die deutschen Behörden legen einen lobenswerten politischen Realismus und echten Sinn für ihre Verantwortung an den Tag und haben bereits 1990 dahingehend geplant, daß bei der ersten Weltausstellung in Deutschland (die vom 1. Juni bis 31. Oktober 2000 in Hannover stattfindet), sieben Jahre nach dem Erdgipfel auch einer breiten Öffentlichkeit erstmalig Gelegenheit geboten werden soll, unterschiedliche Auslegungen des zwischenzeitlich nicht mehr zu ignorierenden Begriffs der nachhaltigen Entwicklung aus ihrer Sicht darzustellen. Knapp 190 Nationen wurden hierzu aufgefordert und eingeladen. Das übergeordnete Thema lautet «Mensch, Natur, Technik: eine neue Welt entsteht» und wurde als Ansatz ausgewählt, um Ideen und Vorstellungen auf verschiedenen Ebenen zu fördern, die klar auf die Ziele der «Agenda 21» als Aktionsprogramm für das 21. Jahrhundert[5] ausgerichtet sind. In Deutschland, wo der ökologische Anspruch in der öffentlichen Meinung sehr ernst genommen wird und neue politische Kräfte an die Macht gebracht hat, gehört es zum guten Ton, wenn von vornherein festgelegt wird, daß auf den 1400 Hektar Ausstellungsgelände ein Gebiet am Stadtrand der 600.000 Einwohner zählenden Messestadt Hannover neugestaltet wird, das bisher zu zwei Dritteln von der Deutschen Messe (einer der meistbesuchten Handelsmessen der Welt) eingenommen wurde. Im Rahmen einer solch beispielhaften Planung sind die rund 50 Nationen bzw. Institutionen, die einen eigenen Pavillon beantragt haben, dazu angehalten, in der Gestaltung der Architektur ihrer Bauten die Machbarkeit nachhaltiger Entwicklung zu demonstrieren, die als Dreh- und Angelpunkt für die Überlegungen und Experimente der Weltausstellung angekündigt worden ist.

hanover's universal exhibition

To mark the year 2000, Germany chose to follow a path very different from that of Great Britain, as manifested in the Millennium Dome. In 1990 the German authorities decided to host their country's first Universal Exhibition in Hanover from 1 June to 30 October 2000. Demonstrating laudable political realism and a sense of their planetary responsibilities, they indeed resolved that – seven years of debate on from the Earth Summit – this should also give the public its first global opportunity to take stock of the various ways in which the now inescapable notion of sustainable development is being managed. To this end, nearly 190 nations were invited to take part. The following unifying theme was agreed: «Man, Nature, and Technology: A New World is born». This approach has been selected to promote across a wide range of fields «ideas and theories clearly directed toward the objectives of Agenda 21» (the operational application of the Rio Declaration) «as the plan of action for the 21st century».[5] In Germany, where ecological considerations have mobilized public opinion and swept new political forces into power, it was considered highly appropriate to decide from the outset that the 280-acre site of the exhibition would in itself, for the most part, actually be an unprecedented operation to recycle a suburban district (i.e. Hanover's Trade Fair, Deustche Messe, one of the most heavily attended in the economic world, which previously occupied two-thirds of the site) located on the outskirts of this city of 600,000 inhabitants. For the fifty or so nations or institutions which had opted for an individual pavilion, the exemplary nature of this planning approach meant building new architectural structures. Using building technologies, they had to illustrate in various innovative ways the feasibility of the very principle of sustainable development being promoted as pivotal to the questioning and experimental nature of this event – in a manner appropriate to an eco-responsible approach.

Modell für den japanischen Pavillon auf der Expo 2000, Shigeru Ban
Model for the japanese pavilion at the Expo 2000, Shigeru Ban

japans neue ethik: shigeru ban

Die rund hundert Bewerberländer wurden aufgefordert, ihre Beiträge nach den Schwerpunkten der thematischen Vorgaben auszurichten. In den meisten Fällen wurden die Anforderungen an Inhalt und Form mißverstanden, verfälscht oder nicht beachtet. Eines der wenigen Länder, das sich den damit vorgegebenen Möglichkeiten und Herausforderungen gestellt hat, ist Japan, ein Land, in dem man bisher wenig Wert auf Formen nachhaltiger Entwicklung gelegt hat. Als Reak-tion auf diese Aufforderung hat Japan Mut gezeigt und will sich mit einer neuen Ethik, einer neuen Botschaft und einem neuen Image präsentieren. Die Vertreter Japans haben sich für den Vorschlag des Architekten Shigeru Ban (Jahrgang 1957) entschieden. In seiner fünfzehnjährigen Laufbahn hat Shigeru Ban eine Architektur entwickelt, bei der die Bauelemente und tragenden Teile ausschließlich aus einem Recycling-Produkt bestehen, nämlich aus Altpapier, das sich in unzähligen, auf allen Kontinenten anzutreffenden Fabriken problemlos zu höchst widerstandsfähigen Kartonzylindern unterschiedlicher Abmessungen verarbeiten läßt. Shigeru Ban hat verschiedene Systeme patentieren lassen, mit denen seine Baukomponenten gegen Wasser, Feuer und sonstige Einwirkungen geschützt sind. Auf der Grundlage seines Know-how einer innovativen und stabilen Bautechnik hat Shigeru Ban für Japan einen Pavillon (3.600 m²) entworfen, der sich sowohl in planerischer als auch in umweltrelevanter und ästhetischer Hinsicht durch seine klare Eleganz auszeichnet. Die Wölbungen und Gegenwölbungen seines Kartongebäudes (25 mm starke Röhren von 12 cm Durchmesser) haben auch eine poetische Dimension. Das gesamte bemerkenswerte Bauvorhaben ist zudem darauf ausgelegt, einen gewerblichen Entsorgungs- und Wiederverwertungskreislauf für eine innovative und umweltgerechte Architektur nutzbar zu machen.

a new ethical approach in japan: shigeru ban

At this stage, the hundred or so candidate countries were invited to make their contributions match this underlying aspiration. In most cases, this requirement relating to principle and form was misunderstood, distorted, or ignored. Japan is one of the rare countries to have fully grasped the advantages and challenges of this opportunity, seizing the opportunity to update its ethical approach, its message, and its image. To this end, Japan's representatives selected the stimulating proposal of the talented young architect, Shigeru Ban (born 1957). In the course of some fifteen years of practice, he has notably become the only builder in the world to develop architectural structural and load-bearing elements made entirely of a recycled and «recyclable» product: the paper waste which many factories, apparently located across all five continents, commonly process into very strong cardboard cylinders of many different sizes. He has patented various systems for improving the resistance of these elements to the risks of water, fire, and other hazards. Using his mastery of this innovative and reliable building system, Shigeru Ban designed a 3,600m² Japanese pavilion of serene elegance. The curves and counter-curves of the cardboard structure (tubes 12 cm in diameter and 25 mm thick) also frame a truly poetic landscape. The whole of this remarkable project was designed to develop an industrial recycling process capable of being widely extended to other eco-progressive buildings.

Prototyp des ZERI-Pavillons in Manizales (Kolumbien), Simón Vélez, 1999. Der Bau eines Prototypen im Maßstab 1:1 war zur Erteilung der Baugenehmigung durch die deutschen Behörden erforderlich und war nur aufgrund der niedrigen Baukosten in Kolumbien möglich.
Prototype for the ZERI pavilion in Manizales (Colombia), Simón Vélez, 1999. A life-size prototype was required by German officials before permission was granted for construction. This was possible only because of the low building costs in Colombia.

die ZERI-strategie

1994 wurden mehrere Werbeagenturen damit beauftragt, für die Expo 2000 in Hannover außerhalb der offiziellen staatlichen Stellen nach Personen, nach Teams, nach Nichtregierungsorganisation oder Pilotprojekten Ausschau zu halten, deren Arbeit der Öffentlichkeit vorgestellt werden sollte. Sabine Mpacko machte im Rahmen dieses Auftrags im Jahr 1995 Gunter Pauli ausfindig, den Gründer und Leiter der Stiftung ZERI (Zero Emissions Research Initiative), einer Vereinigung mit Sitz in Genf, die seit 1996 existiert und das Abfallprinzip verneint: Jeder Ausschuß kann für andere Zwecke genutzt werden. Gunter Pauli ist Wirtschaftsexperte, er stammt aus Belgien und hat im Rahmen seiner praktischen Arbeit eine Ethik entwickelt, die in zahlreichen alternativen Entwicklungsprogrammen für Europa und vor allem für die Dritte Welt zum Ausdruck kommt. Er wurde aufgefordert, für die Expo 2000 in Hannover zehn seiner Projekte auszuwählen, die besonders beispielhaft sind. Mehr als die Hälfte davon haben die kreative Verbindung von Industriekreisläufen zum Thema. Aufgrund der hochwertigen Ansätze der Arbeit von ZERI hat die Expo 2000 Gunter Pauli einen eigenen Pavillon für seine Stiftung angeboten, wie ihn sonst nur ein Land bekommt. Zusätzlich zu diesem Privileg wird ihm (laut Beschluß von Hans-Dieter Zeissner) noch eine weitere Sonderbehandlung gewährt, nämlich eine optimale Lokalisierung an einem der beiden wichtigsten Standorte unmittelbar gegenüber dem japanischen Pavillon. Im vollen Bewußtsein der Bedeutung des ökologischen Anspruchs seines Pavillons und ganz im Sinne von Mc Luhan («the medium is the message») hat Gunter Pauli die optimale Entscheidung für die Gestaltung des ZERI-Pavillons getroffen, indem er ihn bei dem Kolumbianer Simón Vélez aus Bogota in Auftrag gab. Von Simón Vélez' Fähigkeiten konnte ich mir selbst ein Bild machen, als ich 1991 für das Centre Georges Pompidou eine Ausstellung über Kolumbien geplant habe, die die Modernität und das Potential der Bambus-Architektur zum Thema hatte und damit um die schöpferische Persönlichkeit von Simón Vélez angelegt war.

the strategy of ZERI

By 1994, prospecting agents for the Hanover «Expo 2000» were asked to identify throughout the world – outside government circles – individuals, teams, NGOs, or foundations supporting pilot projects in order to invite them to present their work to the public. In 1995, Sabine Mpacko thus identified Gunter Pauli, founder and director of ZERI (the Zero Emissions Research Initiative), a foundation focusing on issues of sustainable development set up in Geneva in 1996, which refuses the concept of waste: Whatever is a leftover of one, is an input for another. In the course of his field missions, this Belgian economist has developed an ethical approach which is integrated into a number of alternative development programs, above all in the Third World. Hanover therefore invited him to select ten of his projects in the light of their capacity to serve as examples and to be replicable. These provide a concrete illustration of the various creative clustering of industries. Given the high quality of these initiatives, Expo 2000 decided that Gunter Pauli's Foundation should benefit from an individual pavilion, just like a State. With this privilege came a sizeable favor: a perfect location (decided by Hans-Dieter Zeissner) on one of the major sites, opposite the Japanese pavilion. Alive to the importance of achieving consistency between the nature of his militant stance and the specific ecological nature of his pavilion, and following McLuhan's concept («the medium is the message»), Pauli selected the ideal person to give an appropriate form to the pavilion: Simón Vélez, based in Bogota, Colombia. I was able to appreciate the latter's talents in person in 1991 when preparing for the Centre Georges Pompidou an exhibition focused on his country, about the «modernity and the potentialities of bamboo furniture and architectural design» and revolving around the personality of this highly creative person. As a result of various unforeseeable circumstances, this exhibition was not able to take place as initially scheduled, but it should soon find a climate stimulating to its delayed opening in the new context described below.

simón vélez und seine projekte in kolumbien

Simón Vélez ist 1949 geboren und der einzige Architekt auf der Welt, der nach fünfzehn Jahren Experimentierphase (so lange brauchte auch Shigeru Ban, um seine Architektur zur Reife zu bringen) das Bauen mit Bambus vollständig beherrscht und damit mit einem Baustoff, der bisher in Fachkreisen trotz seiner besonders guten Eignung für bauliche Zwecke und trotz der Möglichkeiten, die er für die Gestaltung des Wohnumfelds bietet, nicht ausreichend beachtet worden ist. Auf dem ersten internationalen Kolloquium zum Thema neue und kreative Nutzung von Bambus als Rohstoff, das von der UNESCO 1997 in Vietnam veranstaltet wurde, hat Simón Vélez großes Aufsehen erregt, als er seine wichtigsten Bauvorhaben und Bauwerke in Kolumbien vorstellte: eine Reihe unterschiedlichster Wohnbauten (von höchst luxuriös bis höchst sparsam), Brücken mit 40 m Spannweite, eine Vielzahl von Gebäuden für die Landwirtschaft und für die Stadt und als Herausforderung an die technische Machbarkeit einen 46 m hohen Aussichtsturm. Alle gebaut aus dem «Riesengras», das er mit einem ihm angeborenen genialen Sinn für dessen bauliche Verwendungsmöglichkeiten einsetzt. Simón Vélez plante also für die ZERI-Stiftung einen Pavillon aus pflanzlichem Material für Hannover. Sein Entwurf ist ein Rundbau aus Bambus (genauer gesagt ein Raum auf einem zehnseitigen Vieleck) mit 40 Metern Durchmesser, mit einem umlaufenden, sieben Meter ausladenden Vordach, so daß das Gebäude keine Fenster braucht und das Innere auch vor starkem Regen geschützt ist. Das Gebäude steht auf zwei konzentrischen Reihen aus 20 Stützen von 8 bis 14 Metern Höhe und bietet auf zwei Ebenen insgesamt 2.150 m² Nutzfläche (1.650 m² ebenerdig und 500 m² im Halbgeschoß über einem Teil der Grundfläche). Von außen sieht es aus wie ein schlanker Pilz. Der Pilz spielt aufgrund bestimmter Vorzüge auch bei einem Landwirtschaftsprojekt von ZERI eine wichtige Rolle. Boden und Innenausstattung des Pavillons sind passend zum Gebäude aus verschiedenen Bambusarten gefertigt. Bambus aus China (für das Parkett), aus Bali und aus Kolumbien, gestaltet von den beiden Designern Linda Garland, einer in Bali lebenden Irin, und Marcelo Villegas, einem Weggefährten von Simón Vélez im eigenen Land. Ein Meisterwerk der Architektur und des intelligen-

the projects of simón vélez in colombia

Born in 1949 in Manizales (Colombia), Simón Vélez is the only architect in the world who, having devoted himself for some fifteen years to many varied experiments (during the same period in which Shigeru Ban was maturing his own ideas), has completely mastered building with a material until now neglected by the profession, despite its building performances and its remarkable potentialities in terms of architecture or of housing: bamboo. During the first international seminar on «new and creative uses of bamboo resources» held in Vietnam in 1997 by UNESCO, Simón Vélez stole the show by presenting his main projects and achievements in Colombia. These included a varied range of homes (from the most luxurious to the most economical), bridges with a 40-meter span, innumerable agricultural and urban buildings, and finally a real technological challenge: a tower, a 46-meter high observatory accessible to the public on foot. With a virtually innate sense of building genius, all used this «giant grass». At the request of the ZERI Foundation, Vélez therefore designed an «organic» pavilion for Hanover, a circular bamboo structure 40 meters in diameter (or, more precisely, a space based on a 10-sided polygon plan), with a peripheral overhang seven meters wide, thanks to which the building requires no window panes, even in heavy rain. The building rests on two concentric courses of 20 supporting wooden pilasters measuring 8 to 14 meters in height. The pavilion provides two levels totalling 2,150m² of sheltered surface area (1,650 at ground level and 500 on the partial 1st floor mezzanine). The building as a whole may suggest the slender form of a mushroom, a plant some of the virtues of which are highlighted by one of ZERI's agronomic projects. The pavilion's floors and the design of its furniture are in harmony with the structure: bamboos of eloquent diversity – from China (for the parquet floors), from Bali, and from Colombia – are transfigured thanks to the work of two designers: Linda Garland (Irish-born but living in Bali) and Marcelo Villegas, a travelling companion of Simón Vélez in his own country.
In all, an architectural masterpiece, combining building intelligence, elegance, harmony, and economy. In contrast to the expensive excesses of the other Hanover pavilions, the cost of this spectacular structure remains financially modest. Due to this achievement, bamboo can be considered a material in its own right in terms of contemporary creativity. Thus, comparing the

ten Bauens, elegant, harmonisch und wirtschaftlich – im Unterschied zu den kostspieligen Irrungen und Wirrungen der anderen Pavillons auf der Expo 2000 sind die Kosten für den Bambusbau gering. All das ist der Beweis dafür, daß Bambus in Zukunft als zeitgemäßer, vollwertiger, kreativer Baustoff gelten muß. Beim Vergleich des Millennium Dome mit dem ZERI-Pavillon wird auch die arrogante Dünkelhaftigkeit des «Dinosauriers» in Großbritannien deutlich, der vielleicht das letzte Riesenspielzeug einer ökologisch überholten Art ist und dem die intelligente Anpassungsfähigkeit des aus Naturbaustoff errichteten «Pilzes» gegenübersteht. Denn Bambus ist mit Blick auf das Konzept der nachhaltigen Entwicklung ein Schlüsselbaustoff. Die langen Pflanzenrohre wachsen außerordentlich schnell (oftmals bis zu 15 Meter innnerhalb von nur einem Jahr) und sind nach drei weiteren Jahren endgültig in der Struktur gefestigt. Deshalb ist dieses Baumaterial für unterschiedliche Arten der Verwendung am Bau geeignet, deren Vielfalt und Möglichkeiten bisher mit Sicherheit unterschätzt wurden. Innerhalb von vier Jahren lassen sich Baumbusanbauflächen also optimieren, auch in der Stadt oder am Stadtrand, und sorgen in einem konstanten, sich immer wieder erneuernden Zyklus für die Versorgung mit einem in ökologischer Hinsicht beispielhaften Baustoff. Die Weltausstellung im Jahr 2000 kann so für sich in Anspruch nehmen, daß sie den 40 Millionen erwarteten Zuschauern (250.000 pro Tag) die erste Demonstration auf europäischem Boden dieser Denkweise im Bauwesen bietet.

technokratische verzerrungen der ökologischen ethik

Allerdings hat man bei diesen schönen Denkansätzen die Rechnung ohne die Technokraten und ihre Fehlleistungen gemacht. Bei der Planung der Länderpavillons und der anderen Pavillons gerieten die Organisatoren und die Aussteller der Expo 2000 in Konflikt mit den höchst schwerfälligen administrativen, technischen und rechtlichen Stellen, die für Überwachung, Unfallverhütung und Sicherheit zuständig sind. Überwachung, Unfallverhütung und Sicherheit sind natürlich in einer modernen Gesellschaft sehr wichtig, aber, wenn hier allzusehr übertrieben wird, kreativitätstötend. So ist es dann auch gekommen – und keineswegs nur im Einzelfall. Eine jeder Vernunft entbehrende Aufbauschung

Millennium Dome and the ZERI pavilion reveals the arrogant fatuity of the «dinosaur» – the last heavy gadget of an ecologically extinct species? – as opposed to the naturalist capacity of adaptation of the «mushroom». This is even more true, given that bamboo is one of the keys to promoting the principle of sustainable development in architectural practice. Why? Because this long organic stem, widespread in many countries of the world, grows very quickly (often up to fifteen meters during the first year) and acquires its ultimate structural strength some three years later. It is then capable of being used for various building purposes, the potential variety of which have to date been underestimated. In four years, therefore, entire stands of cultivated bamboo can be exploited, even within cities or on their outskirts, providing a constant and renewable cycle of supply of an ecologically exemplary building material. Thus the Universal Exhibition of the year 2000 can take pride in presenting to its anticipated 40 million visitors (250,000 per day) the first demonstration of this building practice in Europe.

technocratic distortions of the ecology ethic

All of this failed to take account of the way in which technocracy would distort these appropriate principles. In designing their national or other pavilions, the organizers and guests of Expo 2000 have had to face the excessively constrictive burdens imposed by the administrative, technical, and legal bodies responsible for standards, prevention, or safety. Undoubtedly, these are important in a modern society, but any significant excess in this area leads to a paralysis of creativity, or even of productivity. This is exactly what happened in all too many cases. The German building norms with unreasonably excessive standards which were imposed on their architects and engineers forced most of the pavilions into architectonic meaninglessness. The result is an

der Auflagen und Bauvorschriften hat die meisten Pavillons zu architektonischer Bedeutungslosigkeit verkommen lassen. Ergebnis ist ein sinnloses Durcheinander von industriell hergestellten Baustoffen, und die Werke der Architekten eignen sich bestenfalls noch als Parodie auf eine Gesellschaft, die sich durch überhöhten Konsum und ungezügelte Verschwendung auszeichnet, einer Gesellschaft, die keinerlei Verantwortung gegenüber ökologischen Werten zeigt, und das angesichts der Tatsache, daß gerade solche Werte für die Expo 2000 als zentraler, thematischer Dreh- und Angelpunkt vorgegeben worden sind. Mehrere bedeutende Vertreter der zeitgenössischen Architektur, die von verschiedenen Regierungen Aufträge für die Expo 2000 erhalten haben, müssen machtlos zusehen, wie ihre Pavillons durch überzogene Auflagen der Bauaufsichtsbehörden abgeändert bzw. entartet werden. Möglicherweise werden die Gründe für eine so strenge Kritik an der Architektur für die Besucher nicht allzu offensichtlich sein, die ab Juni 2000 auf die Weltausstellung kommen, denn in den meisten Pavillons wird die Baustoffüberdosis (vor allem Aluminium, Stahl und Beton mit ihren in höchst energieintensiven und umweltbelastenden Herstellungsprozessen) zumeist hinter neutralen oder manchmal auch Naturstoff-Verkleidungen versteckt. Wer die kaschierte Wahrheit über die tatsächliche Bauweise kennt oder erraten kann, zieht an dieser Stelle unweigerlich Rückschlüsse. Anstatt der experimentellen Dimension Raum zu geben, hielt man in einer Kehrtwendung an ultrakonservativen Gewohnheiten aus herkömmlichen Industrie- und Handelsstrukturen fest. Auch das mitreißende Konzept des japanischen Pavillons ist von Verfälschungen durch den unerquicklichen Interventionismus der Technokraten nicht verschont geblieben. Es sieht sogar ganz im Gegenteil alles danach aus, als hätten es die zuständigen Behörde speziell auf dieses beispielhafte Projekt abgesehen. Gerade der japanische Pavillon ist letztendlich das bedauernswerteste Opfer der Routine bei der Bearbeitung der Anträge auf «Baugenehmigung» durch die örtlichen Bürokraten geworden. Das ist umso betrüblicher, als Shigeru Ban mit Frei Otto (dem Mitplaner der grazilen Spannarchitektur auf dem Münchner Olympiagelände für die Spiele 1972) für sein modellhaftes Projekt einer der berühmtesten deutschen Bauingenieure als Partner zur Seite stand, der für das Vorha-

unwieldy mish-mash of industrialized materials transforming their constructions into caricatures of a society of unbridled over-consumption and waste, a society irresponsible vis à vis the very ecological challenges initially chosen here as a central pivot of creativity. Several great figures of contemporary architecture commissioned by various States thus find their pavilions dictated to or distorted by the abusive constraint of the process of monitoring and constructibility. My severe critical reading (see «Warning» below) of the architectural scene of Expo 2000 may not be so obvious to visitors by June 2000, since, in most pavilions, this overdose of materials (in this case, mainly aluminum, steel, and concrete) will be hidden by neutral or sometimes even natural renders. For those who will know or surmise the hidden structural reality, these architectural lies will then expose the cynicism of the enterprise, contempt for the public thus deceived, and the farce of this supposed celebration of ecology applied to the built environment. The experimental mission of the event has been hijacked in favour of the ultra-conservative applications of a mere industrial and commercial enterprise. As for the meaningful concept of Japan's pavilion, it proved no exception to these kinds of changes as a result of the inappropriate intrusions of technocracy. Indeed, it even seems as if the relevant authorities focused relentlessly on this exemplary building. In the final resort, it emerges as the most regrettable victim of this routine application of «planning permissions» by local bureaucrats. The fact that Shigeru Ban was working in association with the most celebrated German engineer of architectonic structures, Professor Frei Otto (co-author notably of the memorable and slender hanging structures of the Munich 1972 Olympic Games) who, from a scientific point of view, endorsed the architect's plan makes this all the more galling. The latter was forced to abandon an important component of his original project (the peripheral gallery which was to shade the many visitors waiting outside to visit the pavilion). In addition, modifications were imposed upon him which distort the initial boldness of the concept – and this as a result of the plethora of precautions taken to reinforce still further its load-bearing structure. This was despite his having already demonstrated its technological viability in Japan, notably in 1998, when he built a 600 m^2 warehouse at Gifu with a 27-meter free-span parabolic roof. Despite these regrettable alterations, the Japanese pavilion, together with the bamboo

ben seines japanischen Kollegen in wissenschaftlicher Hinsicht als Gewährsmann aufgetreten ist. Shigeru Ban wurde nicht nur gezwungen, mit der umlaufenden Außengalerie, die die im Freien für die Besichtigung des Pavillons anstehenden Besucher vor der Sonne schützen sollte, eine entscheidende Komponente seines Vorhabens aufzugeben. Ihm wurden auch Änderungen zur Auflage gemacht, durch die die ursprüngliche Kühnheit seines Projekts entstellt wird, obwohl zuvor umfassende Vorkehrungen ergriffen worden waren, um das Tragwerk zu verstärken. Die technische Festigkeit seiner Bauten hatte Shigeru Ban eigentlich in Japan schon mehrfach ausreichend unter Beweis gestellt, insbesondere mit der 600 m² Lagerhalle mit ihrem 27 m freitragendem Paraboldach, die er 1998 in Gifu gebaut hat. Dennoch wird der japanische Pavillon trotz aller bedauerlicher Entstellungen zusammen mit dem Bambus-Pavillon eines der beiden einzigen baulichen Experimente mit ökologischem Anspruch sein.

pavilion, will nevertheless be the only two promising building eco-experimentations in Hanover.

Innenansichten des Prototypen für den ZERI-Pavillon in Manizales (Kolumbien), Simón Vélez, 1999
Interior views of the prototype for the ZERI pavilion in Manizales (Colombia), Simón Vélez, 1999

die erfolgsstory des kolumbianischen bambus

Neben dem japanischen Pavillon wird der Pavillon der Stiftung ZERI von Simón Vélez stehen, der – paradoxerweise – der einzige ist, der den Attacken der Bürokraten entkommen konnte. Was nicht heißen soll, daß sie nicht versucht hätten, auch dieses gewagte Projekt zusammenzustreichen. In ihrem Eifer mußte den Behörden gerade der in der technischen Kultur Deutschlands fremde Baustoff Bambus natürlich von vornherein als das ideale exotische Opfer ins Auge stechen. Als die Technokraten im Vorfeld angesichts des Entwurfs für den ZERI-Pavillon ankündigten, daß sie den Antrag auf Baugenehmigung gar nicht erst bearbeiten würden, machten sie folgende, in sich durchaus schlüssige Begründung geltend: In Deutschland sei noch nie etwas aus Bambus gebaut worden. Deshalb gebe es zu diesem Baustoff keine rechtliche Grundlage für Bauvorschriften. Deshalb könne man den Antrag auf Baugenehmigung für den Pavillon nicht bearbeiten. Gunter Pauli reagierte diplomatisch. Er äußerte sich sinngemäß wie folgt: Es sei von deutscher Seite doch politisch sicherlich nicht korrekt, alle Nationen zur Weltausstellung einzuladen und dann bestimmte Besonderheiten nicht zuzulassen, noch dazu, wenn sie sich im übrigen genau mit den ethischen Zielsetzungen der Weltausstellung decken. Deutschland verfüge noch nicht über das technische Know-How für Bambus, in Kolumbien hingegen, das ganz offiziell die Einladung nach Hannover angenommen hat (die kolumbianische Regierung baut im übrigen einen kolumbianischen Pavillon in konventieller Architektur), verfüge man über entsprechende Fertigkeiten. Die seien darüberhinaus im Land gang und gäbe, sowohl als das Erbe alter indianischer Traditionen als auch beim europäischstämmigen Teil der Bevölkerung. Zudem genieße Simón Vélez – auch ein Sprößling dieses soziokulturellen Gemischs – in Südamerika und bei der UNESCO den Ruf einer Autorität in diesem Bereich wegen seiner innovativen Bauten und seiner Fertigkeit in der Verwendung von Bambus als Ökobaustoff. Deshalb schlage er vor, den ZERI–Pavillon zunächst in Originalgröße in Kolumbien aufzubauen, und dann solle ein Team von durch die Behörde ausgewählten deutschen Fachleuten dort die entsprechenden technischen Prüfungen vornehmen. Ausgehend davon könne man dann allfällige Verbesserun-

the eco-saga of colombian bamboo

The ZERI Foundation pavilion built by Simón Vélez is – paradoxically – the only one to have escaped the harassment of the bureaucrats. Alien as it is to German technical culture, bamboo must indeed have seemed to the authorities, castrating knives at the ready, a heaven-sent opportunity to claim another exotic victim. When the technocrats signified their refusal to consider an application for planning permission at the outset of the project, their reasoning was implacable: there has never been any building with bamboo in Germany. Therefore there is no legal building code for this material. Therefore we cannot accept an application for planning permission for this pavilion. QED. Gunter Pauli's reaction was a diplomatic one. He argued his case in roughly these terms: is it not politically incorrect for Germany to invite all the nations of the world and not to take into consideration some of their important and specific qualities, especially those corresponding exactly to the ethical objectives of your Universal Exhibition? Although Germany does not yet have enough technological knowledge of bamboo, Colombia, which has responded officially to Hanover's invitation (its government as it happens is building separately a conventional national pavilion) does have these skills. These are indeed worthy of note, both because of the ancient traditions of the Indians and through the practices of the Europeans integrated into the population. In addition, Simón Vélez – a child of this socio-cultural integration – is a recognised authority both in this part of the world and by UNESCO for his innovative achievements and his building skills using this eco-material. Pauli therefore proposed that the pavilion should be erected in advance, to full scale, in Colombia, and that German specialists should then carry out the technical examinations required with a view to suggesting any improvements necessary and to issuing it with the certifications relating to its strength, solidity, safety, fire-resistance, mold-resistance, etc. which would enable it to be erected to an identical design in Hanover. QED. The bamboo pavilion was finally designed in Colombia by Vélez over a weekend of brain-storming, enriched by ideas from Gunter Pauli, from Paulo Lugari (the initiator and director of the famous eco-development scheme in Gaviotas) and from a charismatic figure in the region: the lawyer and economist Mario Calderon Rivera, a former member of the «Club of Rome». Following this creative

gen vorschlagen und dem Pavillon die Stabilität, Festigkeit, Sicherheit, Feuerbeständigkeit, Verrottungsbeständigkeit, usw. bescheinigen, die erforderlich seien, damit er dann entsprechend in Hannover gebaut werden könne. Simón Vélez schloß die Planung der endgültigen Ausgestaltung des Bambus-Pavillons an einem Brainstorming-Wochenende in Kolumbien ab und wurde dabei unterstützt und beraten von Gunter Pauli und (dem für die ZERI-Aufgaben in Südamerika zuständigen) Carlos Bernal, von Paulo Lugari (siehe unten) und einer charismatischen Persönlichkeit der Region, dem Rechtsanwalt und Wirtschaftsexperten Mario Calderon Rivera, einem ehemaligen Mitglied des «Club of Rome», der in den siebziger und achtziger Jahren erste Definitionsversuche für die Begrifflichkeiten der nachhaltigen Entwicklung anstellte. Nach dem Treffen an besagtem Wochenende wurde der Pavillon im Frühjahr 1999 in Manizales gebaut (einer 600.000 Einwohner zählenden Stadt im Herzen eines Gebiets, in dem vor allem Bambus und Kaffee angebaut werden, wobei der wirtschaftliche Ertrag aus letzterem zur Finanzierung des Bauvorhabens beigetragen hat). Untersuchungen der kolumbianischen Behörden ergaben, daß der Pavillon in dieser Form eigentlich nicht baubar sei. Hochkarätige Kapazitäten aus Deutschland kamen daraufhin zum Ortstermin: Professor Aicher vom Otto-Graf-Institut Stuttgart, der Ingenieur Josef Lindemann aus Hannover und Professor Klaus Steffens von der Universität Bremen (vor kurzem bekannt geworden durch seinen entscheidenden Beitrag in Zusammenarbeit mit Norman Foster zur Umgestaltung des Reichtstagsgebäudes in Berlin für den neuen Bundestag). Auftrag der Fachleute war es, die verschiedenen Eigenschaften dieses befremdlichen Architekturobjekts zu testen und zu messen, dessen Baustoff in ihrem Wissens- und Erfahrungsschatz nicht enthalten war. Zunächst waren sie auch von der Persönlichkeit von Simón Vélez beeindruckt, vom Pragmatismus seiner Vorgehensweise und von der Schönheit des Gebäudes an seinem Standort am Rand des Regenwalds. Daneben waren auch die wissenschaftlichen Untersuchungen dazu angetan, daß die Gäste die für sie zunächst (auch im Hinblick auf das hohe Erdbebenrisiko in der dortigen Gegend) überraschenden herausragenden Eigenschaften einer leistungsfähigen und höchst wirtschaftlichen Bautechnik verstehen

outburst, the pavilion was built during spring 1999 in Manizales (a city of 600,000 inhabitants in the heart of a bamboo- and coffee-producing region). Preliminary studies by the Colombian authorities revealed that the building could not, apparently, actually be built in this shape. It was then that Germany's most eminent academics made their appearance: Professor Aicher from the Otto Graf Institute in Stuttgart, the engineer Josef Lindemann from Hanover and Professor Klaus Steffens from the University of Bremen (who recently distinguished himself by his key participation with Norman Foster in the ambitious recycling of the historic Reichstag building in Berlin into the new national parliament). The role of these experts was to test and quantify the various reactions of this strange architectural object, the intrinsic nature of which had hitherto escaped their theoretical and practical knowledge. They were first charmed by the charisma of Vélez's personality, the pragmatism of his approach, and the beauty of the structure erected on the outskirts of the tropical forest. Setting aside such affective considerations, the scientific analyses they carried out in situ led them to understand and to recognize the efficiency of this high-performance and ultra-economic technology. The former quality took into consideration the frequent earthquake risks of the region; the latter is the result of an optimal modernization of the traditional and living skills of the indigenous Indian communities. The efficiency of the process apparently came as a surprise to the European scholars. These men of science (devoid, naturally, of any bias), the best possible ambassadors of Germany's reliability, thus reversed the fate of the bamboo pavilion, allowing it to move on to a new universal destiny in Hanover. By doing so, they put into practice several principles of the «Rio Declaration». Confronted by the unexpected positive and unanimous views of their own experts, the German authorities had no choice but to accept the pavilion (on a temporary basis...) within their boundaries. Like the reed in La Fontaine's fable, when put to the test the bamboo did not break. As the famous, optimistic adage of Christianity would have it: «And the Last shall be First».

und anerkennen lernten, die aus der optimalen Anpassung eines uralten Know-How der indianischen Ureinwohner an die Moderne hervorgegangen ist. Die aus Deutschland angereisten Wissenschaftler, die sich vorurteilsfrei ein ernstzunehmendes und zuverlässiges Urteil gebildet hatten, wendeten das Geschick des kolumbianischen Pavillons und eröffneten ihm eine Zukunft auf der Weltausstellung in Hannover. Angesichts der nicht voraussehbaren einstimmigen Befürwortung durch die eigenen Fachleute konnten die Behörden in Hannover nicht umhin, den Pavillon zuzulassen. Wie das Schilfrohr aus der Fabel von La Fontaine ist auch der Bambus unter dem Druck nicht gebrochen. Und auch vor christlichem Hintergrund gibt es eine bekannte ermutigende Aussage für solche Fälle:
«die letzten werden die ersten sein...»

Der Bau des ZERI-Pavillons in Hannover begann mit der Konstruktion des Dachs.
The construction of the ZERI pavilion in Hanover began with the works on the roof.

das meisterwerk der bambus baumeister

Die für den Bau in Hannover benötigten 3.500 Rohre *Guadua* (so der einheimische Name) wurden in 16 Überseecontainern verschifft, im Frühjahr 2000 nach Hannover gebracht und dort von rund vierzig kolumbianischen Facharbeitern verarbeitet. Vélez selbst sieht sich und handelt eher als Baumeister (in der Art zum Beispiel der Dombaumeister im Mittelalter in Europa) – das heißt er ist vor allem auf der Baustelle anwesend und arbeitet mit seinen Gesellen eng und konstant zusammen – anders als die Mehrzahl der Architekten heute, die oft selbst kaum mehr auf den Plan treten und nur noch die Sklaven allmächtiger Planungsbüros sind.

Im Frühjahr 2000 wird der Bambus-Pavillon auf der Großbaustelle für die Weltausstellung in Hannover gebaut und schon allein dieser Vorgang ist in seiner Art einzigartig. Obwohl die Baustelle es vom Umfang her mit zahlreichen anderen zeitgleich laufenden Bauarbeiten durchaus aufnehmen kann, kommt man hier ohne Kran und ohne schwere Baufahrzeuge aus. Die kolumbianischen Bambus-Handwerker beherrschen die Kunst, ihren Bau ohne Hilfsmittel und ohne mechanische Raffinessen aus eigener Kraft und in unbeirrbarer Konsequenz aufzubauen. Auf der Baustelle erweist sich nicht nur, daß die Verwendung des Baustoffs Bambus aus der Abhängigkeit von einer oftmals übermäßigen Mechanisierung der Arbeitsumwelt befreit, sondern es entstehen dabei immer mehr Arbeitsplätze für Facharbeiter, die wegen ihrer aktiven Mitwirkung und ihrer Kreativität gefragt sind. Schließlich wird der einzige Pavillon auf der Weltausstellung in Hannover, der (sowohl inhaltlich, als auch in bezug auf die Bauweise und die Form) dem Thema «Mensch, Natur, Technik» in vollem Umfang gerecht wird – und der offenbar auch der einzige ist, der in keiner Weise Einschränkungen durch die Behörden auf der planerischen Ebene hinnehmen mußte – letztendlich der Pavillon sein, der aus der einvernehmlichen Partnerschaft der beiden charismatischen Persönlichkeiten eines europäischen Strategen und eines lateinamerikanischen Architekten hervorgeht. Simón Vélez ist auf jeden Fall nach der Erfolgsstory seines Bambuspavillons zukünftig als der Architekt aus der Dritten Welt mit dem stärksten Innovationsgeist anzusehen, insbesondere in bezug auf die Umweltverträg-

the bamboo guild's masterpiece

The 3,500 or so culms, or stems, of *Guadua* (its local name) required were transported in sixteen maritime containers and assembled in spring 2000 in Hanover by some forty skilled Colombian workers, members of a kind of bamboo guild, who had worked for many years to Simón Vélez's demanding standards. He himself thinks and acts like a master builder (somewhat in the manner of the Middle Ages for the building of Europe's cathedrals), i.e. essentially «hands on», in close and constant professional symbiosis with his guild members – unlike the majority of today's architects, who are all too often in thrall to the tyranny of expert committees.

In spring 2000, the bamboo pavilion emerged from the outset as unique of its kind on Hanover's immense exhibition site: the only building to have no need of cranes or other heavy machinery (despite its size, at least equal to that of many others under construction). On this building site, the use of bamboo not only appears to liberate the craftsmen from the often abusive mechanization of the work environment, but in addition it creates many skilled jobs, which promote active participation and creative input. Thus, in the final analysis, this is the only pavilion built for the Universal Exhibition which is completely faithful (in principle and process, as well as in spirit) to the «Rio Declaration», as it is in relation to the theme «Man, Nature, and Technology» set for Hanover. It is the only structure not to have been subjected to any underhand design deals at the hands of the local authorities. It has also been the only one to emerge from the alliance of one charismatic European and one Third World figure: a strategist and an architect, the latter, however, unknown until now to the media and to the profession outside his own country. As a result of this saga, Simón Vélez now finally emerges as the most inventive architect of the Third World, particularly in terms of eco-responsibility. Thanks to him, the South–North dialogue has found new proof of its feasibility: notably to resolve a problem as difficult as adapting building practices to the vital objective of sustainable development. The architect Jean Nouvel (who designed one of the eleven exhibitions inside Hanover's «theme park») is one of the figures of the cultural world elevated by Expo 2000 to the role of media ambassador. Why does this diplomatic game not apply equally to Simón Vélez,

lichkeit. Der Architekt Jean Nouvel, der für Hannover eine der elf Ausstellungen im Themenpark geplant hat, ist eine Persönlichkeit aus dem kulturellen Bereich, der über die Expo 2000 in den Medien die Rolle eines «Botschafters» zugewiesen wurde. Hier stellt sich die Frage, ob eine so diplomatische Funktionszuweisung nicht auch für Simón Vélez gelten sollte, damit er die Schwellenländer und das einzige Projekt vor Ort vertreten kann, das in vollem Umfang der Erklärung von Rio entspricht.

and enable him to represent the emerging nations, when his is the only project in the Exhibition to be entirely in line with the «Rio Declaration»?

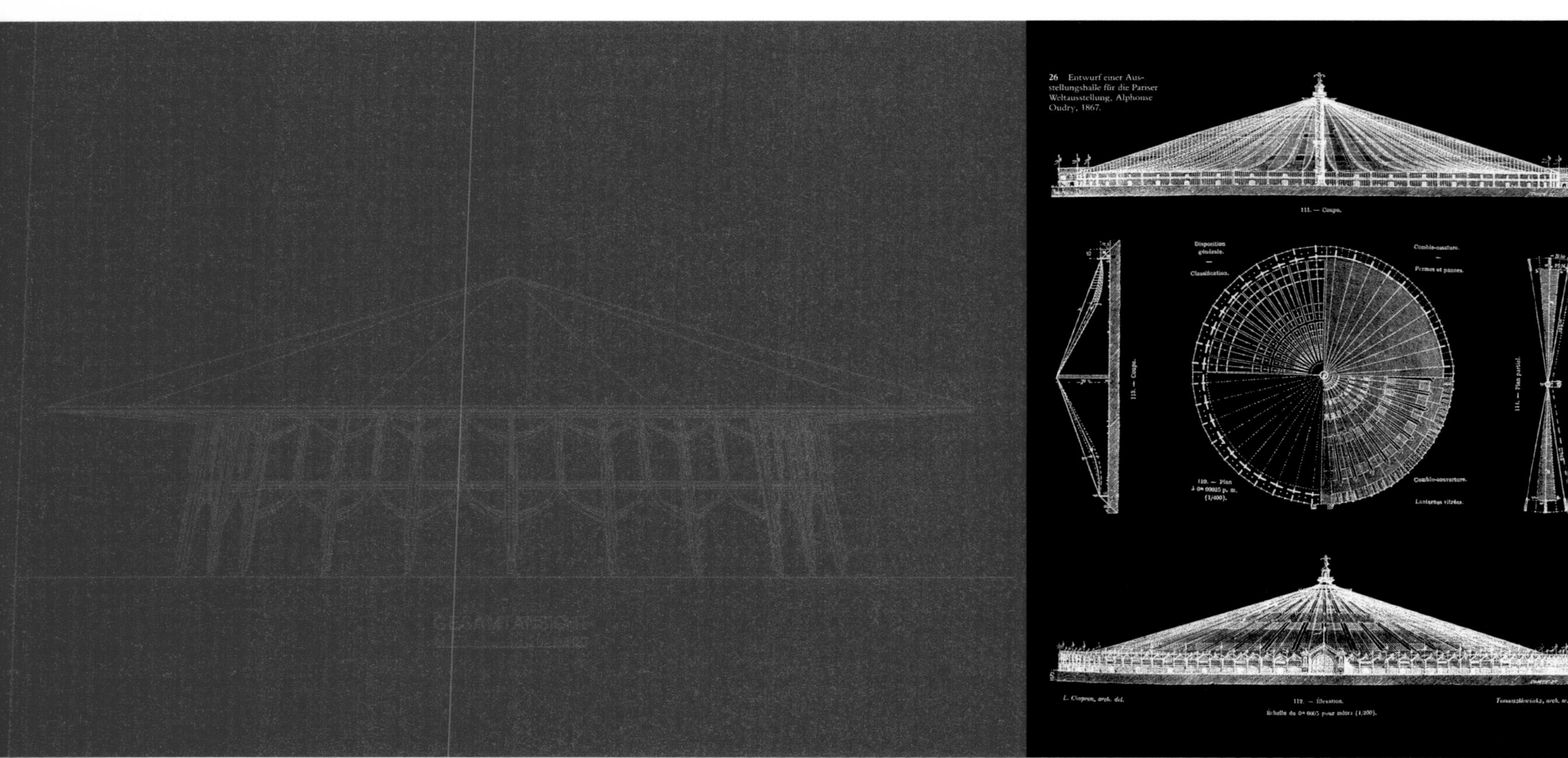

Gesamtansicht des ZERI-Pavillons
General view of the ZERI pavilion

Entwurf einer Ausstellungshalle für die Pariser Weltausstellung, Alphonse Oudry, 1867
Design of exhibition hall for Paris World Fair, Alphonse Oudry, 1867

[6] Das Vitra Design Museum und das Centre Pompidou geben jedes Jahr gemeinsam ein ausführliches Programm über die Seminare und Veranstaltungen heraus, die den ganzen Sommer über in Boisbuchet in Südwestfrankreich stattfinden.

[6] The Vitra Design Museum and the Centre Georges Pompidou jointly publish a detailed annual program of seminars and workshops held throughout the summer on the Boisbuchet site in SW France.

lehm und bambus in europa

Manche behaupten, Vélez sei der Calatrava des Bambus. Abgesehen von der patriarchalisch bevormundenden Konnotation, die sich darin zeigt, daß eine große kreative Persönlichkeit aus der Dritten Welt zwar wahrgenommen, ihr aber gleich ein westlicher Bezugscode zugeordnet wird, der mit ihr gar nichts zu tun hat, hat dieser Vergleich keinen Sinn. Der eine verwendet Baustoffe, die aus einem energieverzehrenden und umweltbelastenden Fertigungsprozeß stammen, der andere nutzt eine in höchstem Maße wirtschaftliche (wenn auch örtlich aufgrund ihrer ländlichen und volkstümlichen Konnotationen wenig geachtete) Ressource, die kurzfristig vollständig erneuerbar ist. Das gilt sowohl für arme Länder, in denen es Bambus im Überfluß gibt, als auch für viele andere Orte, an denen man das Riesengras anbauen kann (Beweis dafür ist der große Bambushain in Anduze in Südfrankreich) oder wohin Bambus importiert werden kann, wie nach Hannover. So geschehen auch im französischen Domaine de Boisbuchet in Lessac in der Charente (zwischen Limoges, Angoulême und Poitiers), wo Alexander von Vegesack, der Direktor des Vitra Design Museums[6] mit europäischen Universitäten und seit 1996 in offizieller Partnerschaft mit dem Centre Georges Pompidou ein Versuchs- und Ausbildungsgelände (mit Besichtigungsmöglichkeit) angelegt hat, auf das er bekannte Forscher, Designer und Architekten einlädt, um dort mit Unterstützung von Studenten verschiedene zukunftsweisende Prototypen zu entwickeln. Hier hat Simón Vélez vor kurzem zwei Bauten aus (aus Kolumbien importiertem) Bambus errichtet, von denen vor allem das sehr kostengünstige Wohnhaus (in Kolumbien rund 5.000 Dollar) interessant ist, das auf zwei Stockwerken 60 m² Wohnfläche bietet. Das ursprüngliche Konzept war darauf ausgerichtet, daß die Ärmsten in seinem Land sich ihr Haus selbst bauen können. Dahinter steht der Anspruch, die zukünftigen Bewohner in die Lage zu versetzen, den Baustoff für ihr Haus an dessen zukünftigem Standort über den Zeitraum von vier Jahren, die er für Wachstum und Reifung braucht, selbst anzubauen. Zudem sind Bambusanpflanzungen eine sinnvolle Form der Bekämpfung der Bodenerosion. So ist aus der Zusammenarbeit zwischen Simón Vélez und Gunter Pauli eine Symbiose zwischen dem Herstellungsvorgang

earth and bamboo in europe

Having only recently discovered the talents of Simón Vélez, a few admirers devised a nickname for him: for them he was a new Calatrava (the famous Catalan architect and engineer settled in Switzerland to whom we owe recent and remarkable buildings in steel and concrete) or, more precisely, the «Calatrava of Bamboo». Apart from the paternalistic connotations of recognizing a great creative talent of the Third World but imposing on him a Western code of reference alien to him, this comparative assimilation makes little sense. One builds using materials resulting from an industrial process which consumes a huge amount of energy and which is hostile to the environment, the other by promoting optimal use of an ultra economic natural resource (although locally dismissed because of its rural and working class connotations) which is entirely renewable in the short term. It is this which gives this process its innovative and auspicious value vis-à-vis a form of eco-development. This option applies equally to poor countries where bamboo grows in abundance, and to many other areas of our planet where the plant can be acclimatized (as shown by the vast bamboo grove of Anduze) or imported as occurred in Hanover. Another example in France is the Domaine de Boisbuchet, at Lessac in the Poitou-Charente region (between Limoges, Angoulême, and Poitiers) where Alexander von Vegesack, Director of Germany's Vitra Design Museum[6] created an experimental and training site together with some European universities and with the official support since 1996 of the Centre Georges Pompidou. This is now going to host a series of workshops each summer, focusing on architectonic systems using natural, renewable resources. Renowned researchers, designers, and architects are invited to attend these, in active participation with students, and develop various prototypes which hold promise for the future. It is here that Simón Vélez recently erected two bamboo structures (using bamboo imported from Colombia) and notably a very low-cost house (approximately 5,000 US dollars in Colombia) which covers 60m², on two levels. This was designed initially to be built by the poorest populations of his country on a self-help basis. In fact, this initiative is part of a more ambitious strategy which consists in the future users assuming responsibility for growing for and by themselves, right on the site of their future houses, the bamboo they will need to build them.

[7] Gunter Pauli: Upsizing: the road to zero emissions. More jobs, more income and no pollution, Greenleaf Publishing, Sheffield, 1998.

[8] CRATerre (Centre international de Recherches et d'Applications pour la construction en Terre), Grenoble. craterre@club-internet.fr.

[7] Gunter Pauli: Upsizing: The Road to Zero Emissions. More Jobs, More Income and No Pollution, Greenleaf Publishing, Sheffield, 1998.

[8] CRATerre (International Centre for Earth Construction), Grenoble. craterre@club-internet.fr.

eines Naturbaustoffs und der Bauausführung entstanden. Ein ganzheitliches Konzept, für das der spanische Begriff der «arquitectura cultivable» mit seinen sowohl landwirtschaftlichen als auch sozialen und poetischen Bedeutungsinhalten steht, und der mit «grow your own house» ins Amerikanische übertragen wurde. Diese Vorgehensweise ist komplementär zu einem anderen Schlüsselbegriff geworden, der zwischenzeitlich fast wie ein Manifest verkündet wird: «global denken, lokal handeln». All das deckt sich mit der Botschaft von Gunter Pauli, die er in seinem letzten Buch «Upsizing: the road to zero emissions»[7] wie folgt auf den Nenner bringt: «making more with less, while generating jobs and reducing pollution». Die Tragstruktur aus Bambus für den Hausprototyp in Boisbuchet wird im Sommer 2000 (zwischen 31. Juli und 31. August) fertiggestellt. Die Außen- und Innenwände werden mit Lehm gearbeitet, so daß das Experimentalhaus die konkrete Verwirklichung eines durch und durch ökologischen Produkts ist, das aus der Kombination zweier Naturbaustoffe – Bambus und Lehm – hervorgegangen ist und aus der neuen Zusammenarbeit zwischen Simón Vélez und der Gruppe CRATerre[8]. CRATerre steht für «Centre de Recherche et d'Application de la Construction en Terre» (Zentrum für angewandte Lehmbauforschung), ist der Ecole d'Architecture de Grenoble (EAG) angeschlossen und wird von seinen Gründern, dem französischen Architekten Patrice Doat und dem belgischen Ingenieur Hugo Houben gemeinsam geleitet. 1998 wurde es von der UNESCO als die weltweit kompetenteste Stelle im Experimental- und Ausbildungsbereich (einen Postgraduiertenstudiengang in diesem Fach gibt es weltweit nur an der EAG) für Lehmarchitektur ausgezeichnet. Das Team ist sowohl in den Entwicklungsländern tätig, wo es zahlreiche Projekte anleitet, als auch in Frankreich. Insbesondere südlich von Lyon, in der neuen Stadt L'Isle d'Abeau hat CRATerre als wissenschaftlicher und technischer Partner für den Bau der 1984 fertiggestellten Siedlung «Domaine de la Terre» gewirkt, einem Experimental-Wohnviertel mit ökologischem Anspruch bestehend aus 62 Sozialwohnungen, die mithilfe verschiedener moderner Lehmbautechniken errichtet wurden. Im Rahmen des Projekts werden Ideen in Echtgröße umgesetzt, die 1980 in der von mir zusammen mit dem leider verstorbenen Heinrich Klotz, dem damaligen Leiter des Architekturmu-

During the four years they need to mature, the bamboo plantations also provide an opportune way of preventing soil erosion. Thus is born out of a collaboration between Simón Vélez and Gunter Pauli, the key – perhaps ultimately the revolutionary? – notion of a form of symbiosis between the act of producing a natural building material and that of putting it to constructive use. An integrating concept, evoked in Spanish – with agronomic, social, and poetic overtones – by the expression «arquitectura cultivable», which is itself transposed into American in the term «Grow your own house». This practice proves to be complementary to another key notion, now almost a manifesto: «thinking globally, acting locally». All of this is part of Gunter Pauli's creed, as summarized in his most recent book, «Upsizing: the road to zero emissions. More jobs, more income and no pollution».[7] At Boisbuchet, in summer 2000, the load-bearing bamboo structure of the housing prototype will be enhanced by the addition of raw earth walls and partitions. These will in the final resort confer on this experimental house the obvious advantage of a globally ecological product resulting from the combined use of two natural materials – bamboo and raw earth – and from a new cooperation between Vélez and the CRATerre group.[8] This «International Centre for Earth Construction», co-founded and co-directed by French architect Patrice Doat and Belgian engineer Hugo Houben within the School of Architecture of Grenoble (EAG), has been recognized – notably in 1998 by UNESCO – as the best focus of international skills in experimenting, professional training (EAG is the only university in the world to offer a post-graduate qualification in this field) and actual building using unfired earth, both in developing countries, where this team steers a number of projects, and in France. Thirty kilometers south of Lyon, in the new town of L'Isle d'Abeau, CRATerre notably played the role of scientific and technical partner in the construction of the «Domaine de la Terre» inaugurated in 1984: an experimental eco-neighbourhood of 62 low-cost social housing units using various modernized techniques for building with raw earth. This pilot operation was initiated by the Centre Georges Pompidou (and selected by the French government as a reference model for the United Nations' International Year of Housing and the Homeless in 1987). The scheme provides a full-scale demonstration of ideas developed in 1980 in the exhibition I produced (in co-production with

[9] **Info zur Wanderausstellung: ruth.eaton@wanadoo.fr. S. auch: Houben, H. und Guillaud, H.: Traité de construction en Terre, Editions Parenthèses, Marseille, 1989.**

[9] For the touring program of the exhibition contact: ruth.eaton@wanadoo.fr. See also: H. Houben, and H. Guillaud: Earth Construction: a comprehensive guide, Intermediate Technology Publications, London, 1994.

seums Frankfurt) organisierten Ausstellung zum Thema «Des architectures de terre ou l'avenir d'une tradition millénaire» («Lehmarchitektur oder die Zukunft einer jahrtausendalten Tradition»)[9] entwickelt wurden. Seit 20 Jahren reist diese Ausstellung durch die Welt, um den Reichtum der Traditionen und vor allem die Zukunft des Naturbaustoffs Lehm mit seinen herausragenden ökologischen und wirtschaftlichen Eigenschaften vorzuführen, der häufig – nicht anders als Bambus – nicht gewürdigt oder unterschätzt wird.

the Frankfurt Deutches Architekurmuseum, then directed by the late lamented Heinrich Klotz) entitled «Des Architectures de Terre; ou l'avenir d'une tradition millénaire [Down to Earth: the future of an ancestral tradition]».[9] This has continued to tour over the last twenty years across all five continents, proving to a very large audience the richness of these traditions and above all their future, thanks to the eco-constructive and low-cost qualities of a natural material which, like bamboo, is still often dismissed or undervalued.

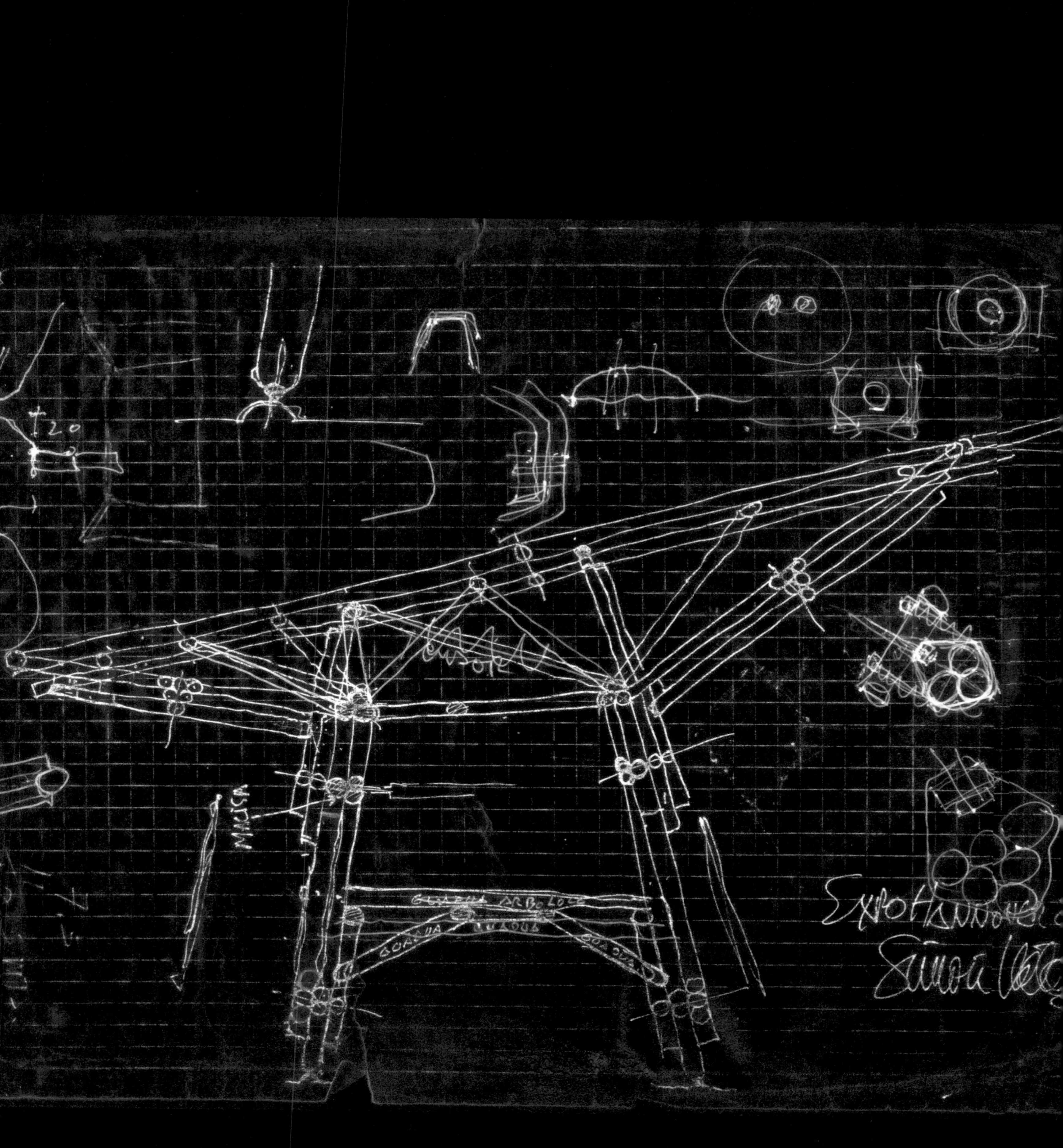

Skizze für den ZERI-Pavillon, Simón Vélez, 1999. Nach dieser Zeichnung wurde der Pavillon gebaut.
Sketch for the ZERI pavilion, Simón Vélez, 1999. The pavilion was built based on this drawing

ergänzungen und ausschlüsse

Die Annäherung zwischen Lehm und Bambus, zwischen CRATerre und Simón Vélez verläuft auch deshalb ganz selbstverständlich und «natürlich», weil jeder der beiden Partner in seinem Bereich das optimale Know-How besitzt. Keiner von den beiden meint jedoch, sein Baustoff schließe die Ergänzung durch andere natürliche oder industrielle Komponenten aus. Sie befürworten im Gegenteil wohlbegründete und sinnvolle Kreuzungen, die einer optimalen Entwicklung eines alternativen Modells im Bau- und Wohnbereich förderlich sind. So fordern beispielsweise sowohl CRATerre als auch Simón Vélez die gemäßigte, aber sinnvolle Verwendung von Zement zur Stabilisierung bei bestimmten Arten des Einsatzes von Lehm und zur Verstärkung der Belastungspunkte des Bambus bei räumlichen Tragekonstruktionen. Die großen Kunst- und Kulturbiennalen in Europa, deren Existenzberechtigung sich aus ihrem Auftrag herleitet, die Öffentlichkeit über einschneidende neue Entwicklungstrends in der Welt zu informieren, schweigen sich über solcherart zukunftsweisende Entwicklungen in dieser Welt aus. Dies trifft vor allem auf die Biennale in Venedig zu, die dieses Jahr, im Jahr 2000, von Massimiliano Fuksas geleitet wird und mit «weniger Ästhetik, mehr Ethik» um ein wichtiges und sinnvolles Thema in der Architektur angelegt ist. Daran, daß das in der Tat sinnvolle Thema letztlich verfehlt wird, ist abzulesen, daß die ethische Annäherung zwischen Architektur, Kunst und Ökologie noch nicht stattgefunden hat. Die innovative Kreativität in der Architektur gerade der aufstrebenden Entwicklungsländer (auch wenn sie sich dabei laut und deutlich für eine ökologische Ethik und gegen die umweltzerstörerischen Prozesse der landläufigen Baumethoden einsetzen) wird nicht berücksichtigt. Shigeru Ban wurde mit seinem Schaffen – das inzwischen Anerkennung und Medienwirksamkeit gewonnen hat – zurecht zur Biennale in Venedig eingeladen (wie weitere knapp 80 Architekten oder Künstler aus dem Städtebau). Simón Vélez hingegen ist – vielleicht aus Fortschrittsfeindlichkeit oder aus Angst vor dem «Unbekannten» – zu dieser Veranstaltung nicht zugelassen worden, obwohl dies für seine berufliche Tätigkeit eine sehr wichtige Plattform wäre.

complementarities and exclusions

The complementarity between earth and bamboo, between CRATerre and Vélez, is all the more «natural» in that each of these two partners now possesses state-of-the-art knowledge of their own field. Neither is naive enough to believe that the material they understand so well should never be used to complement other natural or industrial materials. Nor is either of them an ayatollah of some kind of purist eco-technological creed. On the contrary, they are seeking to achieve reasoned and reasonable «alliances» or «inter-breeding» in order to be able to proceed in the best way with a model of alternative and viable development in the building and housing sector. To take one example of this, CRATerre and Vélez recommend the moderate but precisely dosed use of artificial binders (including cement) to give strength to certain ways of using unfired eart, which is then «stabilized», and to give solidity to bamboo joints in three-dimensional load-bearing structures. The great Biennales of art and culture in Europe – justified by their aim to enlighten the public about major and new trends in the way the world is changing – remain silent on these auspicious eco-evolutions. This applies mainly to the Venice Biennale, steered this year 2000 by Massimiliano Fuksas and devoted to architecture in a key and opportune area: «Less Aesthetics, More Ethics». This lost opportunity notably shows that notions of architectural, artistic, and ecological ethics have yet to come together. Thus the innovative architectural creativity of emerging nations – even when it reflects a noteworthy militant stance in favor of the ethics of ecology and against the environmental corruption of common building practices – is totally ignored. Deservedly, the work of Shigeru Ban – already widely recognized and publicized by the media – has gained the right to be represented (with that of nearly 80 other architects or artists active in urban areas) within the Venice Biennale. Perhaps through inertia or from fear of the «unknown», Simón Vélez has not, however, received accreditation in this context, despite the obvious relation of this to his professional work.

[10] **Yunus, M.: Vers un monde sans pauvreté: l'autobiographie du «banquier des pauvres», Editions Lattès, Paris, 1997. yunus@citecho.net.**

[10] M. Yunus: Vers un monde sans pauvreté: l'autobiographie du «banquier des pauvres». Editions Lattès, Paris, 1997. yunus@citecho.net.

architektonische allianzen

Die Architekten und Entscheidungsträger der armen Länder, die an solchen gesellschaftsrelevanten Diskussionen teilnehmen sollten, werden fast niemals an den runden Tisch geladen, sie werden nicht einmal nach ihrer Meinung gefragt. Die Entwicklungen dort sind im Westen nach wie vor unbekannt oder sogar Gegenstand von Vorurteilen. Die Biennale in Venedig wäre ein geeignetes Formun gewesen, um sich mit der vernachlässigten Dimension der Kreativität und der Ethik in den Entwicklungsländern auseinanderzusetzen. Man hätte mehrere Jahrzehnte zusammenfassend darstellen können, von den bahnbrechenden Umwälzungen bei der Erlangung der Unabhängigkeit in den fünfziger Jahren bis heute. Die Zukunftsperspektiven, die die herausragendsten Vertreter dieser Teile der Erde dabei abgesteckt haben, hätten dabei bekanntgemacht werden können. Und das nicht nur im Sinne von Kultur und Technologie, sondern auch unter Einbeziehung der unumgänglichen sozioökonomischen Herausforderungen. Niemand auf der Welt kann besser erklären als der Wirtschaftsexperte Mohammad Yunus[10] (auch in seinem Buch «Vers un monde sans pauvreté»), wie die Strategie, die er selbst über die Grameen Bank in Bangladesh umgesetzt hat, tatsächlich in der Lage ist, eine stille Revolution einzuleiten, indem sie mit vorbildlichem Einfühlungsvermögen den Ärmsten der Armen Geld leiht, die per definitionem keinerlei Kreditsicherheiten bieten können und damit von den konventionellen Geldinstituten unweigerlich abgelehnt werden. Die seit 1976 bestehende radikale wirtschaftliche Alternative seiner Methode, die den Kreditnehmern vor allem die Möglichkeit eröffnete, sich ein eigenes Haus zu bauen, wird heute in rund fünfzig weiteren armen Ländern weiterpraktiziert und gilt als herausragender Erfolg im Entwicklungssektor. Zahlreiche Institutionen nehmen sich ein Beispiel an seiner Ethik und seiner Methode, der gegenüber die Weltbank lang Zeit Skepsis und Unverständnis bekundet hat. Dieselbe Arroganz des Westens bekommen auch die Architekten aus der Dritten Welt zu spüren, ein Vélez genau so wie seine Kollegen aus Asien oder Afrika, zum Beispiel der talentierte Elie Mouyal aus Marrakech, der geschickt in nunancenreicher Anbindung an die Traditionen seines Landes aus ungebranntem und gebranntem Lehm eine neue marokkani-

from «non-aligned» architecture to «north–south» eco-alliances

The «New Builders» from poor countries likely to be taking part in such debates about the future of our society are hardly ever invited to the discussion table, or even consulted. The specific nature of the paths they follow remain unknown or even dismissed in the West. The Venice Biennale would have been an appropriate forum in which to address this neglected aspect of the creative process and the ethics of developing countries, perhaps covering several decades, since the wave of independences in the 1950s until the present day. This would have brought to light unexpected future prospects which the best of these distant lands have already mapped out. And not only in cultural and technological terms, but also taking account of the inevitable socio-economic challenges coming into play. Nobody in the world is better placed than the economist Muhammad Yunus to explain (as he does in his book «Vers un monde sans pauvreté [Toward a world without poverty]»[10]) how the strategy which he introduced in Bangladesh through the Grameen Bank is capable of performing a silent revolution by lending money, with exemplary tact, to the poorest of the poor. By definition, the latter are totally unable to provide any loan collateral and are therefore invariably rejected by conventional institutions. Launched in 1976, the radical economic alternative of his method (which notably enabled the beneficiaries to access the process of building their homes on a self-help basis) has now been passed on to some fifty other poor countries and is recognized as a remarkable development success. A great many bodies now draw inspiration from the ethics and the method he pioneered, despite the fact that for many years the World Bank expressed its lofty scepticism and incomprehension. The same kind of Western haughtiness affects the architects of the Third World, such as Vélez and so many of his fellows in Asia and Africa. These include, for example, the talented Elie Mouyal from Marrakesh, who skillfully develops a new form of domestic architecture, designed with fired and unfired earth, subtly in tune with the needs of present-day Morocco. All too often the Establishment also reserves a more insidious and more refined condescension – within Europe itself – for groups as inventive and effective as CRATerre, Development Workshop, the Intermediate Technology Group and many more

[11] Fathy, H.: Le Pays d'Utopie, in: La Revue du Caire 24, November 1949, S. 8–35, und Architecture for the Poor: An Experiment in Rural Egypt, University of Chicago Press, Chicago, 1973.

[11] H. Fathy: Le Pays d'Utopie, in: La Revue du Caire 24, November 1949, pp. 8–35, and Architecture for the Poor: An Experiment in Rural Egypt, University of Chicago Press, Chicago, 1973.

sche Architektur geschaffen hat. Zielscheibe einer falschen, höflichen Herablassung des Establishment sind auch – sogar in Europa – innovative und praktisch erfolgreiche Gruppen wie CRATerre, Development Workshop, Intermediate Techonology Group (und viele andere), die ihre Kreativität auf die Problemstellungen armer Länder ausgerichtet haben. Diejenigen, die heute kreativ sind, sind jedoch nicht plötzlich wie die Sterne vom Himmel gefallen. Sie sind ganz im Gegenteil seit rund zwanzig Jahren in eine Entwicklung eingebunden, die in zahlreichen wissenschaftlichen oder volkstümlichen Überlieferungen verwurzelt ist, dies gilt für die Lehmarchitektur genauso wie für die Baumbusarchitektur. Die qualitativ hochwertige Arbeit entstand auch in der Nachfolge mancher Pioniere, die Begründer einer Denkweise ebenso wie einer Arbeitsweise waren, die sich von den vorherrscheenden westlichen und wirtschaftlichen Modellen unterschied. Dahinter stand häufig die Absicht, die Eigenschaften der bei ihnen häufigen natürlichen Rohstoffe in innovative Vorteile zu verwandeln. Die frühen Pioniere stehen im Zusammenhang mit der Konferenz der blockfreien Staaten 1955 in Bandung in Asien, auf der Nehru für Indien, Sukarno für Indonesien und Zhou Enlai für China die Vorkämpfer waren, deren Ideen am meisten Gehör fanden. Zahlreiche kreative Persönlichkeiten haben sich in der Zeit danach bemüht, sich bei ihrer Arbeit aus den Ideen von einer auf Autarkie ausgerichteten Entwicklung inspirieren zu lassen, deren Samen bei dieser historischen Veranstaltung in alle Winde ausgesät worden war. Es ist kein Zufall, daß danach in Ägypten in den fünfziger und sechziger Jahren die Spätwerke des Architekten und Philosophen Hassan Fathy (1900–1989) wie beispielsweise das Dorf Gourna, aber auch seine Streitschriften entstanden (1949 «Le Pays d'Utopie»), vor allem aber auch eines der wichtigsten Bücher zum Themenbereich Gesellschaft und Architektur unter dem Titel «Architecture for the poor – an experiment in rural Egypt».[11] Hassan Fathy gilt sowohl in ethischer als auch in kultureller und technischer Hinsicht als eine der wichtigsten Bezugspersonen für die Architektur Ägyptens. Er war der erste nichtwestliche Architekt, der sich für eine demokratische und ökologische Architektur einsetzte, die mit den vor Ort vorhandenen Ressourcen auskommen sollte. CRATerre und andere Architekten haben dort das Ferment für die ersten Ausformungen ihrer

which focus their creative talents on the problem issues of the poorest countries in the world. And yet all these creative individuals and groups active today have not suddenly appeared on the world scene like a bolt from the blue. They have been around for some twenty years or so, working in a direct line rooted in any number of erudite and popular traditions: this applies to building both with raw earth and with bamboo. The success of their activities also illustrates their links with certain pioneers who were able to introduce a way of thinking as well as of acting which differentiated them from the predominant Western and economic models. In doing so, they were often seeking to make the very best use of the precarious natural resources at their disposal. The work of these more long-standing pioneers seems to follow in the wake of the Conference of Non-Aligned Countries launched in Bandung, Asia, in 1955, in the course of which the militants who received the most attention were Nehru for India, Sukarno for Indonesia, and Chou En Lai for China. Many creative figures sought to sow the seeds of «autarchic development», liberally scattered to the four winds in the course of this historic meeting. It is no coincidence that the works of the mature years of the architect and philosopher Hassan Fathy (1900–89) made their appearance at this time, in the 1950s and 1960s. These included amongst others the pilot village of New Gourna, but also his writings, «Le Pays d'Utopie» and «Architecture for the Poor: An Experiment in Rural Egypt».[11] Fathy was to become a key reference for the reformers of poor countries from a moral, technical, and technological standpoint. He was the first outside the West to develop the theory and practice of a democratic and ecological architecture, deliberately built using only local resources. The Development Workshop group, co-founded in Canada by architect John Norton, and the Egyptian architect Abdel Wahed El-Wakil (born 1943) worked with Fathy in Egypt from the 1960s. CRATerre and many others drew from him the inspiration of their early convictions and practical field work. Hassan Fathy thus acquired the stature of founding father of a system of operational ethics in the Third World Countries wishing to follow a «non-aligned» destiny. The main objective of the Hassan Fathy Institute founded in Rome (in the wake of an international bricklayers' trade union movement led by the American humanist Jack Joyce) is now to develop an innovative policy in favour of ambitious action in the Third World. The

[12] Hassan Fathy Institute, Sustainable Development Task Force: mliles@bacweb.org.

[12] Hassan Fathy Institute, Sustainable Development Task Force: mliles@bacweb.org.

Überzeugungen und für ihre ersten praktischen Ansätze gefunden. Hassan Fathy wurde zum Gründungsvater einer Ethik, die in den armen Ländern wirksam ist, die auf eine «blockfreie» Zukunft hinarbeiten. Das am Ende des 20. Jahrhunderts (im Rahmen einer internationalen Gewerkschaftsbewegung der Maurer unter dem amerikanischen Humanisten Jack Joyce) in Rom gegründete Hassan Fathy Institute hat sich nun als wichtigste Zielsetzung die Entwicklung einer innovativen Strategie zur Aufgabe gemacht, deren Gegenstand anspruchvolle Maßnahmen in der Dritten Welt sind. Im März 2000 wurde in Kairo[12] die «Sustainable Architecture Task Force» des Hassan Fathy Instituts gegründet. Nach dem zweiten Weltkrieg haben sich in Indien unter dem Einfluß der Botschaften Gandhis neue Zielsetzungen herausgebildet. Die Architekten des Kolonialreichs reisten ab und wurden von Talenten wie Lawrence Baker (britischer Kriegsdienstverweigerer, geboren 1917, der nach der Unabhängigkeit indischer Staatsbürger wurde), Raj Rewal (1934) oder Charles Correa (1930) abgelöst. Im selben Atemzug sind auch Francisco Manosa (geboren 1930) von den Philippinen, Muzhural Islam (1925) aus Bangladesh und viele andere Baumeister zu nennen, die mit politischem und sozialem Anspruch auf der Suche nach Eigenständigkeit wirkten. Die erste Vorkämpferin dieser Art von Berufsverständnis in Asien war (die um 1940 geborene) Yasmine Larie aus Pakistan. In Lateinamerika ist der Wettstreit der nationalen bzw. regionalen Architektur auf dem ganzen Kontinent noch stärker ausgeprägt, da dort auch die Unabhängigkeit weiter zurückliegt. Zu nennen sind hier (ohne irgendeinen Anspruch auf Vollständigkeit) in Mexiko Luís Barragán (1902–1988), Carlos Mijares (geboren 1930), Juan Legaretta (1902–1934) und der zum verwechseln ähnlich klingende Ricardo Legoreta (1931), in Brasilien der Landschaftsarchitekt Roberto Burle Marx (1909–1994), Francisco Assis Reis (1926) und der Autodidakt José Zanine (1919), in Kuba Walter Betancourt (1932–1978) und Ricardo Porro (1925) oder auch in Uruguay der Architekt und Ingenieur Eladio Dieste (1917), von dem sehr einfallsreiche Backsteinbauten stammen, die im Lauf des 20. Jahrhunderts entstanden. Wer als «Macher» einer modernen Architektur gelten darf, die eine ernsthafte Alternative zur konservativen Rechtgläubigkeit darstellt und sich zum Vorteil der sogenannten Schwellenländer

Institute's «Sustainable Architecture Task Force» was set up in Cairo in March 2000.[12] Under the galvanizing influence of Gandhi's messages and actions – notably in favor of optimum use of traditional technologies – new professional vocations were to come to light. Following the withdrawal of the architects of the colonial empire, the cause was taken up by Laurie Baker (a British conscientious objector born in 1917 who acquired Indian nationality at independence), Raj Rewal (1934) or Charles Correa (1930). Francisco Manosa (born in 1930) in the Philippines, Muzhural Islam (1925) in Bangladesh and many other politically and socially committed builders in a quest for autarchy followed in the same lineage. In Asia, the first female militant of their professional practice was Yasmine Lari (born c. 1940) in Pakistan. In Latin America, precisely because independence here had come long before, this trend toward emulating national or regional specific architecture seemed to flourish more abundantly throughout the continent: a by no means exhaustive list might include in Mexico Luís Barragán (1902–88), Carolos Mijares (born 1930), Juan Legaretta (1902–34) and his compatriot Ricardo Legoreta (1931); in Brazil the landscape architect Roberto Burle Marx (1909–34), Francisco Asis Reis (1926) and the self-taught José Zanine (1919); in Cuba, Walter Betancourt (1932–94) and Ricardo Porro (1925); in Uruguay, the architect and engineer Eladio Dieste (1917), to whom we owe some of the most inventive brick structures to be erected in the 20th century. It is within the network of this geo-creativity that we must frame the current practitioners of a genuine alternative to Western dominant architecture in the emerging nations. Only North–South and South–North complementarity will be realistic to develop a fair and global practice of sustainable development and a reasonable redefinition of our future. The natural complementarity of raw earth, bamboo, and recycled paper, in this year 2000, is an architectural and technological, economic and ethical metaphor of this form of eco-alliance.

Jean Dethier is Director of Architectural Exhibitions at the Centre Georges Pompidou, Paris.

This article was completed in March 2000 on the basis of a detailed visit to Hanover's Expo 2000 site in February, when the structural elements of the great majority of the pavilions were completed and their finishings were underway. No internal

auswirkt, wird erst in Zukunft zu beurteilen sein. Erst aus der gegenseitigen Ergänzung von Norden nach Süden und von Süden nach Norden wird eine gerechte und globale Beurteilung der nachhaltigen Entwicklung möglich, die in Zukunft ausschlaggebend sein werden, will man an einer Neudefinition der Zukunft unseres Planeten mitwirken. Die natürliche Synthese von Lehm, Bambus und Recyclingpapier steht als Methapher für diese Zukunft.

Jean Dethier ist Kurator für Architektur am Centre Georges Pompidou, Paris.

Vorliegender Beitrag wurde im März 2000 fertiggestellt und gibt die auf einer Besichtigung des Geländes der Expo 2000 in Hannover im Februar 2000 gewonnenen Eindrücke wieder. Die meisten Pavillons waren bereits im Rohbau fertig. Im Innern der Pavillons waren jedoch noch keine Ausstellungen eingerichtet, so daß Kommentare hierzu vollständig fehlen.
Der Verfasser möchte sich bei Hugo Houben für seine wertvollen Anregungen zu den verschiedenen Entwürfen zu vorliegenden Text bedanken. Gedankt sei ebenfalls Mateo Kries, Claire Norton und Alexander von Vegesack.

exhibition, however, had yet been installed; hence the absence here of any comment on either form or content.

The author would like to thank Hugo Houben for his valuable suggestions made during various draft versions of this text. His gratitude extends also to Mateo Kries, Claire Norton, and Alexander von Vegesack.

testbericht / test report

Belastungstest des Etagenbodens im Prototypen des Expo-Pavillons in Manizales (Kolumbien) von Simón Vélez, 1999
Load-bearing test of the floors in the prototype for the Expo Pavilion in Manizales (Colombia), Simón Vélez, 1999

aus dem testbericht zur experimentellen tragsicherheitsbewertung des ZERI-pavillons / excerpt from an experimental evaluation of the load-bearing properties of the ZERI pavilion

klaus steffens

«Die Tragsicherheits- und Gebrauchsfähigkeitsbewertung werden soweit möglich auf der Basis vorhandener Werkstoffkennwerte rechnerisch nachgewiesen. Wegen der großen Imponderabilien (Materialkennwerte, Geometrieabweichungen, Exzentrizitäten, Anschlüsse, Fertigung) sind ergänzende und experimentelle Nachweise der wesentlichen Teile der tragenden Struktur angezeigt. [...] Um das Sicherheitsniveau abzuschätzen, Erfahrungen für Belastungsversuche am Pavillon in Hannover zu gewinnen und eine Baugenehmigung erwirken zu können, werden am Prototyp in Manizales (Kolumbien) Vorversuche durchgeführt. Die Planung und Durchführung der Belastungsversuche erfolgen als Bestandteil des Baugenehmigungsverfahrens in enger Abstimmung mit dem Tragwerksplaner und der Bauaufsichtsbehörde. [...]

Wegen der großen Zahl an Imponderabilien empfiehlt sich, aus Sicherheits- und Kostengründen Belastungsversuche an den primär tragenden Bauteilen in möglichst globaler Form vorzunehmen. Somit werden im Rahmen der Vorversuche folgende Meßorte vorgeschlagen: Kragdach (Versuchsziellast F=6,5 kN), Geschoßdecke Empore (Versuchsziellast 4,0 kN/m≈), Rahmen (Versuchsziellast F=235 kN). [...] Während der Versuchsdurchführung wird die Probelast kontinuierlich bis auf die vorzuhaltende Testlast (= Versuchsziellast) gesteigert.

Testergebnisse:
Die Meßprotokolle zeigen einen gleichmäßigen Verlauf der Kraft-Verformungskurven. In allen Belastungsversuchen wurde die Versuchsziellast ohne beobachtete Besonderheiten erreicht.

Kragdach (Nebenbinder):
Eigengewicht + 0,375kN/m≈ Schnee einschließlich Sicherheitsfaktoren
Empore (Decke Ebene 1):
Eigengewicht + 2,0 kN/m≈ Verkehrslast einschließlich Sicherheitsfaktoren
Rahmen (Horizontalaussteifung):
Eigengewicht + 2,0 kN/m≈ Verkehrslast + fi Windlast oder Eigengewicht + Windlast, beides ohne Sicherheitsfaktoren

Die Testergebnisse (Verformungsmessungen) zeigen einheitlich eine gute Übereinstimmung zwischen Belastungsversuchen und der statischen Berechung. Sie stützen den Schluß,

«Load capacity and viability evaluations are, wherever possible, mathematically proven based on characteristic values for the materials. Given the large number of imponderables (characteristic values for the materials, geometrical deviation, eccentricities, connections, manufacturing), supplementary and experimental proof for the essential parts of the supporting structure are in order. ... So as to estimate the level of safety, and to gain experiential data with which to run load capacity trials at the pavilion in Hanover and to obtain a license for construction, pre-tests were carried out using the prototype in Manizales (Colombia). Planning and execution of the load-bearing trials were handled in close coordination with the roof-planner and the building supervisory authorities. ...

Given the large number of imponderables, it seemed advisable for reasons of safety and costs to conduct the load tests as regards the primary supporting sections on as global a scale as possible. Therefore, we recommend that measurements of the following are taken as part of the pre-tests: cantilever-roof (experimental trial burden: F=6.5 kN), ceiling gallery (experimental trial burden: 4.0 kN/m^2), frame (experimental trial burden: F=235 kN). ... During the test, the trial load will be gradually increased until the planned test-load is reached (experimental trial load).

Test results:
The measurement log shows an even flow of force/deformation curves. In all the load-bearing tests, the experimental trial load was achieved without any peculiarities being detected.

Cantilever roof (side binder):
net weight + 0.375kN/m^2 snow,
including safety edge
Gallery (ceiling level 1):
net weight + 2.0 kN/m^2 traffic load,
including safety edge
Frame (horizontal bracing):
net weight + 2.0 kN/m^2 traffic load + fi wind load or net weight + wind load, both without safety factors.

The test results (working measurements) are all remarkably congruent with load trials and calculations of static load. This supports the conclusion that the load-bearing capacity and

[1] aus: Meier, B.: Zurück in die Zukunft, Zeitungs-artikel im Kurier am Sonntag, Nr. 48, 1999, Bremen

[1] from: Meier, B.: Zurück in die Zukunft, Zeitungsartikel im Kurier am Sonntag, Nr. 48, 1999, Bremen

daß die Tragsicherheit und Gebrauchsfähigkeit des ZERI-Pavillons für die EXPO 2000 in Hannover in Kombination von Bauteilversuchen, statischer Berechnung und Belastungsversuchen gemäß Planung bei vergleichbarer Ausführungsqualität wie in Manizales sicher erreicht werden kann.“

viability of the ZERI Pavilion for Expo 2000 in Hanover – combined with testing of components, static calculations and load testing as planned – can achieve results of a similar quality to those seen in Manizales.»

Prof. Dr. Klaus Steffens ist seit 1980 Leiter des Instituts für experimentelle Statik an der Hochschule Bremen, und führte bereits die experimentelle Tragsicherheitsbewertung beim Umbau des Reichstagsgebäudes in Berlin durch. In einem Zeitungsinterview zeigte sich Steffens «schwer beeindruckt» von dem Zeri-Pavillon und den Perspektiven der Bambus-Architektur.[1]

Prof. Dr Klaus Steffens has been Director of the Experimental Statics Institute at the University of Bremen since.1980 He has conducted experimental evaluations of load-bearing safety at the reconstructed building of the Reichstag in Berlin. In a newspaper interview, Prof. Steffens stated he was «greatly impressed» by the ZERI Pavilion and the future perspectives for bamboo architecture.[1]

Belastungstest im Prototypen des Expo-Pavillons in Manizales (Kolumbien) von Simón Vélez, 1999
Load-bearing test in the prototype for the Expo Pavilion in Manizales (Colombia), Simón Vélez, 1999

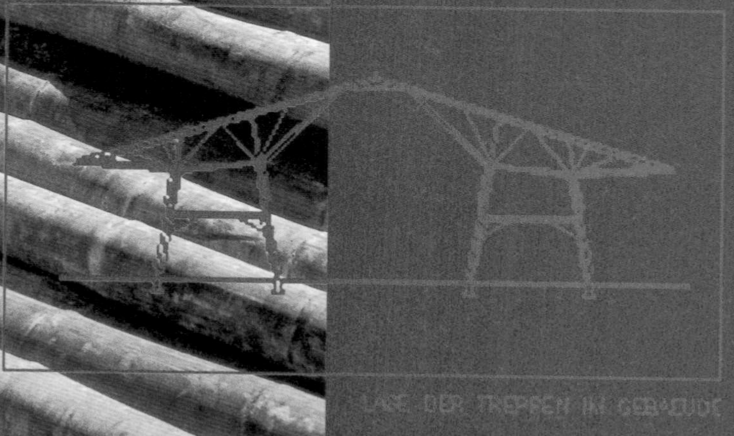

Simón Vélez beim Bau eines Wohnhauses während der Sommer-Workshops des Vitra Design Museums und des Centre Pompidou auf dem Gelände der C.I.R.E.C.A., Boisbuchet (Frankreich), 1999.
Simón Vélez building a residential house during summer workshops by Vitra Design Museum and the Centre Georges Pompidou on C.I.R.E.C.A. premises, Boisbuchet (France), 1999.

Herr Vélez, Ihre Architektur zeugt von Ihrer kolumbianischen Herkunft. Wie hat Ihre Herkunft Sie beeinflusst?

Ich komme aus Manizales, einer sehr jungen Stadt. Die meisten der ersten Häuser wurden dort vor etwa 160 Jahren aus Lehm gebaut, so ähnlich wie die riesigen Mauern, die man in Spanien findet. Kurz nach der Gründung der Stadt gab es ein sehr starkes Erdbeben, das die Bambushäuser am besten überstanden – dadurch nahm die Bambusarchitektur einen großen Aufschwung. Allerdings baute man genauso mit Bambus, wie man vorher mit Lehm gebaut hatte, nämlich ein Haus direkt an das nächste angeschlossen. Die Tatsache, daß die Stadt sehr bald von einem Feuer zerstört wurde, nachdem zu Beginn des letzten Jahrhunderts die Elektrizität eingeführt wurde, zeigte, daß man mit Bambus und Holz eben nicht genauso bauen kann wie mit Erde. Wenn man aus Holz baut, braucht man einen Abstand zwischen den Häusern, ähnlich wie in der Karibik oder auch in Japan, wo man nie zwei Häuser ganz nah beieinander findet.

Wie kamen Sie zur Architektur?

Bereits mein Vater und mein Großvater waren Architekten. Da meine Familie im Goldgeschäft tätig war, konnten sie ihre Kinder zur Ausbildung ins Ausland schicken. So studierte mein Vater Architektur in Washington. Aufgrund des Krieges kamen damals viele Architekten aus Deutschland in die USA, etwa Bauhauslehrer wie Marcel Breuer oder Walter Gropius. Mein Vater war einer der ersten modernen Architekten Kolumbiens und das Haus, in dem ich geboren wurde, zählte in Kolumbien damals zur Avantgarde-Architektur – es war eindeutig von der Bauhaus-Schule beeinflusst.

Wie haben Sie die lokalen Traditionen entdeckt, die ursprüngliche Art und Weise zu bauen?

Ich selbst mußte in Bogotá studieren, wo die Professoren geradezu besessen von der internationalen Architektur und vom Bauhaus waren. In Opposition zu dieser kritiklosen Verehrung und den vielen schlechten Imitationen moderner Architektur habe ich dann begonnen, eine Abneigung dagegen zu entwickeln und mich mehr an der Natur zu orientieren.

Mr Vélez, your architecture bears witness to your Colombian roots. In what way were you influenced by your origins?

I come from Manizales, a very young city. Most of the first houses there were built of clay about 160 years ago, similar to the great walls in Spain. Shortly after the city was founded, there was a large earthquake in which the bamboo houses survived the best. Because of this, bamboo architecture experienced a great surge in popularity. The bamboo structures were built adjoining one another, however, as the clay houses before them had been built. The fact that the city was soon destroyed by a fire after electricity had been introduced at the beginning of last century showed that bamboo could not be used in the same way as clay to build with. Gaps have to be left between wooden buildings, as is the case in the Caribbean or in Japan where no two wooden houses ever stand really close together.

What prompted you to take up architecture?

My father and grandfather were both architects. As my family was involved in the gold business, they were able to send their children overseas to be educated. My father studied architecture in Washington. Because of the war, many German architects came to the United States at that time, for instance Bauhaus teachers like Marcel Breuer and Walter Gropius. My father was one of the first modern Colombian architects and the house in which I was born was considered avant-garde architecture in its day – it was clearly influenced by the Bauhaus.

How did you rediscover local traditions – the original way of building?

I had to study in Bogotá where the professors were utterly taken with the International Style and the Bauhaus. I began, in opposition to this uncritical worship and the many bad imitations of modern architecture, to develop an aversion to Bauhaus and modern architecture, and to focus more on nature.

Wann haben Sie zum ersten Mal mit Bambus gearbeitet?

Ich war auf der Hazienda eines Freundes, wo viel Bambus wächst. Er benötigte einen Stall für seine Pferde und bat mich, Bambus zu verwenden, obwohl ich vorher noch nie mit diesem Material gebaut hatte. Da ich ein großes Überdach plante, mußte ich eine neue Verbindungstechnik für die Bambusstäbe entwickeln, mit der ein solcher Bau möglich war.
Vielleicht genauso wichtig war es für mich, als ich später ein Clubhaus für eine Golfanlage und damit das erste Mal einen Bau für sehr reiche Leute aus Bambus baute. Das war der Beginn der sozialen Aufwertung von Bambus. Nach wie vor mögen allerdings Aufsteiger aus unteren Klassen, wie es in Kolumbien auch viele Drogenbosse sind, keinen Bambus. Da Bambus in Ihren Augen für die Armut steht, der sie entflohen sind, bevorzugen sie Marmor und Stahl.

Sie arbeiten nicht nur mit Bambus, sind aber trotzdem als «Bambusarchitekt» bekannt ...

Es stimmt – den Ruf, den ich habe, verdanke ich dem Bambus. Doch es gibt so etwas wie eine Gemeinde von Bambus-Liebhabern, zu denen ich eigentlich nicht gezählt werden möchte. Als Architekt kann man sich nicht nur mit einem Material befassen. Ich möchte nicht «Bambusarchitekt» genannt werden, denn Bambus ist nur eines der vielen tropischen Materialien, die in Kolumbien mit seiner vielfältigen Natur zu finden sind. Auch der EXPO-Pavillon für die ZERI-Stiftung besteht ja nicht ausschließlich aus Bambus. Man kann ja auch nicht ausschließlich mit Stein bauen oder nur ein «Eisen-» oder «Holzarchitekt» sein.

Was macht den Reiz von Bambus aus?

Da sind einmal die ökologischen Vorteile: Bambus kann viele tropische Hölzer ersetzen und damit zum Schutz des Regenwaldes beitragen, außerdem verarbeitet Bambus mehr CO_2 als die meisten anderen Pflanzen.
Hinzu kommt, daß Bambus sehr kostengünstig und einfach zu verarbeiten ist. In Kolumbien hatten Leute aus niedrigeren Schichten früher sehr schöne Bambushäuser, die heute fast alle verschwunden sind. Heute ziehen sie Betonhäuser

When did you start working with bamboo?

I was on a friend's hacienda where there was a lot of bamboo growing. He needed a stable for his horses and asked me to use bamboo although I had never before worked with this material. As I had a large roof in mind, I had to develop a new technique for joining the bamboo canes so that I could make such a building.
A perhaps equally crucial experience came later, when I was commissioned to build a clubhouse for a golf course – it was the first time I built something from bamboo for rich people. That was when bamboo had just started to become socially acceptable. Social climbers from the lower rungs of society, as with many drug lords in Colombia, still want nothing to do with bamboo. In their eyes it represents the poverty from which they have fled – their preference lies with marble and steel.

You also work with materials other than bamboo, but are nevertheless known as a bamboo architect...

That is correct – the reputation I have is thanks to bamboo. There is something like a community of bamboo lovers to whom I do not really wish to belong. As an architect, you cannot work with a single material. I do not wish to be called a «bamboo architect» for bamboo is only one of many tropical materials you can find in the abundance of nature in Colombia. The Expo Pavilion for the ZERI Foundation is also not made exclusively from bamboo. It is not possible to build just with stone or just in iron, nor is it possible to be a «wood architect».

What constitutes the appeal of bamboo?

For one, the ecological advantages: Bamboo can replace many tropical woods and thus help protect the rainforest. Also, bamboo converts more carbon dioxide than most other plants.
In addition, bamboo is very cost-effective and easy to work with. In Colombia, people from the lower classes used to have beautiful houses made of bamboo, but today such edifices have as good as vanished. The preference now is for concrete houses in spite of the higher cost. The

trotz ihrer höheren Kosten vor. Die Folgen davon konnte man in Kolumbien bei dem Erdbeben von 1999 beobachten – es war kein schweres Erdbeben, richtete aber massive Schäden an den vielen schlecht gebauten Betonhäusern an.
Wie in der alten Architektur liegt der ästhetische Reiz des Bauens mit Bambus in der Beschränkungen durch die Materialien. Aus diesen Begrenzungen durch die materialspezifischen Eigenschaften ergeben sich die Proportionen eines Gebäudes. Das gilt auch für die Schönheit der Bauten von Shigeru Ban, der mit einfachen Kartonröhren wunderschöne Architektur macht. Beton hingegen ist ein Material, das keine Grenzen aufzeigt. Und wenn es keine Grenzen mehr gibt, verliert man den Rhythmus und das Vokabular einer architektonische Sprache.

Wie würden Sie Ihren Baustil bezeichnen?

Ich würde mich als «Dächer-Architekt» definieren. Zuerst entwerfe ich das Dach, und dann, was darunter sein muss. Dächer müssen den Wetterverhältnissen trotzen und sind immer ein Spiegel der jeweiligen Kultur. Leider wurde das Giebeldach mit dem Erfolg der modernen Architektur und des Flachdachs zu einem Symbol der Heimat-Architektur. Doch Frank Gehry ist in gewisser Hinsicht ja auch ein Dächer-Architekt, nur weiß man bei ihm nie, wo das Dach aufhört und die Wand anfängt. Ich mache allerdings genau das Gegenteil von ihm, ich würde nie einen komplizierten Grundriss entwerfen.
Meine Architektur ist eine Architektur der tropischen Breitengrade. In einem Land, in dem es viel regnet, muss man Dächer mit großen Überhängen bauen, wie z. B. in der chinesischen oder in der indonesischen Architektur. Die indonesische Architektur kennenzulernen war ein radikaler Einschnitt in meinem Leben – diese riesigen Bambusdächer, die ohne jegliche Zurückhaltung oder Schüchternheit gebaut werden. Durch den Einfluss von Le Corbusiers Modulor dachte ich immer, dass ein Dach oder ein Raum eine bestimmte Höhe nicht überschreiten dürften. Aber in Indonesien bauen arme Menschen eigenhändig Dächer, die 10, 15 Meter hoch sind! Das ist eine kulturelle Geste: etwas wichtiges schaffen zu wollen, eine Art Exibitionismus ohne Imponiergehabe.

consequences were apparent in the aftermath of the 1999 earthquake – it wasn't a large earthquake, yet the damage to badly built concrete houses was massive.
As with ancient architecture, the appeal in building with bamboo lies with the limitations defined by the material. The limitations inherent in the nature of the material give rise to the proportions of the building. This is also true of the beauty of Shigeru Ban's buildings – wonderful architecture made of simple cardboard tubing. Concrete, on the other hand, is a material without limits. And when there are no limits any more, the rhythm and vocabulary of an architectural idiom get lost.

How would you describe your style of building?

I would define myself as a «roof architect». I design the roof first and then what comes beneath it. Roofs have to withstand weather and always reflect the culture they come from. Unfortunately, thanks to the success of modern architecture and the flat roof, the gable roof has become a symbol of folk architecture. In a way, Frank Gehry is also a roof architect – but with him, you never quite know where the roof stops and the wall begins. What I do is just the opposite. I would never design a complicated ground plan.
My architecture is tropical architecture. In a country where it rains a lot, you have to build roofs with large overhangs like in Chinese or Indonesian architecture. Learning about Indonesian architecture was a radical development in my life – these huge bamboo roofs built without any restraint or reserve. Influenced by Corbusier's «Modulor», I always thought that a roof or a room should not exceed a certain height. But in Indonesia, poor folk build roofs with their own hands that are 10 or 15 meters high! It's a cultural statement: to create something momentous – a sort of exhibitionism without showing off.

▼ **Der erste Bau von Simón Vélez in Europa war dieser Gartenpavillon für C.I.R.E.C.A. in Boisbuchet (Frankreich), der 1998 anläßlich eines Sommer-Workshops des Vitra Design Museums und des Centre Pompidou entstand.**
This garden pavilion for C.I.R.E.C.A. in Boisbuchet (France) was Simón Vélez's first construction in Europe, erected at the summer workshops run by Vitra Design Museum and the Centre Georges Pompidou, 1998.

▼ **Bau eines Wohnhauses während der Sommer-Workshops des Vitra Design Museums und des Centre Pompidou auf dem Gelände der C.I.R.E.C.A., Boisbuchet (Frankreich), 1999.**
Building a residential house during summer workshops by Vitra Design Museum and the Centre Georges Pompidou on C.I.R.E.C.A. premises, Boisbuchet (France), 1999.

Sie wurden aufgrund der starken Symmetrie in einigen Ihrer Werke mit einem klassizistischen Architekten wie Palladio verglichen. Müssen wir wirklich so weit in die Vergangenheit gehen, um Ihre Vorbilder zu finden, oder gibt es auch andere Architekten der heutigen Zeit, die Sie für Ihre Arbeit bewundern, und die vielleicht einen Einfluss auf Sie haben?

Die japanische Architektur hat mich stark beschäftigt und geprägt. Schon die ersten Architekturbücher, die ich sah, waren Bücher über japanische Architektur meines Vaters. Ich möchte zwar selbst keine japanische Architektur machen, aber es ist sicher einer der Gründe, warum ich mich für Materialien wie Bambus, Holz und Stein interessiere. Außerdem bewundere ich die Architekten Greene & Greene, die ja ebenfalls stark von japanischer Architektur beeinflußt waren.
Aber zurück zu Palladio: Wenn man die traditionelle Architektur betrachtet, sieht man, daß die traditionelle Architektur immer versucht, symmetrisch zu sein. Wenn Sie einem Kind Papier und Bleistift geben und ihm sagen, es solle ein Haus malen, dann wird es ein symmetrisches Haus malen. Seltsamerweise wird die asymmetrische Architektur als organische Architektur bezeichnet, dabei strebt in der Natur fast alles danach, symmetrisch zu sein.

Was verstehen Sie unter organischer Architektur?

Organische Architektur, so wie ich sie verstehe, hält das Gleichgewicht zwischen mineralischen Bestandteilen, also Stein und Metall, und den pflanzlichen Bestandteilen. Das können wir aus der japanischen Architektur lernen. Es gibt dort ein perfektes Gleichgewicht zwischen mineralischen und pflanzlichen Bestandteilen. Um Architektur zu betreiben, braucht man meiner Meinung nach einen gewissen Sinn fürs Kulinarische, um ein Gleichgewicht zwischen diesen Bestandteilen herstellen zu können.

Wie plant und baut man ein Gebäude aus Bambus?

Mein Büro der letzten drei Monate befindet sich in diesem Heft. In dieses Heft zeichne ich und aus diesen Zeichungen entstehen dann die Entwürfe. Manchmal gebe ich sie an Freunde, die

The strict symmetry in some of your works has been compared to classicist architects like Palladio. Is it really necessary to go so far back to find your mentors, or are there other present-day architects whose work you admire and who have an influence on you?

Japanese architecture has greatly interested and influenced me. The first architecture books I laid eyes on were books of my father's on Japanese architecture. I do not want to make Japanese architecture myself, but it is definitely one of the reasons why I choose bamboo, wood, and stone as materials. I also admire the architecture of Greene & Greene, and they were likewise strongly influenced by Japanese architecture.
But let's return to Palladio: When you look at traditional architecture, you see that it always reveals an attempt to be symmetrical. If you put a pencil and paper in the hand of a child and ask him or her to draw a house, the child will draw something symmetrical. Curiously enough, asymmetrical architecture is described as organic architecture although everything in nature strives to be symmetrical.

What does organic architecture mean to you?

Organic architecture, as I understand it, maintains a balance between mineral components like stone and metal, on the one hand, and plant components, on the other. This is something we can learn from Japanese architecture. In Japan, you can find the perfect balance between mineral and plant elements. In my opinion, to be an architect you need a certain culinary sense to compose the proper balance between these components.

How does one plan and build a bamboo construction?

My office for the last three months is inside this book. I make sketches in this book and these become my designs. Sometimes I give them to friends who digitize them on a computer – for the

sie dann in den Computer eingeben, doch diese Computerbilder sind nur dazu da, den Bauherren zu überzeugen. Tatsächlich arbeite ich nur mit meinen Zeichnungen. Der Expo-Pavillon wird von kolumbianischen Arbeitern nur auf der Grundlage von zwei DIN A4-Handzeichnungen gebaut.

Was ist mit der statischen Berechnung, wie sie hier in Europa erforderlich ist?

In Kolumbien ist das nicht die Hauptsache – dort kann die Erfahrung vielfach die statische Vorausberechnung ersetzen, weil die Auflagen dies erlauben. Ich glaube, dass ich im Vergleich mit westlichen Architekten meines Alters zu denjenigen gehöre, die die meisten unterschiedlichen Projekte realisiert haben – bislang über hundert. In Europa wäre das nicht möglich, weil die Tätigkeit des Architekten dort viel teurer und formalisierter ist.
Aber ich arbeite dennoch nach einer naturwissenschaftlichen Methode – dem trial and error-Prinzip. Ich experimentiere in realen Dimensionen und lasse bei jedem Entwurf immer einen gewissen Spielraum für Versuche. Und ich fühle mich wohler, wenn ich mich selbst als Ingenieur bezeichne und wenn ich sehr einfache Grundrisse entwerfe, die nur «wenig Architektur» enthalten.

Die Ästhetik Ihrer Architektur basiert also auf dem Material wie Bambus und seiner fachgerechten Anwendung?

Genau. Es gibt beispielweise ein grundlegendes Prinzip, das es mir erlaubt, die großen Überhänge für so schwere Dächer zu bauen. Ich habe entdeckt, wie man Bambus auf Zug belasten kann, indem ich stabile Zugverbindungen entwickelt habe. Ich habe beim Experimentieren die letzten Kammern des Bambusstabes mit Beton gefüllt und darin Metallelemente eingelassen. Über diese ließen sich die Stäbe verbinden, wobei der Zug auf die stabilen Trennwände des Stabes weitergeben wurde. Auf Zug ist Bambus extrem belastbar.
Für druckbelastete Konstruktionen braucht man anstatt einem etwa sieben Bambusstäbe. Doch auch hier fand ich eine Lösung: Man fügt mehrere Stäbe zusammen, obwohl nur einer die Last trägt. Die anderen versteifen diese Stütze gegen

sole purpose of convincing the developers. I only work with my drawings. The Expo Pavilion was built by Colombian workers on the basis of hand-drawn sketches covering two A4 sheets.

What is the situation as regards calculations of static properties and engineering reports such as are required here in Europe?

This is not the most important issue in Colombia where perhaps experience replaces such calculations and reports, as conditions allow this. I believe that, compared with European architects of my age, I have probably produced more pieces of different architecture – over 100 edifices to date. This would not be possible in Europe as architects work much more formally and because it is more expensive. It is not as if in my work I do not use a scientific approach, namely trial and error. I experiment in real dimensions and always leave a certain scope for this in my designs. And it feels better to call myself an engineer and to design very simple ground plans which contain «a small amount of architecture».

The aesthetics of your architecture is based on the material, such as bamboo, and its specialized use?

Exactly. There is, for example, a fundamental principle which enables me to build the large overhangs for such heavy roofs. I have discovered how bamboo can withstand tensile pressure if connected by tensile joints. I experimented with filling the last chambers of the bamboo cane with concrete and set metal elements into the concrete. The poles could thus be joined with these elements with the tension then distributed through to the chamber walls of the cane.
Bamboo has great tensile strength. For high-load-bearing constructions, say, seven bamboo poles are used instead of one. But I have found a solution for this too: a number of poles are connected together, but only one bears the weight. The others stabilize the support against sideways breakages. Complex support structures like this from a material

Das 1999 von Simón Vélez für C.I.R.E.C.A. in Boisbuchet (Frankreich) gebaute Wohnhaus basiert auf einem Haus für den sozialen Wohnungsbau, das Vélez 1999 entwickelte.
The house built by Simón Vélez for C.I.R.E.C.A. in Boisbuchet (France) in 1999, which was developed as low-cost housing.

seitliches Wegbrechen. Solche komplexen Tragwerksstrukturen aus einem Material wie Bambus sind natürlich nur mit sehr qualifizierten Arbeitern möglich, denn sie müssen handwerklich perfekt ausgeführt sein.

such as bamboo are only possible when the workers are highly qualified – the craftsmanship has to be executed to perfection.

Ein Problem der Bambusarchitektur ist ihre Lebensdauer ...

One problem with bamboo architecture is its life-span ...

In Manizales gibt es Häuser aus Bambus, die 100 Jahre alt sind. Das Einzige, was dort gehalten hat, ist der Bambus. Auch in Japan gibt es ein reichhaltiges Wissen, was die Behandlung von Bambus gegen Witterungseinflüsse und Schädlinge betrifft.
Der beste Schutz ist aber immer noch ein guter Entwurf. So kann man durch Überhänge die Stäbe vor Feuchtigkeit schützen und mit Betonsockeln kann man sie vom feuchten Boden fernhalten.

There are bamboo houses in Manizales that are 100 years old. The only thing that remains of them is the bamboo. In Japan, too, there is an abundance of knowledge on how to treat bamboo against weather and pests. The best protection, however, is a good design. Overhangs can be used to make sure the poles don't get damp, with concrete bases supplying the protection from underneath.

Könnte man auf diese Weise Bambus auch in Europa verwenden?

Could bamboo then be used in Europe?

Sicher, und nachdem wir jetzt den Expo-Pavillon gebaut haben, sind die Türen dafür weit offen. Ich glaube, daß es an der Zeit ist, daß man solche Materialien nach Europa importiert. High-Tech-Architektur besteht schließlich nicht nur aus Titan und Aluminium, man kann auch einfache High-Tech-Architektur mit natürlichen Materialien machen. Das ist ja das Besondere an Bambus: Es ist von Natur aus ein High-Tech-Material. Das Verhältnis zwischen Gewicht und Stärke ist besser als bei den meisten modernen High-Tech-Materialien. Warum sollte man also nicht direkt die Vorteile der Natur nutzen und aus der Natur lernen? In Kolumbien importieren wir ja schließlich auch Materialien aus Europa und aus Nordamerika.

Of course, and now that we have built the Expo pavilion, the doors are wide open. I believe it is time to transport such materials to Europe. After all, high-tech architecture isn't only made from titanium and aluminum, it can also be made from natural materials. That is what is so special about bamboo: It is inherently a high-tech material. The relationship of weight to strength is far better than most modern high-tech materials. So why shouldn't we just take advantage of what nature offers and learn from her? After all, in Colombia we also import materials from Europe and North America.

Wie sind Sie darauf gekommen, einen Bambuspavillon für Hannover zu bauen?

How did you come to build a bamboo pavilion for the Hanover Expo?

Der Pavillon wird von der ZERI-Stiftung mit ihrem Leiter Gunter Pauli finanziert. Ich habe ihn vor 5 Jahren in Indonesien bei einer Einladung der Designerin Linda Garland auf Bali kennengelernt. Damals sprach ich noch kein Englisch, weil ich noch nie aus Kolumbien herausgekommen war. Bambus paßte genau zu dem Grundgedanken der ZERI-Stiftung, natürliche Kreisläufe sinnvoll und kreativ zu nutzen.

The pavilion was sponsored by the ZERI Foundation and its director Gunter Pauli. I first got to know him five years ago in Indonesia when we were both invited by the designer Linda Garland in Bali. At that time I didn't speak any English as I had never been out of Colombia before. Bamboo fits perfectly with the basic principle of the ZERI Foundation – natural cycles put to intelligent and creative use.

Als ZERI vor drei Jahren ein Platz auf der Expo Hannover zugesprochen wurde, kam Pauli nach Kolumbien. Auf der Basis seiner Grundidee entwarf ich den Pavillon.

Das Gespräch führte Mateo Kries im Januar 2000.

When ZERI was promised a place at the Hanover Expo three years ago, Pauli came to Colombia. I designed the pavilion based on his underlying concept.

Interview by Mateo Kries, January 2000.

simón vélez – biografie und werkübersicht / simón vélez – biography and works

Fabrikhalle in Pensilvania (Kolumbien) im Bau, Simón Vélez, 1993
Factory hall under construction in Pensilvania (Colombia), Simón Vélez, 1993

Unter den Bauten und Projekten von Simón Vélez sind auch zahlreiche unentgeltliche oder kaum dokumentierte Entwürfe des Architekten. Dies liegt daran, daß in Kolumbien – wie in vielen Ländern des Südens - der Baubetrieb und die Architektentätigkeit weniger formalisiert und kostenintensiv als in den Industrieländern ist. Den Baustoff Bambus verwendete Simón Vélez ab Mitte der achtziger Jahre.
Die vorliegende Übersicht wurde von Liliana Villegas in Zusammenarbeit mit dem Architekten und seinen Familienangehörigen sowie Mitarbeitern zusammengestellt. Aufgrund der großen Anzahl von Projekten ist sie als Übersicht zu verstehen, für deren Vollständigkeit keine Gewähr übernommen werden kann. Sofern keine Länderangaben genannt sind, befinden sich alle genannten Orte in Kolumbien.

Among Simón Vélez's buildings and projects, there are countless he created free of charge or on which documentation is very sparse. The reason for this is that in Columbia – as in many countries in the Southern hemisphere – construction and architectural work are less formalized and cost-intensive than in the industrialized countries. Simón Vélez has been using bamboo for his buildings since the mid-1980s.
The overview here was compiled by Liliana Villegas together with Vélez himself as well as members of his family and his staff. Owing to the large number of projects he has been involved in, the reader should regard it as an overview which lays no claim to completeness. If no other country is stated, the places in question are in Columbia.

1949	**Geboren in Manizales (Kolumbien), am 2. Februar 1949**	Born in Manizales (Columbia), on February 2, 1949
1968-1975	**Architektur- und Kunststudium an der Universidad de los Andes, Bogotá**	Studies architecture and art at Universidad de los Andes, Bogotá
1970	**Haus Andorra in der Provinz Guajira**	Designs the Andorra House in Guajira Province
1971	**Haus Don Diego für Jaime Laserna, Magdalena. Beginn des Baus am eigenen Wohnhaus in La Candelaria/Bogotá. Seit 1971 plant und erweitert Vélez sein eigenes Wohnhaus, das in einer großen Grünfläche in der Altstadt von Bogotá gelegen ist.**	Creates the Don Diego House for Jaime Laserna, Magdalena. Starts work on his own residence in La Candelaria/Bogotá. As of 1971, plans and expands his own residence, which is located in a broad greenbelt in the old town of Bogotá.
1972	**Wohnhäuser für das INDERENA (Instituto Nacional de Recursos Naturales) in den Nationalparks Tairona/Magdalena, Nevado del Ruiz/Caldas und Tuparro/Orinoco. Diese Bauten wurden aus den lokal verfügbaren Hölzern gebaut.**	Residential buildings for INDERENA (Instituto Nacional de Recursos Naturales) in the Tairona/Magdalena, Nevado del Ruiz/Caldas and Tuparro/Orinoco National Parks. These buildings were made using woods available locally.
1973	**Haus Rio Piedras, Magdalena**	Rio Piedras House, Magdalena
1974	**Haus Hernandez, Bogotá**	Hernandez House, Bogotá
	Haus Gutierrez, La Calera/Bogotá	Gutierrez House, La Calera/Bogotá
	Haus Jenaro Mejia, La Candelaria/Bogota	Jenaro Mejia House, La Candelaria/Bogota
	Aussichtsturm Valenzuela, La Candelaria/ Bogotá	Valenzuela Belvedere, La Candelaria/Bogotá
1975	**Haus Montoya, Suba/Bogotá**	Montoya House, Suba/Bogotá
1976	**Haus Gomez Escobar, Nilo/Cundinamarca**	Gomez Escobar House, Nilo/Cundinamarca
	Haus Velilla, La Floresta/Bogotá	Velilla House, La Floresta/Bogotá
1977	**Haus Santa Fé, Santa Fé de Antioquia**	Santa Fé House, Santa Fé de Antioquia
	Haus Marulanda, Pereira	Marulanda House, Pereira
	Haus Hanne, Isla Latifundio/Islas del Rosario	Hanne House, Isla Latifundio/Islas del Rosario
	Haus/Werkstatt Marlen Hoffman, Bogotá	Marlen Hoffman House and Workshop, Bogotá
1978	**Ospina-Gebäude, Medellín**	Ospina Building, Medellín
	Haus Cortez Ortiz, La Dorada/Caldas	Cortez Ortiz House, La Dorada/Caldas
	Haus Castro, El Placer	Castro House, El Placer

	Aussichtsturm Andres Echavarría, Cartagena	Andres Echavarría Belvedere, Cartagena
	Fabrikhalle und Büros für COLHAP, Bogotá	Factory building and offices for COLHAP, Bogotá
1979	**Wohnungseinheiten für CRAMSA, Barrio Galán/Manizales**	Apartment blocks for CRAMSA, Barrio Galán/Manizales
	Hotel Pesca, Bahia Cupica/Chocó	Hotel Pesca, Bahia Cupica/Chocó
	Projekt für ein Haus in Tumaco	Project for a house in Tumaco
	Tankstelle, Via Chinchiná/Manizales	Gas station, Via Chinchiná/Manizales
1980	**Haus in La María/Cali**	House in La María/Cali
	Projekt für einen Busbahnhof, Manizales	Project for a bus terminus, Manizales
1981	**Haus Uribe Holguín, San Andrés**	Uribe Holguín House, San Andrés
	Haus D'Acosta, La Gloria Magdalena	D'Acosta House, La Gloria Magdalena
1982	**Haus Bruckman, Cota**	Bruckman House, Cota
1982-86	**Santagueda-Kapelle, Caldas**	Santagueda Chapel, Caldas
1983	**Projekt für Coorporación Forestal de Caldas**	Project for Coorporación Forestal de Caldas
	Sporthalle für die Universidad Autónoma, Manizales	Sports hall for Universidad Autónoma, Manizales
	Projekt Haus Tigreros, Circasia	Project: Tigreros House, Circasia
	Projekt Hangar Pedrito, La Nubia/Manizales	Hangar Pedrito House, La Nubia/Manizales
1984	**Haus Salazar Gutierrez, Manizales**	Salazar Gutierrez House, Manizales
	Projekt für eine Fußgängerbrücke, Club Campestre, Pereira	Project for a pedestrian bridge/overpass, Club Campestre, Pereira
	Projekt Haus Cárdenas-Ochoa, Los Morros/Bogotá	Project: Cárdenas-Ochoa House, Los Morros/Bogotá
1985	**Bar/Restaurant «Caballo Loco», Manizales/Caldas**	Bar/Restaurant «Caballo Loco», Manizales/Caldas
	Bühnenbild für «La Balada del Café Triste» am Teatro Libre de Bogotá	Stage set for «La Balada del Café Triste» at the Teatro Libre de Bogotá
1986	**Projekt Haus Hernando Caicedo, Tumaco**	Project: Hernando Caicedo House, Tumaco
1987	**Projekt für den Sitz einer Theatergruppe, Manizales**	Project for the premises for a theater group, Manizales
	Projekt Haus am Golf von Urabá	Project: House on the Gulf of Urabá
	Bühnenbild für «Un muro en el Jardín», Teatro Libre de Bogotá	Stage set for «Un muro en el Jardín» at the Teatro Libre de Bogotá
1990	**Wohnhaus, Islas del Rosario**	Private residence, Islas del Rosario
1991	**Haus Alto de las Palmas, Medellín**	Alto de las Palmas House, Medellín
1992	**Haus Chia**	Chia House
	Hauptgebäude, Clubhäuser und Wohnhäuser für den Country-Club Peñalisa in Girardot/Tolima (bis 1997)	Main building, club houses and residential buildings for the Peñalisa Country Club in Girardot/Tolima (until 1997)
1993	**Aussichtsturm im Parque de la Cultura Cafetera in Montenegro/Quindio (mit Marcelo Villegas)**	Parque de la Cultura Cafetera Belvedere in Montenegro/Quindio (with Marcelo Villegas)
	Fabrikhalle und Häuser in Pensilvania, Caldas	Factory building and houses in Pensilvania, Caldas
	Büros der Firma Descafecol, Manizales	Offices for the Descafecol company, Manizales
	Haus Pedro Mejia, Cali	Pedro Mejia House, Cali
	Keramikatelier Sofos	Ceramics studio, Sofos
1995	**Hauptsitz des Bauunternehmens Melendez, Cali**	Company head office for the Melendez construction corporation, Cali
	Hauptsitz für eine Plantage, Tumaco/Chocó (bis 1999)	Head office for a plantation, Tumaco/Chocó (until 1999)
1996	**Wohnhaus, Anapoima/Tolima**	Residential building, Anapoima/Tolima
1997	**Establo de ordeño, Sofos/Tabio**	Establo de ordeño, Sofos/Tabio
	Haus Sesquilé	Sesquilé House
	Galerie Quinta, Bogotá	Quinta Gallery, Bogotá

	Haus «Plantamos», Usaquén	«Plantamos» House, Usaquén
	Inneineinrichtung für das Apartment Lorenzo Kling, Bogotá	Interior design for Apartment Lorenzo Kling, Bogotá
	Inneneinrichtung für das Apartment Stewart, Florida (USA)	Interior design for Apartment Stewart, Florida (USA)
	Projekt einer Zirkusschule für den «Cirque du soleil»	Project: circus school for the «Cirque du soleil»
	Leitung eines Seminars an der Berkeley University, Kalifornien (USA) und an der Universität von Seattle (USA)	Chairs a seminar at the University of California in Berkeley (USA) and at the University of Seattle (USA)
1998	**Haus Martha Muller, Tabio**	Martha Muller House, Tabio
	Wohnhaus, La Calera/Bogotá	Private residence, La Calera/Bogotá
	Haus in Arbelaez/Fusagasugá	House in Arbelaez/Fusagasugá
	Projekt für die Fundación Batuta, Bogotá	Project: for Fundación Batuta, Bogotá
	Leitung eines Workshops des Vitra Design Museums, des Centre Georges Pompidou und der C.I.R.E.C.A. in Boisbuchet (Frankreich) sowie Konstruktion eines Gartenpavillons	Heads a workshop organized by Vitra Design Museum, Centre Georges Pompidou and C.I.R.E.C.A. in Boisbuchet (France) and builds a garden pavilion
	Leitung von Seminaren an der Universität von Caracas (Venezuela)	Leads seminars at the University of Caracas (Venezuela)
1999	**Haus Franco, La Calera/Bogotá**	Franco House, La Calera/Bogotá
	Haus Steve Jensen, Chia (im Bau)	Steve Jensen House, Chia (im Bau)
	Haus und Atelier Jacanamijoy, Bogotá	Jacanamijoy House and Studio, Bogotá
	Entwicklung eines Hauses für den sozialen Wohnungsbau	Develops a council house
	Inneneinrichtung Apartment Monica Hoyos, Bogotá	Interior design for Apartment Monica Hoyos, Bogotá
	Prototyp des Pavillons für die ZERI Foundation in Manizales, Kolumbien	Prototype of the pavilion for the ZERI Foundation in Manizales, Columbia
	Restaurant Angra dos Reis, Rio de Janeiro (Brasilien)	Restaurant Angra dos Reis, Rio de Janeiro (Brazil)
	Konstruktion eines Hauses aus Bambus für C.I.R.E.C.A in Boisbuchet (Frankreich) anläßlich eines Workshops des Vitra Design Museums und des Centre Georges Pompidou	Designs a bamboo house for C.I.R.E.C.A. in Boisbuchet (France) on the occasion of a workshop held by Vitra Design Museum and Centre Georges Pompidou
2000	**Pavillon für die ZERI Foundation auf der Expo 2000, Hannover (Deutschland)**	Pavilion for the ZERI Foundation at Expo 2000, Hanover (Germany)
	Konstruktion eines Hauses aus Bambus für C.I.R.E.C.A in Boisbuchet (Frankreich) anläßlich eines Workshops des Vitra Design Museums und des Centre Georges Pompidou	Designs a bamboo house for C.I.R.E.C.A. in Boisbuchet (France) on the occasion of a workshop organized by Vitra Design Museum and Centre Georges Pompidou
	Projekt für eine Brücke für das Bob-Marley-Museum in Jamaica	Project: bridge for the Bob Marley Museum in Jamaica
	Projekt für einen Aussichtsturm im Parque Nacional de la Guadua in Pereira/Risaralda	Project: belvedere in Parque Nacional de la Guadua in Pereira/Risaralda
	Haus Kahn, Cabrera/Dominikanische Republik	Kahn House, Cabrera/Dominican Republic

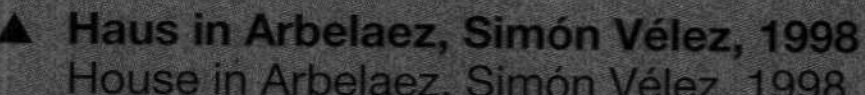

▲ **Haus in Arbelaez, Simón Vélez, 1998**
House in Arbelaez, Simón Vélez, 1998

▼ **Galerie Quinta in Bogotá, Simón Vélez, 1997**

▲ **Haus La Calera in Bogotá, Simón Vélez, 1997/98**
La Calera House in Bogota, Simón Vélez, 1997–8

▼ **Freizeitzentrum Peñalisa in Girardot, Simón Vélez, 1992/97**
Country Club Peñalisa in Girardot, Simón Vélez, 1992–7.

▲ **Halle in Fusagasugá, Simón Vélez, 1994**
Hall in Fusagasugá, Simón Vélez, 1994

▼ **Haus Luis Salazar in Manizales (Kolumbien), Simón Vélez, 1984-87**
The Luis Salazar House in Manizales (Colombia), Simón Vélez, 1984–7

▲ **Das Wohnhaus von Simón Vélez, von ihm 1986 erbaut, befindet sich in der Altstadt von Bogotá. Eingebettet in einen großen Garten, liegt es im Innern eines großen Häuserkomplexes.**
Simón Vélez's residential house which he built himself in 1986 lies in the old center of Bogotá. Nestled into a sizeable garden, it is located inside a large housing complex.

Freizeitzentrum Peñalisa in Girardot, Simón Vélez, 1992/97. Das monumentale Dach dieses Hauptgebäudes eines Freizeitzentrums war bis zum ZERI-Pavillon die größte existierende Bambusstruktur.
Country Club Peñalisa in Girardot, Simón Vélez, 1992–7. The monumental roof of this main building at a country club was the largest existing bamboo structure until the construction of the ZERI pavilion

grundelemente
basic elements

Kathedrale von Laon (Frankreich), nach 1170
Laon Cathedral (France), after 1170

Illustration zu einer Theorie, die Elemente der gotischen Architektur auf den Holzbau zurückführt, James Hall, 1797
Illustration of a theory which derives the elements of Gothic architecture from wooden buildings, James Hall, 1797

[1] **Nähere Informationen hierzu in: Pieper, J.: Steinerne Bäume und künstliches Astwerk – die gotischen Theorien des James Hall (1761 - 1832), Beitrag in Graefe, R.: Zur Geschichte des Konstruierens, Wiesbaden, 1977**

[2] **Harada, J.: The Lesson of Japanese Architecture, The Studio, London 1936, S. 21**

[1] For more information on this, see: J. Pieper: Steinerne Bäume und künstliches Astwerk – die gotischen Theorien des James Hall (1761–1832), contribution in R. Graefe: Zur Geschichte des Konstruierens, Wiesbaden, 1997.

[2] J. Harada: The Lesson of Japanese Architecture, The Studio, London 1936, p. 21.

Mit ihren mächtigen Dachkonstruktionen betonen die Bauten von Simón Vélez in besonderem Maße die Funktion der Stütze. Vélez setzt dafür nicht nur einzelne Stäbe ein, sondern entwickelte für die großen Dimensionen seiner Bauten ein Stützsystem aus mehreren, zu einem Bündel miteinander verbundenen Stäben. Dabei werden die Stäbe parallel aneinander befestigt, von denen aber nur ein oder zwei auf einem Betonfundament ruhen. Die restlichen Stäbe geben die an ihrem oberen Ende aufgenommenen Kräfte an den Mittelstab weiter und stabilisieren ihn gleichzeitig gegen seitliches Wegbrechen. Oftmals erhöht eine leichte Neigung der Stützen nach innen die Stabilität.
Das Stützsystem von Simón Vélez erinnert an die vertikal gerippten, entmaterialisiert wirkenden Pfeiler der gotischen Kathedralen. Dieser Zusammenhang könnte durchaus funktional begründet sein, denn Theorien wie etwa die des Engländers James Hall von 1797 leiten sowohl Säulenrippen als auch Gewölbe gotischer Bauwerke daraus her, daß zuvor gebündelte und gebogenen Weidenzweige für vergleichbare Zwecke verwendet wurden.[1]
Ebenso wie Simón Vélez nutzt auch der japanische Architekt Shigeru Ban die Stabilität und Leichtigkeit von runden Hohlraumkörpern, allerdings bei einem anderen Material, das ebenso zukunftsweisend wie Bambus sein könnte: Kartonröhren.
Bambus eignet sich hervorragend als Stütze, weil er durch die Trennwände der einzelnen Segmente auf natürliche Weise versteift wird. Da Bambus anfällig gegen Bodenfeuchtigkeit und Insekten ist, werden Bambusstützen oft mit Füßen aus Gestein oder Beton vor direktem Bodenkontakt geschützt.
In der japanischen Architektur besteht etwa die naturbelassene, meist sorgfältig inszenierte Stütze oft aus Bambus, die den zeremoniellen Tokanoma-Bereich markiert. Diese Stütze setzt innenarchitektonische Akzente und soll innerhalb der strengen japanischen Architektur den Respekt vor der organische Bauweise der Natur symbolisieren.[2] Bei anderen japanische Gebäuden wird das Tragwerk des Dachs über einen Keil mit einer Bambusstütze verbunden, der in den aufgespaltenen Stab eingelassen wurde – auch hier wird die Funktion der Stütze anschaulich hervorgehoben.

With their massive roof structures, Simón Vélez's creations particularly emphasize the function of supports. The sheer size of his buildings require special supports so, in addition to using individual canes, Vélez also developed a load-bearing structure made up of several canes joined together to form a bundle. The canes are fastened to one another lengthwise, but only one of them rests on a concrete base. The remaining canes transfer the forces absorbed at their upper ends to the central support while likewise stabilizing it, preventing it from sideways breakage. Often the stability is enhanced by opting for supports that slope slightly inwards.
Simón Vélez's load-bearing system is reminiscent of the vertically ribbed, seemingly weightless pillars gracing Gothic cathedrals. Quite possibly there is a practical reason for this connection. Indeed, theories such as that of Englishman James Hall of 1797 suggest that ribbed pillars and the vaults of Gothic buildings derived from the earlier form of bundles of bent willow branches which were used for a similar purpose.[1]
Like Simón Vélez, Japanese architect Shigeru Ban also makes use of the sturdiness and lightness of round, hollow bodies – albeit with a different material, and one which could prove to be just as pioneering as bamboo. He prefers to coat cardboard tubes with Teflon to enhance their resistance to wear and tear.
Bamboo makes for an excellent support, since it has an inherent stiffness owing to the natural subdivision into individual segments. As bamboo is susceptible to ground moisture and insects, bamboo supports are often fitted with feet of stone or concrete to protect them from direct contact with the ground.
In Japanese architecture, bamboo is often used as the material for the untreated, usually carefully set support which marks the ceremonial tokonoma area. Within the framework of Japan's strict architectural code, it symbolizes respect for the organic structure of nature whilst also functioning as part of the interior design.[2] In other Japanese buildings, the roof-bearing structure is connected to a bamboo support via a wedge inserted into the split support – here, too, the function of the support is visually emphasized.

Der für besondere Anlässe genutzte Tokanoma-Raum mit Bambusstütze in einem traditionellen japanischen Wohnhaus
The tokanoma room in a traditional residence. Built with bamboo supports, it was used for special occasions

ambusstützen am Katsura-Kaiserpalast in Kyoto (Japan), 1615-24
amboo supports at the Katsura Imperial Palace in Kyoto (Japan), 1615–24

Shugaku-Villa in Kyoto (Japan)

King's College Chapel, Cambridge (England), 1446–1515

Prototyp des ZERI-Pavillons in Manizales (Kolumbien), Simón Vélez, 1999
Prototype of the ZERI pavilion in Manizales (Colombia), Simón Vélez, 1999

Haus in Arbelaez , Simón Vélez, 1998. Detailansicht
House in Arbelaez, Simón Vélez, 1998. Detailed view

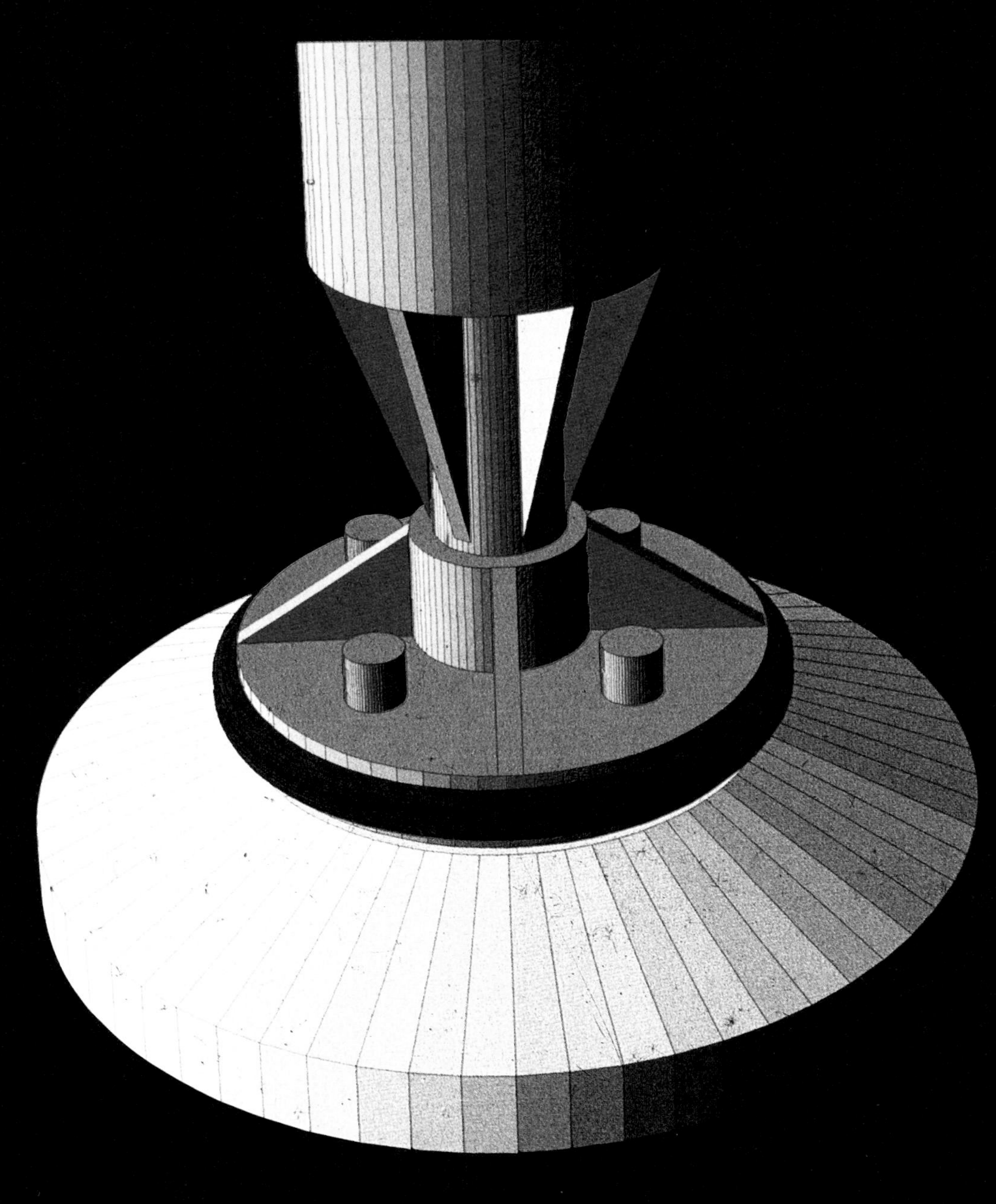

Sockel für das Tragwerk des Betriebsgebäudes der British Rail, Waterloo (England), Nicholas Grimshaw, 1990. Computeranimation
Base for the support structure of the British Rail operations building, Waterloo (England), Nicholas Grimshaw, 1990. Computer animation

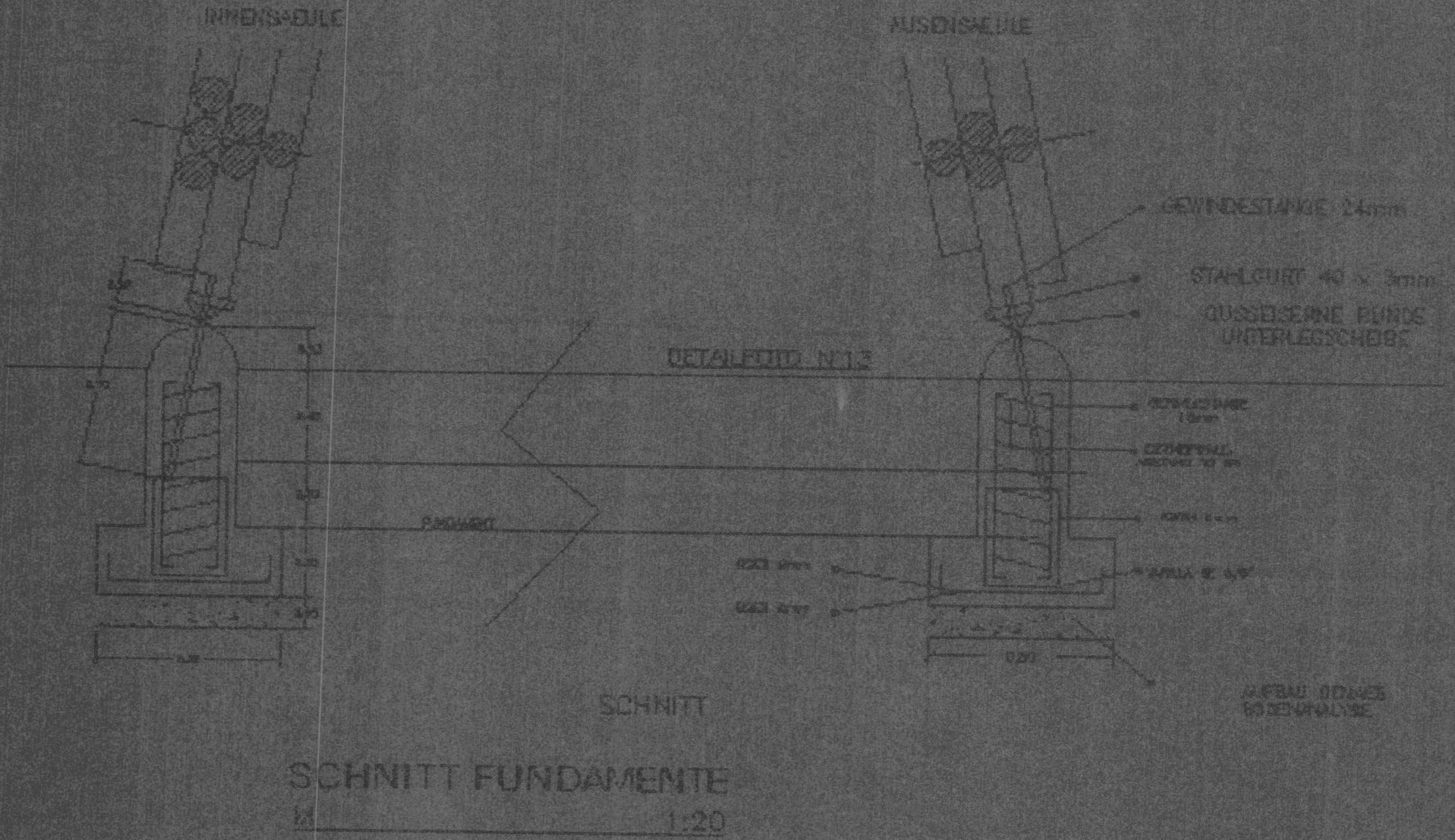

INNENSAEULE

AUSENSAEULE

GEWINDESTANGE 24mm

STAHLGURT 40 x 3mm

GUSSEISERNE RUNDE UNTERLEGSCHEIBE

DETAILFOTO N°1.3

SCHNITT

AUFBAU GEMÄSS BODENANALYSE

SCHNITT FUNDAMENTE

M 1:20

Tragwerkssockel für den Zeri-Pavillon, Simón Vélez, 2000. Hier verwendete Simón Vélez zum ersten Mal Aliso-Holz
Supporting base for the ZERI pavilion, Simón Vélez, 2000. In this case, Simón Vélez used aliso wood for the first time

Hamburger Flughafen, Von Gerkan, 1993
Hamburg Airport, Von Gerkan, 1993

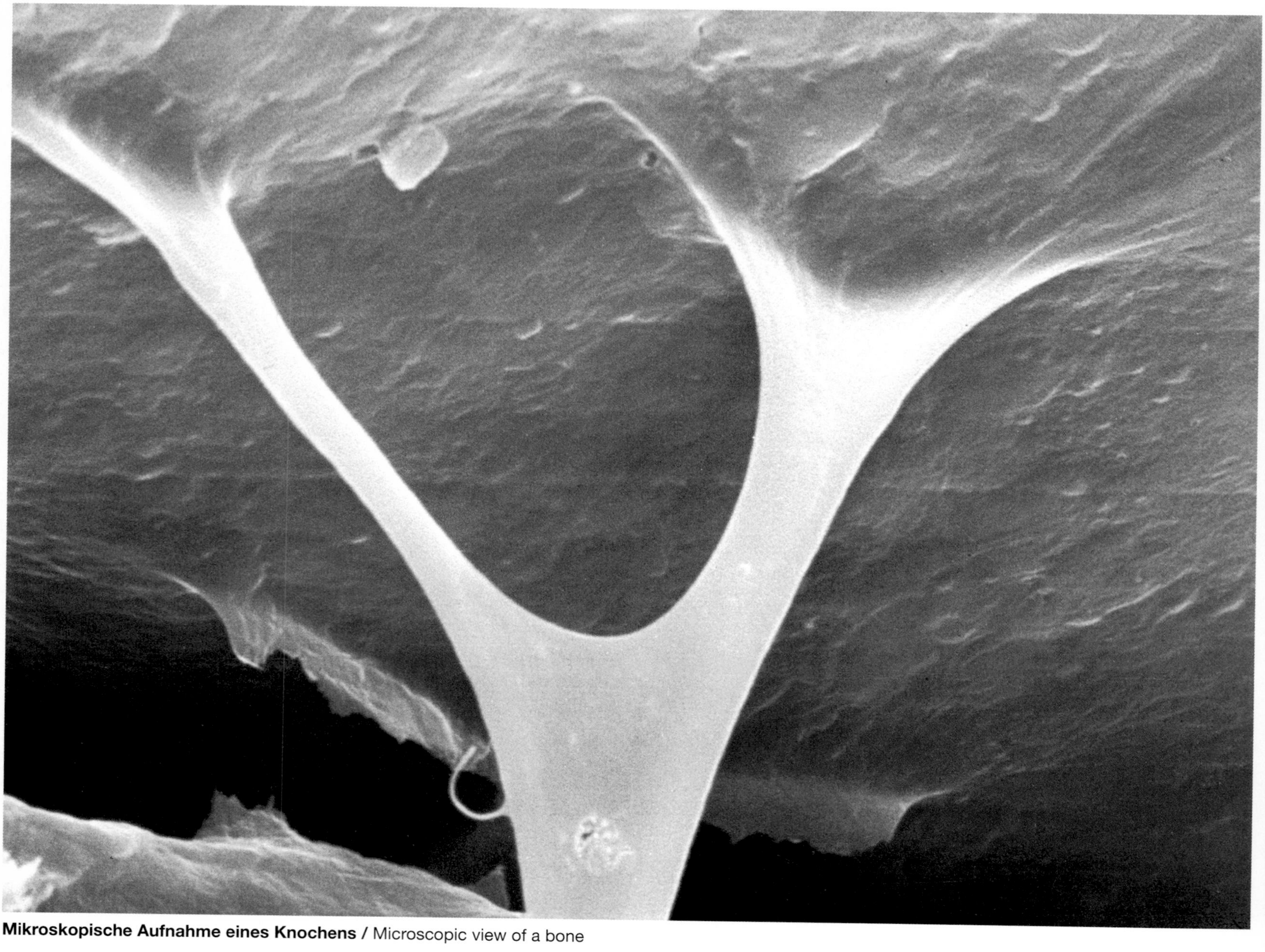

Mikroskopische Aufnahme eines Knochens / Microscopic view of a bone

Prototyp des Expo-Pavillons in Manizales (Kolumbien), Simón Vélez, 1999
Prototype of the Expo pavilion in Manizales (Colombia), Simón Vélez, 1999

Die gebogenen Träger aus Bambuswurzeln am Prototypen für den Expo-Pavillon in Manizales (Kolumbien), Simón Vélez, 1999
The curved supports made of bamboo roots in the Expo pavilion prototype in Manizales (Colombia), Simón Vélez, 1999

die wand / the wall

Es gibt zahlreiche Arten, Bambus für Häuserwände zu verwenden. Die einfachsten Prinzipien sind die Blockwand oder Palisadenwand aus vertikal angeordneten, ganzen Stäben. Ein anderes wichtiges Bauelement für Wandkonstruktionen sind zu Leisten aufgespaltene Bambusstäbe. Diese können vertikal oder horizontal angeordnet bzw. geflochten, teilweise auch als ganze Wandelemente vorgefertigt werden. Ein weiteres Prinzip ist schließlich das Ausfüllen von Wandstrukturen aus Bambus mit Blättern oder Fasern, bei dem teilweise kunstvolle Muster entstehen.
Skelettkonstruktionen aus Bambus können auch mit Lehm ausgefacht oder Wände aus Bambusmatten einfach verputzt werden – Verfahren, die bei vielen Projekten für den sozialen Wohnungsbau in Lateinamerika angewandt werden. Simón Vélez entwickelte daraus für seinen Eigenbedarf eine innovative Materialkombination: er facht Skelettkonstruktionen mit Beton aus.
Auch für Zäune und andere freistehende Wände wird Bambus vielfach verwendet. Palisadenzäune, Zäune aus Flechtmatten mit oder ohne eingeflochtene Blätter oder Zweige sowie kunstvolle Verbindungen zeugen davon.

There are numerous ways in which bamboo can be used for outside walls. The simplest technique is to create a block or palisade wall of vertically arranged, whole canes. Alternatively, bamboo canes split into strips form an important building element for wall structures. The latter can be either arranged vertically or horizontally, interwoven, and in some instances produced as complete prefabricated wall elements. An additional method is to fill bamboo wall structures with leaves or fibers which can result in ornate patterns.
Moreover, skeletal constructions made of bamboo can be filled with clay, or walls of bamboo matting can be simply plastered – both processes are readily encountered in low-cost housing projects in Latin America. Simón Vélez has developed an innovative combination of materials for his own purposes: he fills skeletal structures with concrete.
Bamboo is likewise often the material of choice for fences and self-supporting walls, as is manifested by palisade fences, fences of woven matting, with or without woven leaves or branches, as well as ornate joints.

Umzäunung des Katsura-Kaiserpalasts in Kyoto (Japan), 1615-24
Fence surrounding Katsura Imperial Palace in Kyoto (Japan), 1615–24

Fassade des finnischen Pavillons für die Weltausstellung in Paris (Frankreich), Alvar Aalto, 1939
Facade of the Finnish Pavilion for the World Fair in Paris (France), Alvar Aalto, 1939

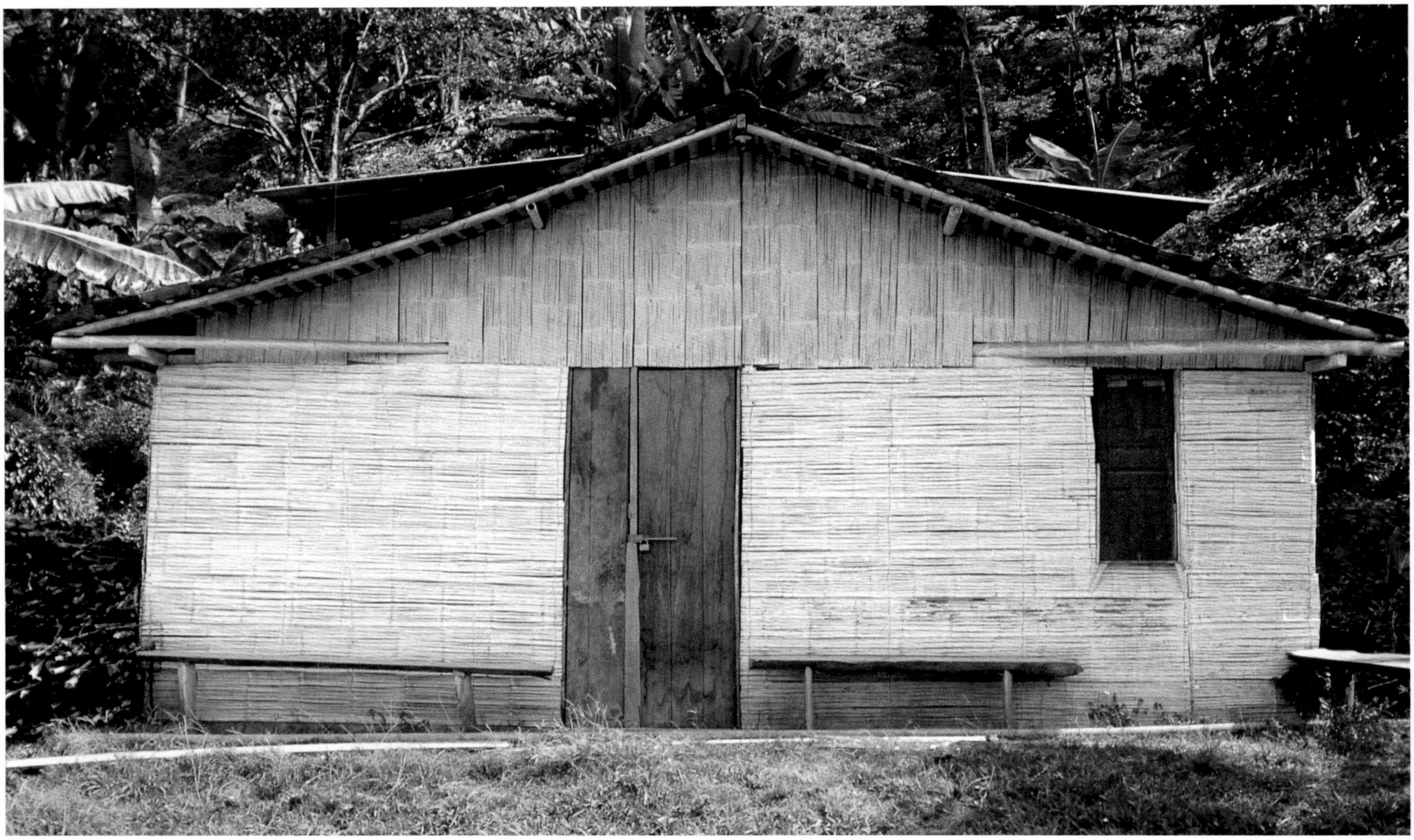

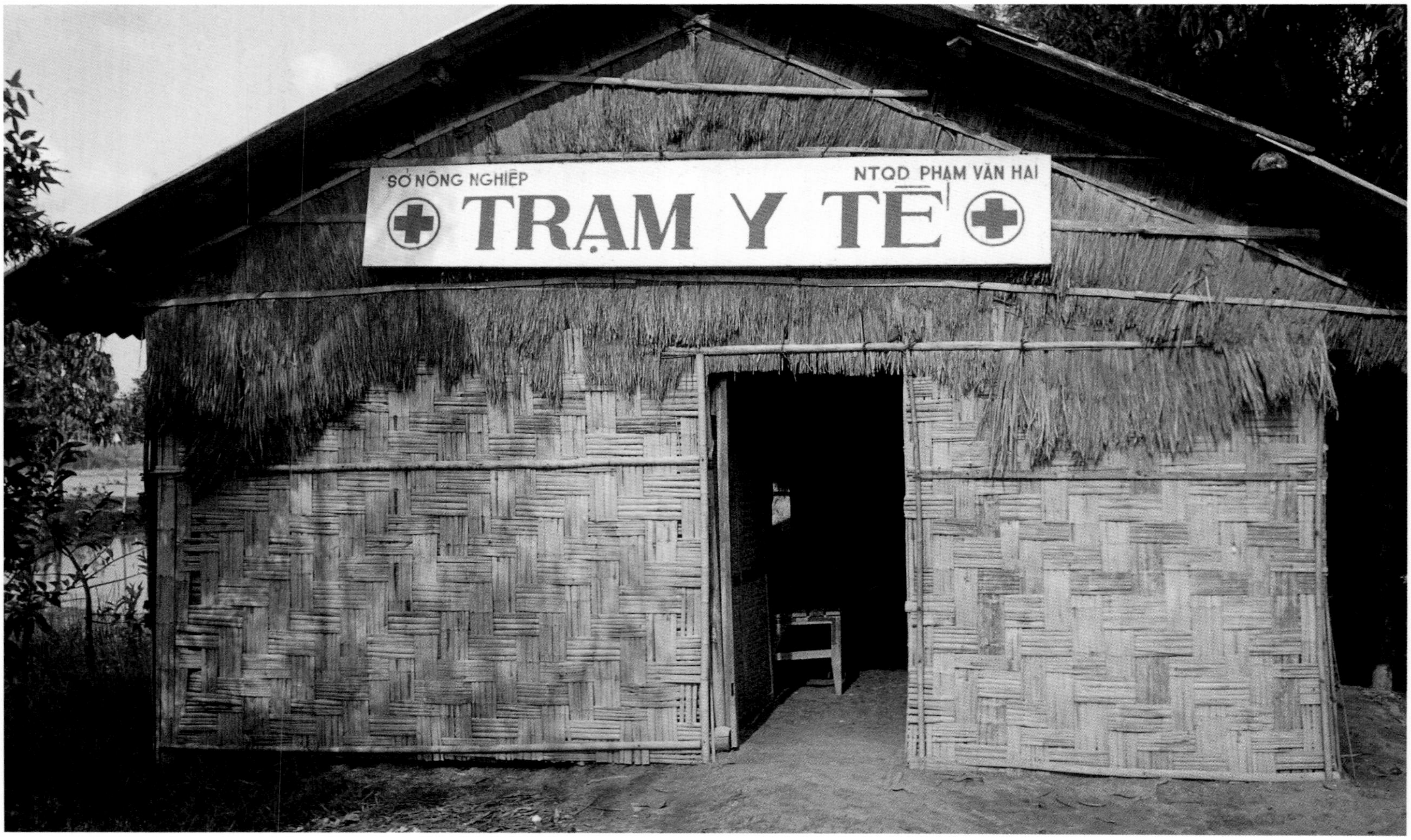
SỞ NÔNG NGHIỆP
NTQD PHẠM VĂN HAI
TRẠM Y TẾ

Jurte der Turkmenen mit Bambusverkleidung, um 1970
Turkmenian yurt with bamboo panelling, 1970

工棚防火
安全第一
卫生

Galerie MDS, Shigeru Ban, Tokyo, 1994 / MDS Gallery, Shigeru Ban, Tokyo, 1994

Hütten aus gespaltenem Bambus in Äthiopien / Huts made of split bamboo in Ethiopia

das fenster, die tür / the window, the door

Moderne Gebäude aus Bambus wie die von Simón Vélez sind meist mit modernen, standardisierten Fenstern ausgestattet. In vielen tropischen Ländern hingegen, in denen die Architektur nicht in erster Linie vor Kälte schützen muß, bestehen die Fenster traditioneller Bambusbauten aus einfachen Öffnungen, die der Belüftung und dem Lichteinfall dienen.

Oft ist der Unterschied zwischen Wand und Fenster kaum betont, etwa bei ornamentalen Rastern in japanische Häusern oder halbkreisförmig angeordneten Bambusstäben, die lediglich einen Sicht- und Einbruchschutz darstellen. Zwischen den weniger dicht angeordneten Stäben in der Fensterzone entsteht ein kunstvolles Spiel aus Licht und Schatten. Schließlich existieren auch Schiebe- und Kippfenster aus Bambus, die an einem bzw. zwei Stäben aufgehängt sind.

Modern bamboo buildings of the kind constructed by Simón Vélez are generally fitted with modern, standardized windows. However, in many tropical countries, where the main function of architecture is not to provide protection from the cold, the windows in traditional bamboo buildings are simple apertures which enhance ventilation and the presence of natural light inside.

Often the difference between wall and window is barely emphasized, as in the case of ornamental lattices in Japanese houses or bamboo canes arranged in a semicircle, which are only intended to act as a visual screen and prevent burglaries. The attractive interplay of light and shadow is produced through the less compactly arranged canes in the window area. And, finally, sliding bamboo shutters or hinged windows (suspended on one or two canes) are also to be encountered.

▲ **Bambushaus auf den Phillipinen, 1976**
Bamboo house in the Philippines, 1976

▼ **Bambusfenster in einem Haus in Hokkaido (Japan)**
Bamboo window in a house in Hokkaido (Japan)

Der Prototyp für den Zeri-Pavillon in Manizales (Kolumbien), Simón Vélez, 1999
Prototype for the ZERI pavilion in Manizales (Colombia), Simón Vélez, 1999

Kansai International Airport in Osaka (Japan), Renzo Piano, 1990–94

die verbindung / the connection

Bambusverbindung aus Metall des japanischen Architekten Shoei Yoh
Bamboo connection in metal by japanese architect Shoei Yoh

[1] aus: Einfaches Bauen mit Bambus, Wohnhäuser im Goldenen Dreieck, in: Detail, 1/1993.

[1] From: Einfaches Bauen mit bamboo, Wohnhäuser im Goldenen Dreieck, in: Detail, 1/1993.

Aufgrund der Hohlkörperstruktur von Bambus müssen Verbindungen bei Konstruktionen aus diesem Material grundlegend anders gelöst werden als bei Holz. Nägel und Schrauben kommen aufgrund der Spittergefahr nicht in Frage, außerdem müssen die immer unterschiedlichen Durchmesser der Bambusstäbe berücksichtigt werden. In den sorgfältig gewählten und ausgeführten Verbindungen jedoch kommen die Vorteile von Bambus gegenüber Holz erst richtig zum Tragen.
Es existiert eine unüberschaubare Vielfalt von Verbindungen für Bambusstäbe, von denen viele neben der konstruktiven Funktion einen eigenen ästhetischen Wert haben. Ihre Bandbreite reicht von einfachen Steck-, Binde- und Klebetechniken über kombinierte Lösungen bis hin zu den komplexen Verbindungen in den Bauten von Simón Vélez, bei denen die verbundenen Enden der Bambusstäbe oft mit Beton ausgefüllt sind. Zu den Grundformen der Verbindungen zählen die Parallelverbindungen, die orthogonalen Verbindungen und die Winkelverbindungen, die oft in komplexer Weise verbunden werden, wobei sich 8 bis 10 Stäbe in einem gemeinsamen Punkt treffen können.
Verbindungen wurden, wie der deutsche Name sagt, ursprünglich gebunden, so daß sie bei Bedarf gelöst oder nachgezogen werden konnten. Für Bindetechniken werden bei traditionellen Bambusbauten Seile und Stricke aus Bambusrinde, aus Bast-, Kokos- und Sagopalmenfasern verwendet, heute kommen natürlich auch synthetische Materialien und Draht zum Einsatz. Ein Beispiel für den nomadischen Ursprung der Bindetechniken findet sich z. B. bei den Bewohnern des Goldenen Dreiecks, das Teile Südwest-Chinas, Burmas und Nordthailands umfaßt. Sie bleiben nur so lange an einem Wohnort, wie die in intensiver Monokultur bewirtschafteten Felder genügend Ertrag bringen. Alle 10-15 Jahre ziehen sie weiter und suchen einen neuen Siedlungsort, wobei sie das Skelett ihres Hauses aus Bambus demontieren und am neuen Standort wiederaufbauen.[1]
Für Steckverbindungen ist Bambus aufgrund seiner Hohlkörperstruktur besonders geeignet. Oft sollen stabilisierende Zapfen oder Seilbünde die Steckverbindungen zusätzlich stabilisieren. In Deutschland wurde ein System von Aufsätzen für Bambusstäbe entwickelt, das standardisierte Verbindungen von Bambusstäben ermöglicht. Das LOTDP (Laboratory of Training and

Given that bamboo is hollow, connections in edifices made of this material call for a totally different approach than is customary with building in wood. Nails and screws are out of the question because of the innate danger of splintering; moreover, it is necessary to allow for the fact that bamboo canes are always of varying diameters. In this context it must be said that the carefully selected connections deployed testify fully to the advantages of bamboo over wood.
A whole host of methods exists for connecting bamboo canes. Many of them, in addition to their practical function, also have an intrinsic aesthetic value. The spectrum ranges from simple bolt/pin, lashing, and adhesive techniques via combined solutions through to the complex methods employed in Simón Vélez's buildings – there, the lashed ends of the bamboo canes are often filled with concrete. Parallel connections, orthogonal connections, and angle joints are amongst the most commonly used shapes. The latter are often bound in a complex manner so that between eight and ten canes converge at one single point.
Originally connections were bound so that if necessary they could later be loosened or tightened. In traditional bamboo buildings, ropes and cords of bamboo rind, of raffia, coconut, and sago palm fibers are employed. Needless to say, today synthetic materials and wire ties are also used. The original binding techniques stem from nomadic cultures such as the inhabitants of the Golden Triangle (which incorporates parts of SW China, Burma and North Thailand). The inhabitants of that region remain in one place only as long as the fields, worked using intensive monoculture, provide sufficient food. Every 10 to 15 years the people move on and search for a new settlement area. On leaving, they simply dismantle the frameworks of their bamboo houses, then re-erect them at the new location chosen.[1] Thanks to its hollow interior, bamboo is especially suited to pin-and-socket connection. Often stabilizing pegs or rope ties make for greater sturdiness. In Germany, a system of tops for bamboo canes has been developed, allowing standardized linkage. The LOTDP (Laboratory of Training and Development of Prototypes) in Rio de Janeiro has developed a technique for connecting bamboo canes in constructions entailing heavy load-bearing: a cap on the end of the cane (which can be tightened as required) absorbs the pressure and passes it on down through the cane. Iron bands or connecting elements of other materials such as wood or

Development of Prototypes) in Rio de Janeiro hat ein Verbindungssystem für Bambusstäbe in druckbelasteten Konstruktionen entwickelt, bei dem eine Kappe auf dem Stabende den Druck an diesen weitergibt und verspannt werden kann. Auch Eisenbinder oder Verbindungselemente aus anderen Materialien wie Holz oder Preßspan werden bei Verbindungen von Bambusstäben verwendet, ebenso wie Klebetechniken.

Simón Vélez hat aus den traditionellen Verfahren eine Technik entwickelt, die an Verbindungen in Gebäuden der High-Tech-Architektur erinnert. Da Bambus eine enorm hohe Zugfestigkeit besitzt, entwickelte Vélez ein System insbesondere für zugbelastete Konstruktionen. Er füllt die Endkammern der zu verbindenden Bambusstäbe mit Beton aus und läßt darin Metallelemente parallel zur Stabrichtung ein, über die die Teile verbunden werden. Ein Großteil der auftretenden Kräfte wird so auf die stabilen Zwischenwände der Stäbe übertragen und das Splittern, wie es bei hohlen Stäben möglich ist, wird verhindert. Diese Verbindungen können zudem auseinandergenommen oder nachgezogen werden.

Auch der italienische Architekt Renzo Piano schätzt die Eigenschaften von Bambus und hat mit Strukturen aus Bambusstäben experimentiert. Seine Ansätze für komplexe Verbindungen von Bambusstäben bestehen aus Leichtmetallteilen wie Rohren oder Platten, die teilweise in die Bambusstäbe eingelassen, teilweise mit ihnen verbunden sind. So entsteht die Möglichkeit von Schnittstellen, über die Bambus auf innovative Weise in Leichtmetallkonstruktionen integriert werden kann.

pressboard are also used to join bamboo canes, as are adhesive methods.

Inspired by traditional usages, Simón Vélez has developed a technique bringing to mind the joints in high-tech buildings. Since bamboo has an enormous tensile strength, Vélez developed a system especially for constructions subject to tensile vectors. First, the end sections of the bamboo canes to be bound are filled with concrete; into the concrete he inserts metal elements parallel to the run of the cane. The parts can then be connected using the metal links. Consequently, a high proportion of the force to which the cane is subject at the end is transferred to the sturdy dividing walls of the canes, and the splintering which normally occurs in hollow canes is avoided. What is more, such connections can be dismantled and/or adjusted.

Italian architect Renzo Piano also appreciates the qualities of bamboo and has experimented with bamboo cane edifices. The methods he has devised for connecting bamboo canes involve light metal components such as tubes or plates, which are sometimes inserted into the canes, sometimes connected to them. In this manner, bamboo can be integrated into light metal constructions in an innovative way.

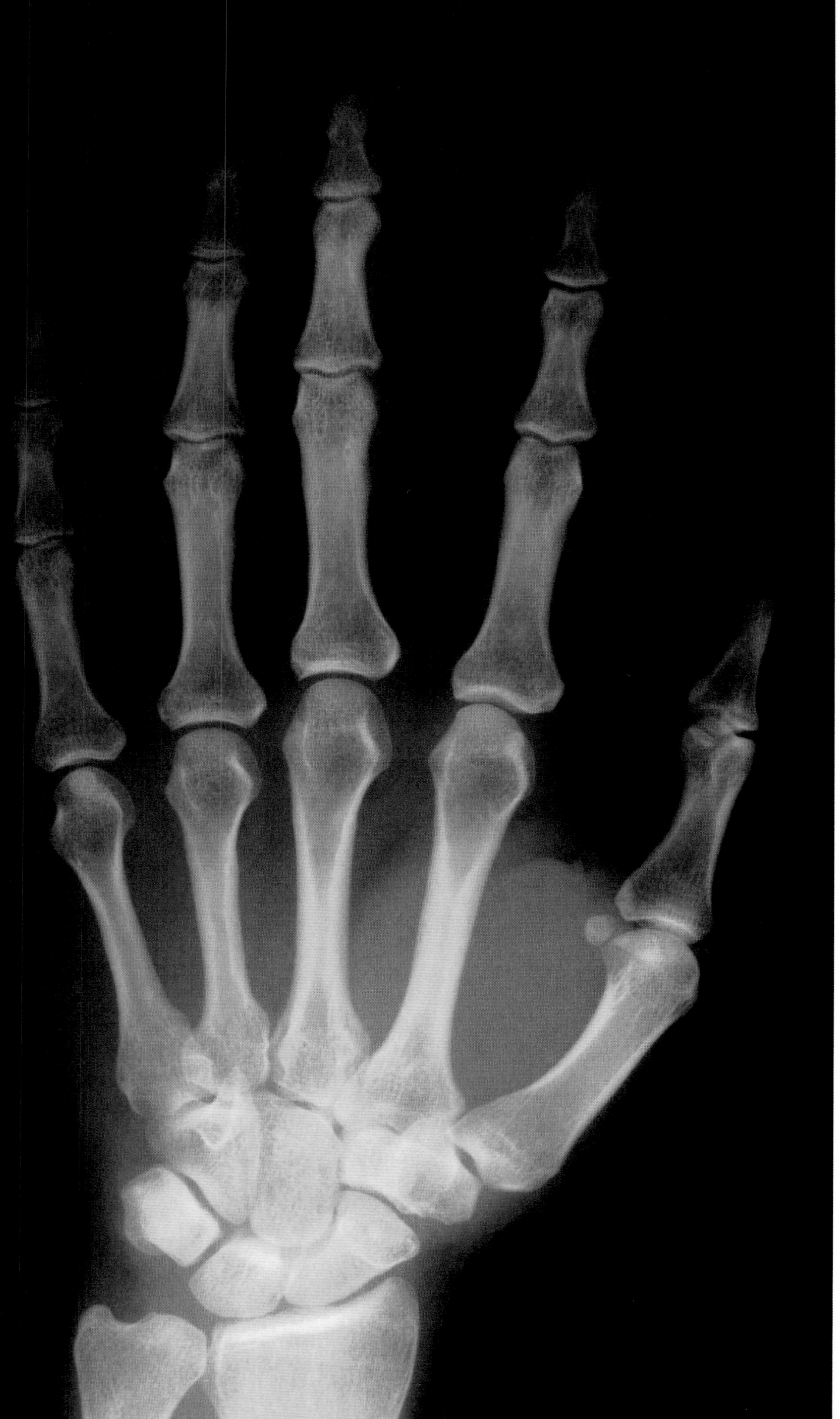

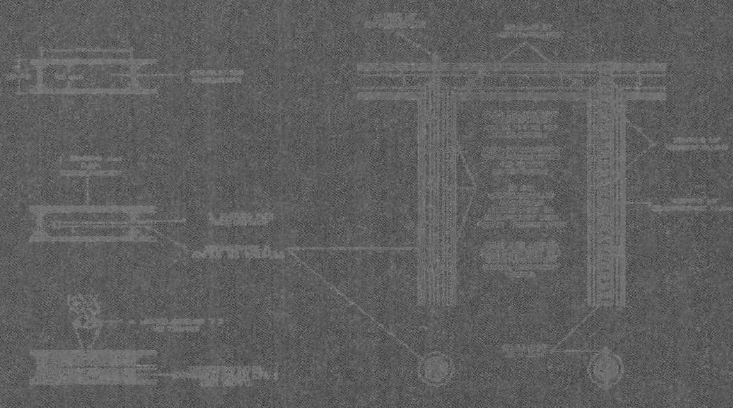

Bei den von Simón Vélez entwickelten Verbindungen für Bambusstäbe werden die Enden der Stäbe mit Beton ausgefüllt und mit Metallelementen verbunden.
In the system of bamboo joints developed by Simón Vélez, the end of the canes are filled with concrete and joined with elements made of metal.

Experimente mit Bambusverbindungen, Renzo Piano, 1997
Experiments with methods for connecting bamboo canes, Renzo Piano, 1997

RENZO
PADRE PIO PROTEGGIMI
1:1
1:5
1:10
1:20
1:50
1:100
1:200
1:500
1:1000
1:2000
1:5000

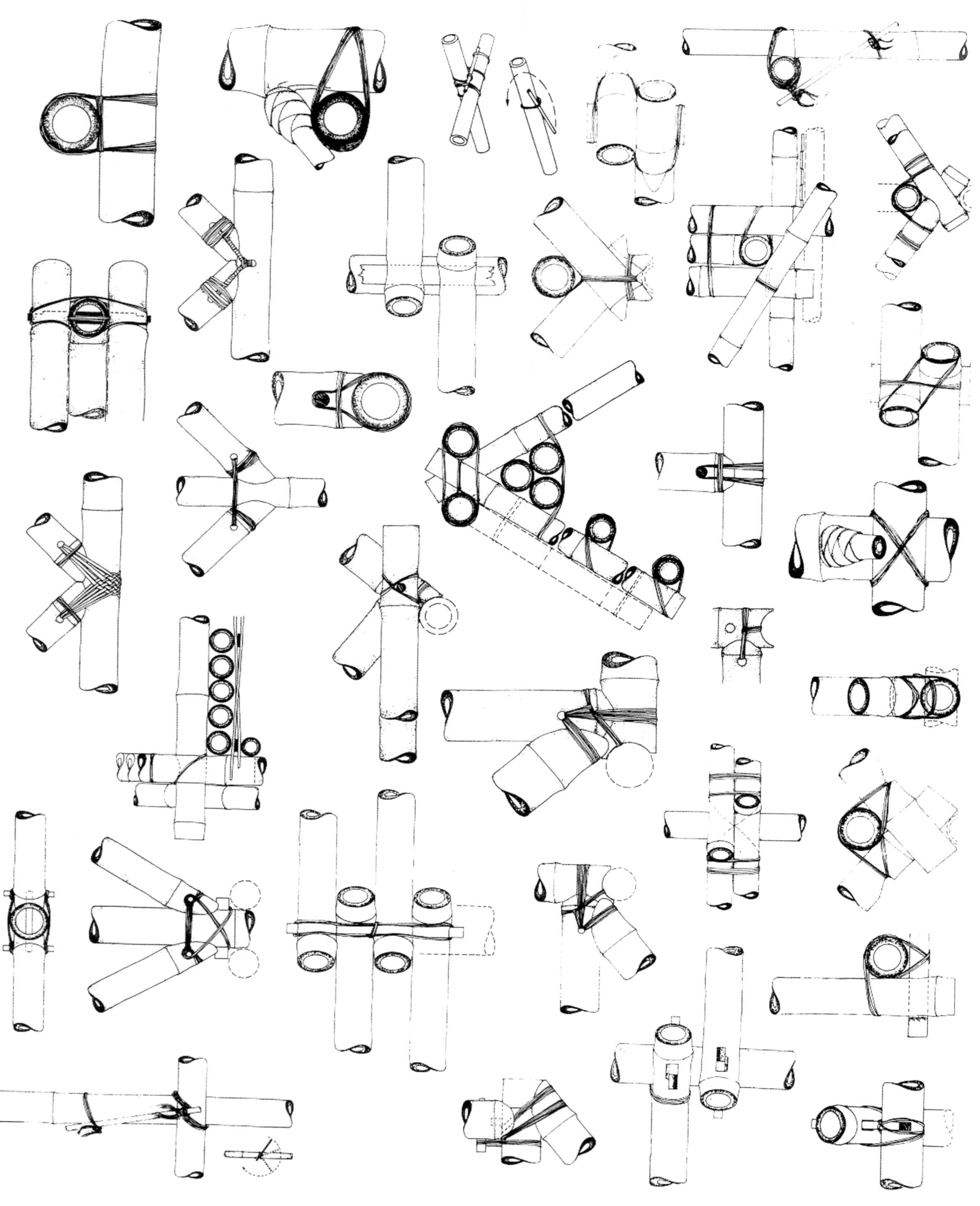

Verbindungen und Säulenquerschnitte des ZERI-Pavillons, Simón Vélez, 2000.
Connections and column sections of the ZERI pavilion, Simón Vélez, 2000.

Auf Malekula (Neue Hebriden) / On Malekula (New Hebrides)

Japanische Eisfischer bauen einen Windschutz auf dem Hachinohe-See
Japanese ice fishermen build a wind-protection wall on Hachinohe Lake

der boden / the floor

Installation «With the wind» für das Naoshima Art Museum, Hiroshi Teshigahara, 1993
Installation «With the wind» for the Naoshima Art Museum, Hiroshi Teshigahara, 1993

Zum Schutz gegen Bodenfeuchtigkeit und Ungeziefer, aber auch weil der Boden im Glauben vieler Völker die Behausung negativer Kräfte ist, werden Bodenkonstruktionen aus Bambus oft aufgeständert.
Der einfachste Boden aus Bambus besteht aus ganzen Bambusstäben, die parallel angeordnet und teilweise durch dekorative Seilbindungen zusammengehalten werden. Auch Leisten aus Bambus oder Bambusmatten werden verwendet. Eine neue Anwendung ist das Bambusparkett, dessen Festigkeit diejenige von marktüblichem Holzparkett übertreffen kann.
Der japanische Künstler Hiroshi Teshigahara hat aus Bambusleisten, die auf dem Boden angeordnet sind, kunstvolle Bühnenbilder und Landschaftsskulpturen geschaffen. Mit den wechselnden Laufrichtungen der Leisten und dem Changieren der leicht gerundeten, samtenen Oberflächen im Sonnenlicht entstehen visuelle Effekte, die an Kunstwerke der Op-Art erinnern – allerdings ins Monumentale gesteigert.

As protection against rising damp and insects (and also in keeping with the common belief that the ground houses negative forces), bamboo floor constructions are often raised on stilts.
The simplest bamboo floors consist of whole bamboo canes which are arranged parallel to one another and are sometimes held together with decorative cord arrangements. Strips of bamboo or bamboo mats are also used. A relatively new idea is bamboo parquet which is sometimes more durable than the normal wooden parquet.
Japanese artist Hiroshi Teshigahara uses bamboo strips arranged on the floor to create ornate stage sets and landscape sculptures. The alternating direction of the strips and the shimmering of the gently rounded, velvety surfaces in the sunlight give rise to visual effects reminiscent of Op Art works – albeit on a monumental scale.

Shogetsutei-Teehaus am Daigoji-Tempel in Kyoto (Japan)
Shogetsutei – traditional tea-house at Daigoji Temple in Kyoto (Japan)

Bambusbrücke in Kolumbien / Bamboo bridge in Colombia

Vorbereitung eines Verstecks aus Bambus vor einer Tigerjagd auf Sumatra (Indonesien)
Preparing a bamboo hide-out before a tiger hunt in Sumatra (Indonesia)

das dach / the roof

Umzug in Guinea
Moving house in Guinea

Dachkonstruktion des ZERI-Pavillons, Simón Vélez, 1999
Roof construction of the ZERI pavilion, Simón Vélez, 1999

[1] s. Hidalgo, O.: Nuevas técnicas de construcción con bambú, Bogotá, 1978, S. 26

[1] See O. Hidalgo: Nuevas técnicas de construcción con bambú, Bogotá, 1978, p. 26.

Nicht umsonst bezeichnet sich Simón Vélez als einen «Architekten der Dächer». Bei seinen Bauten sind die mächtigen Dächer das dominierende Element – in der Kulisse der kolumbianischen Anden scheinen sie frei zu schweben und rufen El Lissitzkys «Wolkenbügel» in Erinnerung.
Wie dieses nie realisierte Projekt geben sie dem Kragprinzip Ausdruck, ein Leitmotiv in Architektur und Design der klassischen Moderne, das die Überwindung der Schwerkraft dank einer ausgereiften Ingenieurskunst propagierte.
Den eher konventionellen Typus des Giebeldachs und einen großen Erfahrungsschatz für dessen Konstruktion übernahm Vélez aus der Tradition des kolumbianischen Kaffeeanbaugebiets. Aufgrund der großen Verarbeitungslänge von Bambusstämmen der Gattung *Guadua angustifolia* erreichen manche Dachkonstruktionen in seinen Bauten Spannweiten bis zu 30 Metern. Für Leimbinderkonstruktionen mit der gleichen Leistungsfähigkeit wäre ein erheblich höherer Materialaufwand nötig. Die Dachüberstände von bis zu 9 Metern schützen das Tragwerk vor Witterungseinflüssen und spenden in der tropischen Hitze Schatten.

Möglicherweise wurde Bambus schon vor dem Tonziegel als Dachbedeckung verwendet. Darauf verweist die These, die Form des klassischen Dachziegels sei nach dem Vorbild von längsseitig halbierten Bambusstäben entstanden. Noch heute werden viele Dächer in tropischen Ländern mit Bambusschindeln gedeckt.

Darüberhinaus existiert für die Verwendung als Dacheindeckung von Bambusbauten eine große Vielfalt an weiteren Möglichkeiten – von Gras, Palmblättern bis zu Lanzettschindeln, Bambusspänen oder Fasersträhnen. Auch bei Dachkonstruktionen kommen parallel angeordnete Stäbe zum Einsatz, deren Seilbund als dekorativ-strukturierendes Element betont wird.

Auch Kuppeldächer, entweder mit rundem oder zwiebelförmigem Abschluß, werden aus Bambus gefertigt. Es wäre also gut möglich, daß Kuppeln wie die des indischen Taj Mahal in der hinduistischen Kultur auf Vorbilder aus gebogenen Bambusstäben zurückgehen.[1] Auch das chinesische Pagodendach wird auf Bambuskonstruktionen zurückgeführt, die sich unter der Last der Schindeln bogen. Noch heute werden in China Pavillons mit Tragwerken aus Bambus gebaut.

It is not for nothing that Simón Vélez calls himself an «architect of roofs». The dominating element of his buildings is always the enormous roof. Set against the backdrop of the Colombian Andes, his roofs appear to float in mid-air and call to mind El Lissitzky's «sky arch». Like this project, which was never realized, Vélez's roofs make use of cantilevering – a leitmotif in classic Modernist architecture and design, which propagated the overcoming of gravity thanks to a highly advanced engineering method.

Vélez took the inspiration for his rather conventional gable roofs and drew on a wealth of experience for their construction from the tradition of the Colombian coffee- growing area. Given the length of processed bamboo trunks of the genus *Guadua angustifolia*, some roof structures in his buildings span 30 meters. Far greater material inputs would have been necessary for glue-bound constructions with comparable properties. Roof projects up to nine meters protect the support structure from the influences of the weather and provide shade from the tropical heat.

It is possible that bamboo preceded clay tiles as a material for roof coverings. There is a theory that the form of the classic roofing tile is based on bamboo canes halved lengthwise. And indeed, today many roofs in tropical countries are covered with bamboo shingles.

In addition, there exists a great diversity of alternative roof coverings for bamboo buildings – from grass, palm leaves to lancet shingles, bamboo shavings, or strips of fiber. Bamboo canes arranged parallel to one another are also used in roof constructions, whereby the cord binding them is emphasized as a decorative, structural element.

Domed roofs, either with a round top or Moorish domes, are also made of bamboo. As such, it is quite possible that in Hindu culture domes such as those in the Taj Mahal in India derive from constructions made of bent bamboo canes.[1] The Chinese pagoda roof can likewise be traced back to bamboo structures, which gave way under the weight of shingles. Pavilions in China continue to be made with support structures of bamboo.

Finally, experiments have been conducted on the use of bamboo for roof constructions comprising grid shell structures and geodesic domes. In this

Schließlich werden mit Bambus auch Dachkonstruktionen aus Gitterschalen und geodätischen Kuppeln erprobt. So führten Yona Friedman und Eda Schaur in den siebziger Jahren auf den Philipinen das Projekt «Roofs for People» durch, bei dem auf der Basis von Bambus Dachkonstruktionen entwickelt werden sollten, die Schutz gegen Nässe, Wind und Hitze bieten und gleichzeitig ästhetisch interessant waren. Es wurde ein Prototyp für das «Museums für einfache Technologie» erprobt, dessen Prinzip in weitere Projekten in Indien aufgenommen wurde.
Wie die Bauten von Simón Vélez zeigen, ist das Dach auch von großer Bedeutung für den Bau von Balkonen. In tropischen Ländern mit hohen Niederschlägen werden Balkone durch große Dachüberhänge geschützt. Balkone gelten hier als Statussymbol der Mittelklasse, denn sie zeugen bereits von einem komfortorientierten Lebensstil.

context, during the 1970s Yona Friedman and Eda Schaur ran a project in the Philippines entitled «Roofs for People» in which roof constructions based on bamboo were to be developed offering protection against the wet, wind, and heat – and were simultaneously aesthetically appealing.
As the buildings of Simón Vélez demonstrate, the roof is also of great importance for the construction of balconies. In tropical countries, the balconies need protecting by deep roof overhangs. Here, balconies are regarded as a sign of a middle-class lifestyle, since they are not required for sheer necessity.

Dachkonstruktion des Wohnhauses für C.I.R.E.C.A. in Boisbuchet (Frankreich), Simón Vélez, 1999
Roof construction of house for C.I.R.E.C.A. in Boisbuchet (France), Simón Vélez, 1999

Bambusdächer in Fukuoka (Japan), Shoei Yoh, 1989
Bamboo roofs in Fukuoka (Japan), Shoei Yoh, 1989

▶ **Dach des Katsura-Kaiserpalasts in Kyoto (Japan), 1615-24**
Roof of Katsura Imperial Palace in Kyoto Japan), 1615–24

▲ **Bambus-Pavillon in China**
Bamboo pavilion in China

▶ **Provisorische Unterkunft aus Bambusmatten nach einem Unwetter in Pakistan**
Makeshift accommodation from bamboo mats after a storm in Pakistan

▼ **Ahnenhaus (Tongkonan) in Lemo/Tana Tora (Indonesien)**
Ancestral house (Tongkonan) in Lemo/ Tana Tora (Indonesia)

▲ **Haus Luis Salazar in Manizales (Kolumbien), Simón Vélez, 1984-87**
Luis Salazar house in Manizales (Colombia), Simón Vélez, 1984–7

▶ **Dach eines Koshikake-Hauses in Japan**
Koshikake house roof in Japan

▼ **Reisspeicher in Sade, Süd-Lombok (Indonesien)**
Rice storehouse in Sade, southern Lombok (Indonesia)

Haus Luis Salazar in Manizales (Kolumbien) während des Baus, Simón Vélez, 1984-87
Luis Salazar house in Manizales (Colombia) during construction, Simón Vélez, 1984–7

▲ **Skelett einer Bambushütte am Malawisee, Tansania**
Skeleton of bamboo hut at Lake Malawi, Tanzania

▲▼ **Bambusskelett eines Hauses der Yawalapiti noch ohne Grasbedeckung, Brasilien**
Bamboo skeleton of a Yawalapiti house before it is covered with grass, Brazil

meta-architektur / meta-architecture

Bambus wird auch für große offene und exponierte Konstruktionen benutzt – etwa für Baugerüste, Wellenbrecher, Leitungssysteme, Brücken oder als Überdachung öffentlicher Räume. Manche Völker bauen aus Bambus zeremonielle Strukturen, die einen geheiligten Raum markieren und als Versammlungsort dienen. Ein Beispiel dafür ist das Dawi, ein Zeremonienhaus für Männer in Neu-Guinea, das bis zu 80 Fuß hoch wird. Überdachte Märkte, wie etwa die Souks in arabischen Ländern, werden oft mit Bambusmatten oder einfachen Bambusstäben überdacht.

Spektakulär sind die Baugerüste aus Bambus, wie sie seit jeher in asiatischen Ländern benutzt werden. In boomenden Metropolen wie Hong Kong oder Shanghai wachsen diese Gerüste teilweise bis zu 70 Stockwerke hoch und für Außenarbeiten an oberen Stockwerken improvisiert man scheinbar freischwebende Gerüste. Bambusmatten werden hier auch als Verkleidung für ganze Gebäude eingesetzt. Nach einem Taifun sieht man in asiatischen Großstädten oft das gleiche Bild: die Stahlgerüste sind zerstört, während die Bambusgerüste, zwar etwas verzogen, stehen geblieben sind. Kein Wunder, denn die Gerüste aus Bambus sind um ein Vielfaches elastischer als vergleichbare Strukturen aus Stahl.

Bamboo is often used for large, open, and exposed constructions – such as scaffolding, breakwaters, pipelines, bridges, or roofing over public spaces. Some peoples use bamboo to build ceremonial structures which mark a sacred area and serve as a place of gathering. One such example is the dawi, a ceremonial house for men from New Guinea which is up to 25 meters high. Covered markets such as souks in Arabic countries often feature bamboo matting or bamboo canes as a roofing material.

The bamboo scaffolding used since time immemorial in Asian countries is highly spectacular. In booming metropolises such as Hong Kong or Shanghai such constructions can be up to 70 stories high. For work on the exterior of upper storeys, scaffolding is improvised that from below seems actually to be floating. Bamboo matting is also often used as covering for entire buildings. In the aftermath of a typhoon in large Asian cities, the picture tends to be the same: the steel scaffolding is destroyed and the bamboo counterparts, while somewhat warped, are still standing. Hardly surprising, since bamboo scaffolding is much more elastic than comparable structures of steel.

Wasserleitung aus Bambus in Hong Kong, vor 1843
Bamboo water pipe in Hong Kong, before 1843

▲ **Hängebrücke in Tierradentro/Cauca (Kolumbien)**
Hanging bridge in Tierradentro, Cauca (Colombia)

▼ **Fischernetze in Kerala (Indien)**
Fishing net in Kerala (India)

▼ **Bambusstruktur eines Versammlungshauses in Maipua (Neu-Guinea)**
Bamboo structure of a meeting house in Maipua (New Guinea)

Bambusstrukturen in Holland, Anton Versteegde, 1997
Bamboo structures in Holland, Anton Versteegde, 1997

Bambusstrukturen, Anton Versteegde, 1997 / Bamboo structures, Anton Versteegde, 1997

▲ **Bambusgerüst an der Kathedrale von Manizales (Kolumbien), vor 1936**
Bamboo scaffolding on the Manizales Cathedral (Colombia), before 1936

▼ **Renovierungsarbeiten am Taj Mahal-Palast in Agra (Indien)**
Renovation work on the Taj Mahal Palace in Agra (India)

▲ **Renovierungsarbeiten am hängenden Kloster Xuangkongsi (China)**
Renovation work on the hanging monastery, Xuangkongsi (China)

Bambusmatten dienen in asiatischen Metropolen auch zur Verkleidung von Baugerüsten
Bamboo matting is also used in Asian cities to cover scaffolding

grow your own ...

... house

«on 500 m^2 of land you can harvest a house each year»

Günter Pauli

Bambus ist die am schnellsten wachsende Pflanze der Welt. Er kann um ein Drittel schneller als der «schnellste Baum» wachsen, und manche Arten erreichen ein Wachstum von über einem Meter täglich. Bereits im Alter von vier bis fünf Jahren sind die Bambusstäbe für Bauzwecke erntereif. Dank der Schnellwüchsigkeit ist der Substanzertrag (das Gewicht pro Bodenfläche und Jahr) bis zu 25 mal höher als bei Bauholz. Auf einem Hektar Anbaufläche kann ein jährlicher Ertrag von 22 bis 44 Tonnen erzielt werden. In den Tropen kann auf einer Fläche von 20 x 20 m innerhalb von 5 Jahren Bambus für zwei Häuser von 8 x 8 m wachsen. Da Bambus sich über sein Wurzelsystem (die Rhizome) vermehrt, wächst er nach der Ernte sofort nach, während ein Wald nach dem Einschlag aufwendig wieder aufgeforstet werden muß. Bambus für den Eigenbedarf kann von Dorfverbänden, ja selbst von einzelnen Familien angepflanzt werden und die Kenntnisse darüber, wie mit Bambus gebaut wird, sind in vielen Kulturen unentbehrliches Allgemeinwissen. Schließlich ist die typische asiatische oder lateinamerikanische Bambushütte prädestiniert für den Eigenbau. Sie ist als Einraum- oder mit einer Küchenzone als Zweiraumwohnung angelegt und soll als mehr oder weniger hoch aufgeständerter Bau Schutz bieten vor Wetter, vor Geistern, vor Tieren und Menschen. Ihre Einzelbestandteile sind Rohre, Rohrhälften, Latten, Stäbe, Leisten, Bretter und ihre Vorteile liegen in der Möglichkeit der Vorfertigung, im einfachen Montagebau, in der leichten Auswechselbarkeit von Einzelteilen, der leichten Demontage und der Wiederverwertbarkeit. Der Charakter dieser Hütten ist ephemer und improvisiert, aber immer geprägt von der Erfahrung ganzer Generationen. Moderne Materialien wie Bleche oder Kunststoffe werden mühelos in diese traditionellen Baukonzepte integriert.

Wo der Bewohner selbst am Bau seines Hauses beteiligt ist, entwickelt er zu diesem oft eine enge, spirituelle Beziehung. In vielen Kulturen symbolisieren die Behausungen den gesamten Kosmos und werden auch als Behausung von Geistern gesehen, die vor negativen Kräften schützen. Bambus steht hier für eine symbiotische Lebensform und eine ganzheitliche, menschennahe und nachhaltige Architektur, die sich in diesen Eigenschaften grundlegend von der anonymen und standardisierten Bauweise der modernen Architektur unterscheidet.

Bamboo is the quickest growing plant in the world. It can grow a good 30 per cent more quickly than the «fastest tree» – in fact, some varieties grow more than one meter each day. Bamboo canes are already suitable for use as a construction material after only five to eight years; in some instances after as little as three years. Thanks to its rapid growth, the yield (weight per acreage and year) is up to 25 times higher than that of timber. Bamboo planted on one hectare of ground offers an annual yield of between 22 and 44 metric tons. In the tropics, within the space of only five years it is possible to grow enough bamboo on a 20 x 20 m piece of land to build two houses measuring 8 x 8 m. Since bamboo is propagated via its root system (rhizomes), it begins growing again immediately after being harvested. By contrast, a forest, once it has been felled, requires intensive reforestation. Bamboo can be planted by village communities, indeed even by individual families growing it for their own needs. And knowing how to use bamboo for building purposes is an indispensable element of general knowledge in many cultures. Moreover, the typical Asian or Latin American bamboo hut is easily constructed. Designed as a single-room or two-room dwelling (with a kitchen area), and on higher or lower stilts, it is intended to provide protection against the weather, spirits, animals, and people. The dwelling comprises bamboo canes, halved canes, slats, beading, strips, and boards. Its advantages are that it can be prefabricated, is easily assembled and dismantled, individual elements are readily replaced, and finally it is recyclable. These huts have an ephemeral and improvized feel to them, yet their appearance testifies to the experience of entire generations. Modern materials such as metals or plastics can easily be integrated into these traditional building concepts.

When the inhabitants of a house are themselves involved in its construction, they often develop a close, spiritual relationship to it. In many cultures, dwellings symbolize the entire cosmos and are also seen as the house of the spirits who provide protection against hostile forces. In this context, bamboo stands for a symbiotic way of life and for a holistic, sustainable architecture which caters to people's needs – characteristics which clearly distinguish it from the anonymous and standardized style of modern architecture.

Bambuspflanze in China, um 1866
Bamboo plant in China, around 1866

[1] aus: Grober, U.: «Der Erfinder der Nachhaltigkeit» in: Die Zeit Nr. 48, 25.11.99

[1] From U. Grober: «Der Erfinder der Nachhaltigkeit» in: Die Zeit Nr. 48, 25 November 1999.

Der Begriff der Nachhaltigkeit wurde erstmals 1713 von dem Deutschen Carl von Carlowitz in seinem forstwissenschaftlichen Buch «Sylvicultura Oeconomica» verwendet und bezeichnet einen ökologisch und ökonomisch langfristig sinnvollen Umgang mit natürlichen Ressourcen.[1] Er wurde auf der Klimakonferenz 1992 in Rio de Janeiro in der sogenannten Agenda 21 als Leitbild für unseren zukünftigen Umgang mit der Umwelt definiert. Bambus ist ein Musterbeispiel in Sachen Nachhaltigkeit – sowohl in bezug auf die wachsende Pflanze als auch bei der Verwendung als Baumaterial.
Die Gefahr, den Boden mit dem Anbau von Monokulturen auszulaugen, ist bei Bambushainen geringer als bei Holz. Nach dem Fällen wachsen Bambusstäbe, anders als Hölzer, schnell nach, weil sie sich über ein unterirdisches Wurzelsystem vermehren. In jedem Stadium des Pflanzenwuchses gibt es für Bambus eine Verwendung. Und bei der Verarbeitung von Bambus fällt kaum Abfall oder Ausschuß an, denn das Entrinden erübrigt sich und die Blätter können verfüttert werden. Ein weiterer Vorteil von Bambus besteht darin, daß umweltschädigende Transportwege vielerorts wegfallen, weil Bambus dort «vor der Tür» wächst. Auch können Bauten aus Bambus leicht recycelt oder demontiert werden, Einzelteile lassen sich problemlos auswechseln – Qualitäten, die in der westlichen Architektur erst in jüngster Vergangenheit angestrebt werden und die mit herkömmlichen Materialien oftmals schwer zu realisieren sind.
Laut Prognosen wird der zukünftige Holzbedarf in den asiatischen Ländern das Angebot bei weitem übersteigen. Um zu verhindern, daß dies die Abholzung der Regenwälder weiter vorantreibt, soll in China ein nationales Programm entwikkelt werden, das die Verwendung von Bambus als Ersatz für Tropenhölzer fördert – ein Forschungsansatz von globaler Bedeutung.

Ein anderes Beispiel für das Substitutionspotential von Bambus kommt aus Indien: Würde dort ein Viertel des Sperrholzbedarfs durch Bambusmatten ersetzt werden, was technisch leicht möglich wäre, so würde dies 400.000 Kubikmeter Rundholz bzw. 11.000 Hektar Wald jährlich vor der Zerstörung bewahren und in den extrem armen indischen Dörfern etwa 1.200 Arbeitsplätze für die dortige Bevölkerung schaffen.

The expression «sustainability» was first used in 1713 by the German Carl von Carlowitz in his forestry book «Sylvicultura Oeconomica» and refers to the ecologically and economically meaningful long-term handling of natural resources.[1] In 1992, at the World Climate Summit in Rio de Janeiro, the term was defined in Agenda 21 as a guideline for our future treatment of the environment. Bamboo is a prime example of sustainability – with respect to both the plant itself and its use as a building material.
Soil leaching – an inevitable consequence of monocultural farming – is less a danger for bamboo groves than for timber. Bamboo often grows in mixed cultures – as can be seen, for example, in the ZERI Pavilion, which is built of materials which grow in direct proximity to bamboo in Colombia: aliso, arboloco (a type of sunflower), and chusque. Unlike timber, after felling, bamboo canes grow again quickly because they are propagated by an underground root system. At every stage of the plant's growth there is a use for bamboo. Moreover, processing bamboo produces virtually no waste, since it need not be stripped of bark and the leaves can be used as fodder.
A further advantage of bamboo is that in many cases environmentally damaging transport is unnecessary, since bamboo grows «on the doorstep». What is more, buildings of bamboo can be easily recycled or dismantled and it is easy to replace individual components – such criteria have only recently emerged in Western architecture and are often difficult to meet using conventional materials.
According to forecasts, the future demand for wood in Asian countries will far exceed supply. In order to prevent this leading to even more rapid destruction of the rainforests, China is working to develop a national program to promote the use of bamboo as a substitute for tropical woods – a scientific approach of global significance.

In India, it would likewise be possible to use bamboo as a substitute: If one quarter of plywood needs were to be covered by bamboo matting instead – and this would be simple to achieve in technical terms – then some 400,000 cubic meters of logs or 11,000 hectares of forest would be spared each year. Equally important, in the extremely poor Indian villages it would create some 1,200 jobs for the local population.

Aufschluß über die Nachhaltigkeit von Bambus gibt auch ein Vergleich der Energiebilanzen verschiedener Baustoffe (also die Energie, die benötigt wird, um eine Einheit eines Baustoffs einer bestimmten Belastbarkeit zu produzieren):

Beton	**240**
Stahl	**1500**
Holz	**80**
Bambus	**30**

(Einheiten: MJ/m³ pro N/mm²; aus Janssen, J.A.: Bamboo research at the Eindhoven University of Technology, Eindhoven 1990, S. 15)

A comparison of the energy balances of various building materials (in other words, the energy required to produce a unit of a building material with a certain level of load-bearing capacity) gives an idea of the sustainability of bamboo:

Concrete	240
Steel	1,500
Wood	80
Bamboo	30

(Units: MJ/m³ per N/mm²; from J.A. Janssen: Bamboo Research at the Eindhoven University of Technology, Eindhoven 1990, p. 15)

Bambushain in Malaysia, um 1930
Bamboo grove in Malaysia, around 1930

botanik und nutzung von bambus / botany and the use of bamboo

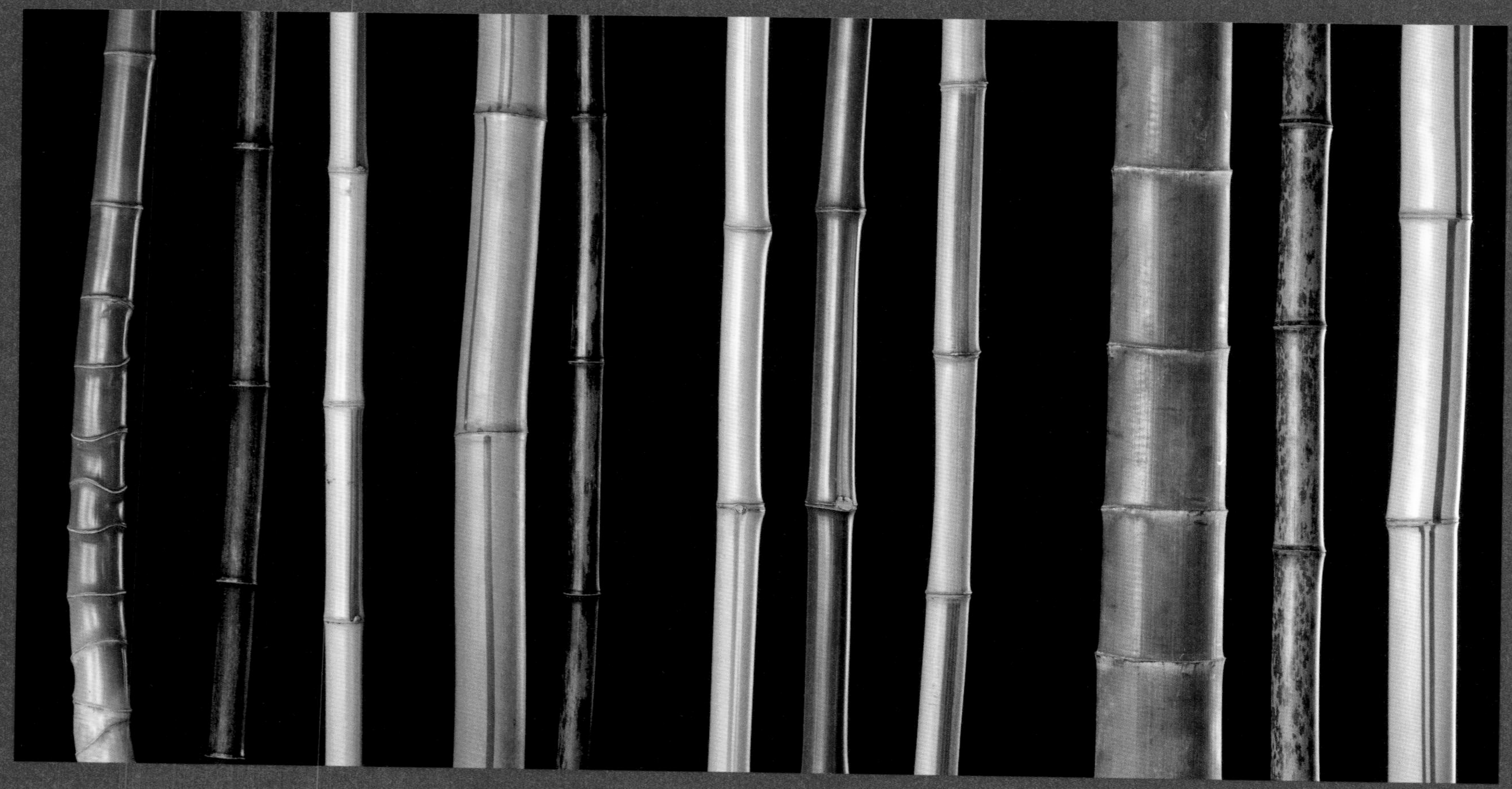

Verschiedene Phyllostachys-Bambusarten
Various types of phyllostachys bamboo

botanik und nutzung von bambus / botany and the use of bamboo

walter liese

Der Bambus gehört zu den weltweit am meisten genutzten Pflanzen. Er ist die Existenzgrundlage für über 1 Milliarde Menschen, zumeist in ländlichen Bereichen der ärmeren Entwicklungsländer. Rund 1.300 Bambusarten von 75 Gattungen bedecken etwa 25 Mill. ha in tropischen und subtropischen sowie zu 10% in temperierten Zonen.
Bambus gehört botanisch zu den Gräsern und bildet daher seine Halme je nach dem Wuchstyp des Rhizoms oder Wurzelstocks. Das Rhizom ist das unterirdisch wachsende Sprosssystem und wie die überirdischen Sprosse in Internodien und Nodien (Knoten) gegliedert. Als leptomorpher Typ kann es sich großflächig ausdehnen oder als pachymorpher Typ horstförmig wachsen. Leptomorphe oder auch monopodiale Bambusse haben ein langes, schlankes Rhizom mit einem Jahreszuwachs bis zu 6 m und sind daher stark wuchernd. Die neuen Halme bilden sich aus Seitenknospen an den Nodien, wodurch ein Bambuswald einzelner Halme entsteht, wie er für temperierte Klimazonen in Ostasien typisch ist. Die in Europa wachsenden Bambussen gehören zu diesen. Verbreitete Gattungen sind Arundinaria, Fargesia, Melocanna, Phyllostachys, Schizostachyum und Semiarundinaria.
Das pachymorphe oder sympodiale Rhizom der in den wärmeren Tropen beheimateten Bambusse ist kurz, gestaucht, von charakteristisch gebogener Form und ohne längere Ausläufer. Daher sind diese Arten horstförmig gestaltet, mit dichten Gruppen aus 20 bis zu 100 Halmen. Zu ihnen gehören die Gattungen Bambusa, Dendrocalamus, Gigantochloa, Guadua, Oxythenanthera, von denen einige als Riesenbambusse bekannt sind.
Die artspezifische Halmlänge wird in 2–3 Monaten erreicht und beträgt im gemäßigten Klima 2–5 m, bei tropischen Bambusen 20 bis 30 m und mehr. Im wachsenden Halm werden die Zellwände der Fasern und Parenchymzellen verstärkt, wodurch der Halm nach zwei Jahren «erntereif» wird. Auch in den Folgejahren entstehen zusätzliche Wandlamellen, so daß in gut bewirtschafteten Beständen Chinas Halme für technologische Nutzung erst nach vier bis fünf Jahren geerntet werden.
Bambus hat eine hohe Produktionskraft an Biomasse, der wachsende Halm erreicht die höchsten Werte im Pflanzenreich. Der jährliche Zuwachs je ha liegt je nach Art, Standort und

Bamboo is one of the plants most used worldwide. It forms the livelihood of over one billion people, mostly in rural areas in poor, developing countries. Approximately 1,300 varieties of bamboo spread across 75 species cover about 25 million hectares in tropical and sub-tropical regions, and around 10 per cent of temperate zones.

In botanical terms, bamboo belongs to the grass category and thus forms its stem in the same way as rhizomes or root-stock growth types. The rhizome is the shoot system that grows underground and is divided into internodes and nodes like the shoots above ground. The leptomorphic type can spread to cover large areas while the pachymorphic type grows like a thicket. Leptomorphs and also monopodial bamboo types have a long slender rhizome and exhibit rampant growth of up to six meters a year. The new stalks form from side-buds at the nodes which is why a typical East Asian bamboo forest in a temperate zone consists of single canes. The bamboo varieties which grow in Europe are of this type. Common species are arundinaria, fargesia, melocanna, phyllostachys, schizostachyum, and semiarundinaria.
The pachymorphic or sympodiale rhizome which thrives in warmer tropical regions is short, shrubby, with a characteristic arched form and without long offshoots. This is the reason why these varieties appear as bushy dense groups of between 20 and 100 stems. The following species are example of this type: bambusa, dendrocalamus, gigantochloa, guadua, and oxythenanthera – some of which are known as giant bamboo. The typical cane length of 2–5 meters is usually achieved in 2–3 months, in tropical regions 20–30 metres or more are common. In the growing stem, the cell walls of the fibers and parenchyma cells are strengthened so that after two years the cane is ready to harvest. In the following years additional wall lamella are formed, so that in well-managed crops in China canes for technological use are first harvested after four or five years.
Bamboo produces a lot of biomass, the growing cane achieving the highest values for the plant realm. Depending on type, location, and ambient climate, the annual growth rate is 15–25 tonnes of harvestable canes, i.e. 6–12 tonnes of air-dried biomass. Bamboo is a self-regenerating raw material – with production continuing after individual canes have been harvested, thanks to the new shoots which appear each year. The

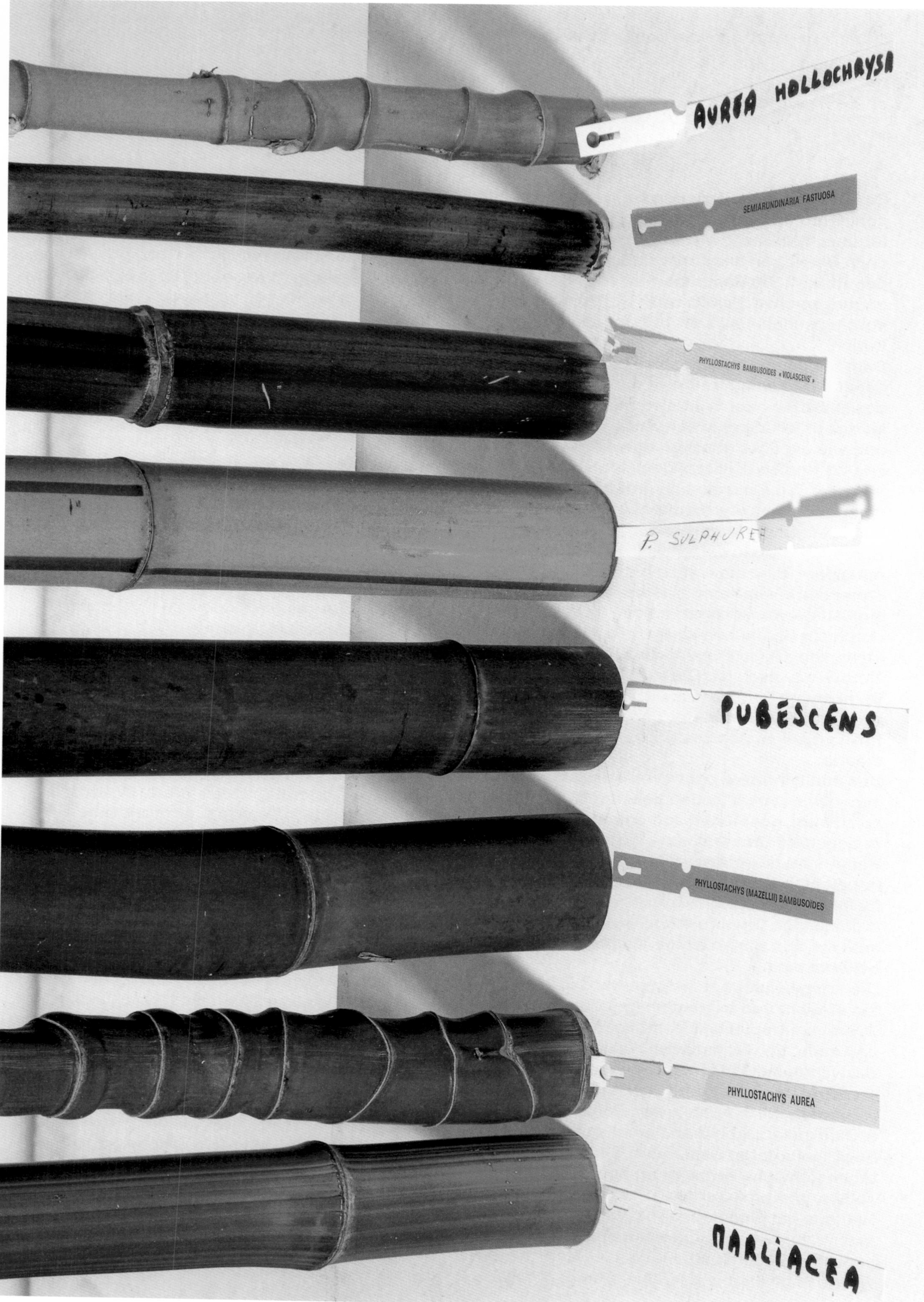
AUREA HOLLOCHRYSA
SEMIARUNDINARIA FASTUOSA
PHYLLOSTACHYS BAMBUSOIDES « VIOLASCENS »
P. SULPHURE
PUBESCENS
PHYLLOSTACHYS (MAZELLII) BAMBUSOIDES
PHYLLOSTACHYS AUREA
MARLIACEA

klimatischen Bedingungen bei 15 bis 25 t erntefrischer Halme, d. h. etwa 6 bis 12 t lufttrockener Biomasse. Bambus ist ein ununterbrochen nachwachsender Rohstoff, dessen Produktion auch nach Ernte der einzelnen Halme durch die jährlich neuen Sprosse voll erhalten bleibt. Die Lebenszeit eines Bestandes wird vor allem durch das großflächig einsetzende Blühen der betreffenden Art bestimmt, dem zumeist das Absterben aller Halme folgt. Die Blühperiode ist artspezifisch, wie bei der in Europa verbreiteten Fargesia murielae nach ca. 100 Jahren.

Bambus ist in Asien und auch anderen Regionen ein unentbehrlicher Rohstoff im Alltagsgebrauch, für den Haushalt, als Nahrungsmittel für Mensch und Tier, in der Landwirtschaft, für Konstruktionen, Möbel, Energie, Musikinstrumente, Medizin, Zellstoff und Papier sowie für viele andere Zwecke. Besonders in den letzten Jahrzehnten wurden viele Kenntnisse über Bewirtschaftung, Eigenschaften und Verarbeitung von Bambus gewonnen, die zu einer breiteren Produktpalette und steigender Wertschätzung geführt haben. So wurde die traditionelle Nutzung der vitaminreichen Bambussprosse erheblich intensiviert und hat in Asien zu einer Exportindustrie mit über 1 Milliarde Dollar Umsatz geführt. In größerem Umfang wird auch die Schutzwirkung von Bambusbeständen genutzt, sei es als Windschutz in der Landwirtschaft oder zur Bodenstabilisierung entlang von Flüssen und entwaldeten Hanglagen. Salztolerantere Arten sollen das sich ausbreitende Ödland entlang der Küste Chinas begrenzen.

Diskutiert wird auch der Gedanke, mit schnell wachsenden Bambusplantagen nachhaltig die Holz- sowie Zellstoffindustrie zu versorgen, um hierdurch die tropischen Wälder zu schonen. Doch enthält der Bambushalm anders als ein Baumstamm wegen seines großen inneren Hohlraumes nur etwa 50 % Masse, die zudem nur 45 % Faseranteil hat. Hinzu kommen Probleme bei Pflege, Ernte, Transport, Lagerung und Verarbeitung. Die sich örtlich kräftig entwickelnde Bambusverarbeitung hat mitunter bereits zu einem Mangel an ausreichender Quantität und Qualität geführt.

Der wichtige Sektor der handwerklichen Bearbeitung im ländlichen Bereich hat hohe Bedeutung zur Arbeitsbeschaffung, erforderlich sind jedoch besseres Management, Qualitätskontrolle, Rationalisierung und Entwicklung hochwertiger Produkte.

life-span of a crop is mainly determined by the large-scale blooming of the particular plant type, after which all the canes usually die off. The flowering period depends on the plant type, e.g. the fargesia murielae, widespread in Europe, blooms after about 100 years.

In Asia and in other areas as well, bamboo is an essential raw material which is used on a daily basis in the household, as nutrition for man and animals, in farming, for construction, furniture, energy, musical instruments, medicine, cellulose, and paper, as well as for many other purposes. In particular in the last few decades much knowledge has been gained on the farming, properties, and use of bamboo, and this has led to an increased range of products and heightened valuation. The traditional use of vitamin-rich bamboo has greatly intensified and become an export industry worth over 1 billion US dollars. In a wider sense, bamboo crops are used as wind-protection in farming or to stabilize river banks and forested hillsides. Salt-tolerant types are being used to limit the expanding wastelands along the coast of China.

Whether fast-growing bamboo can be used enduringly to supply the wood and cellulose industries and thus protect tropical forests is a topic of discussion at present. After all, a bamboo cane, unlike a tree trunk, contains only about 50 per cent mass, because of its large hollow center which, in addition, is only 45 per cent fiber. There are also problems with care, harvest, transport, storage, and processing. The fast-growing rate of bamboo processing in local areas has also led to shortfalls in quantity and quality. Hand-processing bamboo is an important sector in rural areas as it sources many jobs. However, there need to be better management, quality control, rationalization, and development of high-quality products.

In construction in particular, bamboo has been an essential material since time immemorial. Attention must be paid here to possible biological hazards. As structural elements, simple buildings, often made of spanned bamboo or woven matting, are easy to replace. Fungus can be prevented by applying building technology to control dampness, but chemical substances are generally required to control insects. A possible alternative is on the horizon: «fumigation under controlled conditions», a method developed from the Japanese tradition and put into practice for the 4,000 bamboo canes used

Besonders für Konstruktionen ist Bambus seit jeher ein unentbehrliches Material. Zu beachten sind hier die möglichen biologischen Gefahren. Einfache Bauten, oft aus gespaltenem Bambus oder geflochtenen Matten lassen sich leichter auswechseln als konstruktive Elemente. Ein Pilzbefall kann bautechnisch durch Abhalten der Feuchtigkeit verhindert werden, gegen Insekten ist meist der Einsatz chemischer Mittel erforderlich. Eine mögliche Alternative zeichnet sich ab mit dem «Räuchern unter kontollierten Bedingungen», einer aus der japanischen Tradition entwickelten Methode, die praktisch bei den 4000 Bambushalmen des von Simón Vélez konstruierten ZERI-Pavillons auf der Expo in Hannover eingesetzt wird.
Die weltweite Verbreitung und Nutzung von Bambus beflügelt die Vorstellung, auch in Europa Bambus in größerem Umfang anzubauen und als Biomasse oder konstruktiv zu nutzen. Im südlichen Europa gedeihen entsprechende Arten prächtig und in nördlichen Bereichen können die in den Nachkriegsjahren besonders aus China eingeführten Arten auch kältere Winter überdauern. Von der Europäischen Gemeinschaft (EG) wird daher ein Projekt «Bamboo for Europe» gefördert, um die Möglichkeiten eines Anbaues auf ertragsarmen Böden im südlichen Europa sowie die Chancen einer ökonomischen Verwertung der produzierten Biomasse zu erproben.
Bambus als Rohstoff ist noch weitgehend zugänglich und preiswert, weil die örtlichen Löhne gering sind. Es ist eine verpflichtende Aufgabe, diese Situation zu verbessern, wodurch der Bambus teurer und weniger verfügbar würde. So zeigen Länder mit hohem Lohnniveau, wie Japan und Taiwan, ein Verarmen der «Bambuskultur». Dies beeinflusst die vielerorts bestehende Konkurrenzsituation zum universeller verwendbaren Holz, wobei auch Imitate aus Plastik mit «Bamboo-look» Markanteile gewinnen werden. Vereinzelt gilt schon die Umkehrung des Ausspruchs, Bambus sei «das Holz des armen Mannes», denn nur Wohlhabende können sich noch echten Bambus leisten.

Prof. Dr. Walter Liese lehrte von 1963 bis 1991 am Institut für Holzbiologie der Universität Hamburg und erforscht Bambus seit den fünziger Jahren. Er gilt auf seinem Arbeitsgebiet als einer der besten Bambuskenner.

in the ZERI Pavilion at Expo 2000 Hanover.
The worldwide spread and use of bamboo has fired the idea of producing large quantities of bamboo in Europe as well, and using it for biomass or for building purposes. In southern Europe, certain types of bamboo are flourishing and in northern regions the species which were introduced largely from China after the war are surviving the colder winters. The European Union is thus sponsoring a project called «Bamboo for Europe» to test the possibilities of planting crops on unproductive soil in southern Europe and of using the biomass for ecological purposes.

Bamboo is, in the main, a readily available and inexpensive raw material wherever local wages tend to be low. We are duty-bound to improve this situation, which will of course make bamboo more expensive and less available. In countries with higher wage costs, such as Japan and Taiwan, the «bamboo culture» is drying up. This has an impact on the existing competitive situation in many places with universally usable wood, with plastic bamboo imitations also gaining more market share. In a few cases, the saying is once more valid that «bamboo is the poor man's wood», as only the well-off are able to afford real bamboo.

Prof. Dr Walter Liese lectured at the Institute for Wood Biology at Hamburg University from 1963 to 1991. He is one of the most knowledgeable experts in the field of bamboo.

zuschnitt und verarbeitung / cutting and processing

Transport von Bambusstangen in Thailand
Transporting bamboo poles in Thailand

Bambushändler in Tokyo (Japan)
Bamboo handler in Tokyo (Japan)

Nach etwa dreißig Tagen können Bambussprossen als Lebensmittel verwendet werden. Körbe und andere Flechtwaren werden aus Bambusstäben von 6 Monaten bis einem Jahr gefertigt, etwa zweijährige Bambusstäbe können gespalten und als Streifen geflochten werden. Für Bauzwecke muß der Bambus mindestens drei Jahre, besser jedoch fünf Jahre alt sein. Simón Vélez bevorzugt Bambus, der nicht älter als 6 Jahre ist, weil seine Stabilität danach abnimmt. Er verwendet für seine Bauwerke Bambus der Art *Guadua augustifolia*, den er gleich nach der Ernte auf seine Qualität untersucht. Anschließend läßt er ihn für zwei bis drei Monate trocknen, bis 90% der Feuchtigkeit ausgetreten sind.

Meist wird Bambus im Morgengrauen und wenn der Mond in seinem letzten Viertel steht geerntet, weil er dann am trockensten ist. Dann kann er besser altern und ist am resistentesten gegen den Befall durch Insekten und Pilze. So wie auch in Europa früher Holz transportiert wurde, finden die Bambusstäbe oft noch heute ihren Weg zur Weiterverarbeitung: Sie werden zu Flößen zusammengebunden und flußabwärts getrieben. Im Wasser sind sie zudem vor Schädlingen geschützt.

Da der größte Nachteil von Bambus in der Anfälligkeit gegenüber Insekten und Pilzen liegt, wurden zahlreiche Verfahren entwickelt, um Bambus dagegen zu schützen. Dazu zählen neben dem Wässern das Einkalken oder Erhitzen bzw. Räuchern. Auch zum Schutz vor Feuer existieren Verfahren, die die Brennbarkeit der Bambusstäbe reduzieren.

Bereits im 16. Jahrhundert wurde in Japan ein Räuchersystem entwickelt, daß den Bambus schützt, und nach dem seither fast alle Bambusgebäude in Japan behandelt wurden. Nach dem Zweiten Weltkrieg wurde in Japan ein weitaus effektiveres, aber auch teureres Verfahren entwickelt. Dabei wird der Bambus leicht erhitzt, so daß er seine pyrolytische Säure ausschwitzt. Diese sammelt sich, verdampft und behandelt wiederum die Oberfläche der Stäbe. Um die Kosten für diesen aufwändigen Prozeß zu senken und ihn an die kolumbianischen Bambusarten anzupassen, wurden in Kolumbien auf Initiative der ZERI-Stiftung einfachere Vorrichtungen entwickelt. Dazu zählt eine Anlage von Antonio Giraldo die am teuersten aber auch am effektivsten ist und von der Gesellschaft für Technische Zusammenarbeit (GTZ) unterstützt

After some 30 days, bamboo sprouts can be used as food. Baskets and other woven goods can be made from the bamboo canes after between six months and one year; roughly two-year-old bamboo canes can be split and the strips woven. For building purposes, bamboo must be at least three years old, better still five years old. Simón Vélez prefers bamboo which is not more than six years old, as thereafter it becomes less sturdy. For his construction work, he uses bamboo of the *Guadua augustifolia* species, which he examines immediately after harvesting to ascertain its quality. Subsequently, he lets the bamboo dry for two to three months, until 90 per cent of the moisture has evaporated.

Bamboo is normally harvested at dawn and when the moon is in its final phase, as it is then most dry. In this state, it can age better and is most resistant to insects or fungus. Today, bamboo canes are often transported for further processing in the same manner that timber was once transported in Europe: They are bound together to form rafts and floated downstream. Being in water also protects them from pests.

Since the greatest disadvantage of bamboo lies in its susceptibility to damage by insects and fungus, numerous methods have been developed to protect bamboo. In addition to immersion, these methods include coating with lime slurry, heating, or smoking. There are also methods which reduce the flammability of bamboo canes, thereby providing protection against fire.

As early as the 16th century, in Japan a system of smoking bamboo was developed in order to protect the wood, and ever since all bamboo buildings in Kyoto have been treated this way. After World War II, a far more effective but also more expensive process was developed in Japan. It involves slightly heating the bamboo in order to sweat out the pyrolytic acids. These accumulate, evaporate, and then serve to treat the surface of the canes. In order to lower the costs of this elaborate process and to adapt it to the types of bamboo found in Colombia, the ZERI Foundation had simple facilities for such a treatment of the canes developed in Colombia. This includes the unit created by Antonio Giraldo; it is the most complicated, but also the most effective, and has been supported by GTZ, the German Society for Technical Cooperation. Gabriel German Londono, owner of the largest Colombian bamboo plantation, has developed a rather less elaborate construction, and designer Marcelo Villegas has devised a smaller unit tailored to his needs.

wird. Gabriel German Londono, Besitzer der größten kolumbianischen Bambusplantage, entwickelte daraus ein einfacheres Verfahren und der Möbeldesigner Marcelo Villegas eine Anlage für kleinere Bambusstäbe.
Neben der Verwendung von – meist nachbehandelten – Rundstäben ist die Spaltung der Stäbe in Bambuslatten die geläufigste Methode der Weiterverarbeitung. Dabei werden die Bambusstäbe mit einer speziellen Vorrichtung parallel zur den Fasern in mehrere Leisten geteilt. Auch das Aufbiegen von Stäben parallel zur Laufrichtung wird praktiziert.
Aus Bambusleisten werden schließlich Matten, Körbe, Möbel oder industrielle Halbware hergestellt, wobei der Vielfalt an Mustern und Formen kaum Grenzen gesetzt sind. Weitere Verarbeitungsformen sind etwa Bambusspäne, die zu Preßspanplatten verarbeitet werden. Auch Laminate aus Bambus sowie der Verbund mit anderen Materialien zu hochwertigen Kompositen werden heute entwickelt. Für das Verformen von Schichtholz aus Bambus wird die Außenseite des Stabes auf die konvexe, also die Seite innerhalb der Biegekurve gelegt. Schichtholz aus Bambus, das sogenannte «plyboo» oder «lamboo» hat ähnliche Eigenschaften wie Schichtholz aus normalem Holz, ist allerdings sehr viel elastischer. In China wurde es z. B. im Zweiten Weltkrieg für den Flugzeugbau verwendet.

In addition to the use of – mostly refined – rounded canes, the most common processing method is to split canes into bamboo slats. This involves using a special device to divide the bamboo canes into several strips along the line of the grain. Another practice is to bend canes up, in line with the grain.
Bamboo strips are subsequently used to fashion matting, baskets, furniture, or semi-finished industrial goods and there are scarcely limits to the diversity of patterns and shapes created. In addition, shavings are processed to form pressboards. Other developments include bamboo laminates as well as combinations of bamboo with other materials to create high-quality composite materials. In order to mold bamboo plywood, the outer side of the cane is placed on the convex side, i.e. inside the bending curve. Bamboo plywood, known as plyboo or lamboo, has similar qualities to the plywood made from normal wood, but is much more elastic. In China, it was used in World War II for airplane construction.

Nur wenn der Bambus genau über einer Trennwand abgeschlagen wird, behält er seine Feuchtigkeit und kann dann neue Triebe produzieren. Bei der Ernte von Bambussprößlingen soll der Feuchtigkeitsgehalt im Sproß möglich hoch sein, was ein Regeneration der Pflanze verhindert.
Only if bamboo is cut exactly above the end of a partition does it retain its moisture after harvesting and can thus produce new shoots. During the harvest of bamboo shoots, the moisture content of the shoots must, by contrast, be as high as possible, and this prevents the plant from regenerating

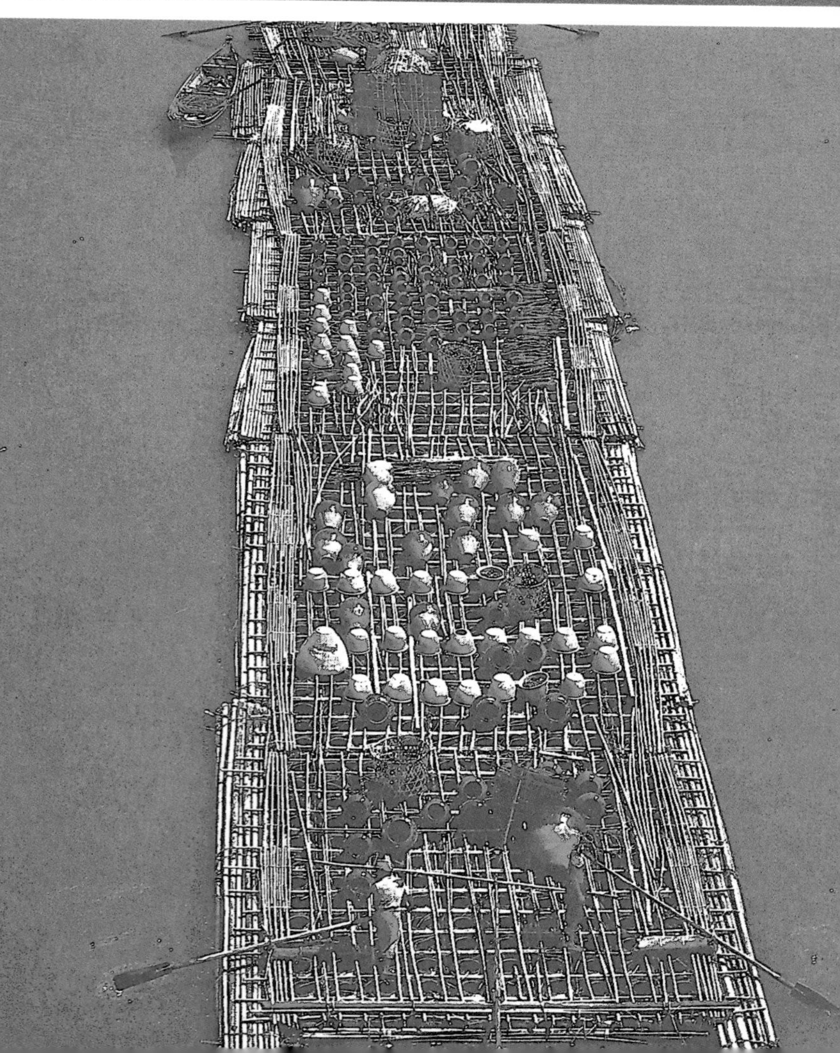

Papierherstellung aus Bambus in China: Einweichen des Bambus in Wasserbehältern. Holzschnitt von Sung Ying Hsing, 1634.
Manufacturing paper in China: the bamboo is soaked in vats of water. Wood print, Sung Ying Hsing, 1634

Kochen der Bambusstengel in einer Mischung aus reinem Wasser und Kalk.
The bamboo canes are boiled in a mixture of pure water and lime

Ofen für das Räuchern von Bambusstäben in Armenia/Quindio, entwickelt von Antonio Giraldo, 1999
Oven used for smoke-impregnating bamboo poles in Armenia/Quindio, developed by Antonio Giraldo, 1999

▶ **Anlage zur Behandlung von Bambusstäben, Gabriel German Londoño.**
Construction for impregnating bamboo poles, Gabriel German Londoño.
▲ **Ofen zur Behandlung von Bambusstäben, Marcelo Villegas, Manizales.**
Oven used for impregnating bamboo poles, Marcelo Villegas, Manizales.

▲ **Spalten von Bambusstäben in Indien**
Split bamboo poles in India

▶ **Transport von Bambusstangen in einer Papierfabrik in Bangladesh**
Transporting bamboo poles in a paper factory in Bangladesh

▼ **Trocknen von Bambusstangen**
Drying bamboo poles

▶ **Bambusstangen zum Transport, Thailand**
Bamboo poles for transport, Thailand

▼ **Trocknen von Bambusstangen**
Drying bamboo poles

▶ **Bambusstangen zum Transport, Thailar**
Bamboo poles for transport, Thailand

▲ **Herstellung von Hüten aus Bambusfasern auf Java**
Making huts from bamboo fiber in Java

▶ **Bambusfurnier**
Bamboo veneer

▲ **Herstellung von Bambusmatten in Indonesien**
Making bamboo mats in Indonesia

▶ **Dreischichtiges Massiv-Bambus-Parkett der Firma Elephant Parkett**
Three-layer solid bamboo parquet floor produced by Elephant Parkett

▲ **Herstellung von Sonnenrollos in Taiwan**
Making sunshades in Taiwan

das «global village» ist aus bambus / the «global village» is made of bamboo

[1] aus Liese, W.: Bamboo – Present, Past, Future, Skript eines Vortrags auf dem Internationalen Bambus-Kongress in Costa Rica 1998

[2] Farelly, D.: The book of bamboo, San Francisco, 1984

[1] From W. Liese: Bamboo – Present, Past, Future, Skript eines Vortrags auf dem Internationalen Bambus-Kongress in Costa Rica, 1998.

[2] D. Farelly: The Book of Bamboo, San Francisco, 1984.

Rund 20 Mio. Tonnen Bambus werden jährlich geerntet. Das entspricht etwa 8 Mio. km oder 200 mal den Erdumfang an Bambusstäben.[1] Der durchschnittliche Pro-Kopf-Verbrauch in Asien liegt bei 12 kg pro Jahr – eine gigantische Menge, bedenkt man die Bevölkerung Asiens. In manchen Regionen Asiens oder Lateinamerikas wird mit Bambuswerkzeugen gearbeitet, Möbel und Häuser werden aus Bambus gefertigt, aus Bambusfasern wird Papier hergestellt und Bambus ist Nahrung für Mensch und Tier.
David Farelly listet in seinem «Book of bamboo» 1000 Verwendungszwecke von Bambus auf – von A wie «acupuncture needles» und «airplane skins» bis Z wie «zithers».[2]

Bambus prägt in vielen Ländern das Landschaftsbild – nicht nur aufgrund ausgedehnter Bambushaine, sondern auch in Form von Zäunen, Windbarrieren, Wasserleitungen, Wellenbrechern, Baugerüsten, Windmühlen, Ställen und Gebäuden. In Indonesien bestanden 1956 35% aller Häuser ausschliesslich aus Bambus und weitere 35% aus einer Mischbauweise aus Bambus und Holz. In Bangladesh und Burma wurden 1945 60% aller Häuser aus Bambus errichtet und auf den Phillipinen sind es 90%.

Während die Bambusforschung in China und Japan stärker die agrartechnischen Aspekte und die Anwendung im Kunsthandwerk hervorhebt, wird in den anderen Ländern, insbesondere in Lateinamerika, gezielt die Anwendung von Bambus im Bauwesen untersucht. Eine koordinierte internationale Erforschung der Möglichkeiten von Bambus nahm 1980 ihren Anfang, als das International Research and Development Center in Singapur einen Workshop über die Bambusforschung organisierte, auf dem sich erstmals Bambusspezialisten aus vierzehn Ländern trafen.

Around 20 million tons of bamboo are harvested annually. That is roughly equal to some 8 million km of bamboo canes (or 200 times the earth's circumference).[1] The average per capita consumption in Asia is about 12 kg per year – a colossal amount when one considers the size of Asia's population. In some regions of Asia or Latin America, tools fashioned of bamboo are used, furniture and houses are made of bamboo, paper is made of bamboo fibers and bamboo is food for man and beast.
In his «Book of Bamboo», David Farelly lists 1,000 uses for bamboo – ranging from A as in «acupuncture needles» and «airplane skins» to Z as in «zithers».[2]

In many countries, bamboo dominates the landscape: in addition to extensive bamboo groves, it occurs as fences, windbreaks, water pipes, breakwaters, scaffolding, windmills, stalls, and buildings. In 1956, in Indonesia 35 per cent of all houses were made solely of bamboo and an additional 35 per cent of a mixture of bamboo and wood. In 1945, in Bangladesh and Burma 60 per cent of all houses were made of bamboo and on the Philippines the figure stands at 90 per cent.

While bamboo research in China and Japan places greater emphasis on agricultural utilization and the plant's use in arts and crafts, other countries, especially in Latin America, focus on deploying bamboo for construction purposes. In 1980, the International Research and Development Center in Singapore organized a workshop on bamboo research which was attended by bamboo specialists from 14 countries. It marked the start of coordinated international research on the uses of bamboo.

Bambus als Brennholz im Hochland von Äthiopien / Bamboo used as firewood in the Ethiopian highlands

Kinder auf Bambusstelzen in Japan
Children on bamboo stilts in Japan

▶ **Muttertag in Costa Rica**
Mothers' day in Costa Rica

▼ **In Asien werden aus gespaltenen Bambusstäben Tierkäfige hergestellt.**
In Asia, split bamboo is used to make animal cages

▲ **Bambusmöbel in Bali**
Bamboo furniture in Bali

▶ **Bambusmöbel auf dem äthiopischen Hochland**
Bamboo furniture in the Ethiopian highlands

▲ **Bambusmöbel in China**
Bamboo furniture in China

▼ **Fischreusen aus Bambus, Vietnam**
Bamboo fish traps, Vietnam

Japanische Handwerker bei der Herstellung und Bemalung von Akari-Lampen, die aus Reispapier und gespaltenen Bambusstäben bestehen, um 1870
Japanese craftsmen making and painting Akari lamps of rice paper and split bamboo, around 1870

Der Mönch der buddhistischen Kamu-So-Sekte in Japan trägt einen Korb auf dem Kopf und spielt auf einer Bambusflöte heilige Musik.
This Buddhist monk from the Kamu-So sect in Japan carries a basket on his head and plays healing music on his bamboo flute

[1] **aus: Takama, S.: Die wunderbare Welt des Bambus, Köln, 1983, S. 230**

[1] From S. Takama: Die wunderbare Welt des Bambus, Köln, 1983, p. 230.

Bambus ist seit jeher Gegenstand der Verehrung vieler Kulturen. Aus Bambus (auf Sanskrit «venu») wird in der vedischen Tradition die Hütte gebaut, in der religiöse Riten vollzogen werden. Mit einem Bambusstab muß auch die Erde ausgegraben werden, aus der der Behälter gemacht wird, in dem man das heilige Feuer entzündet. Nach einer indischen Legende flüchtete sich Agni, der Gott des Feuers, im Streit mit anderen Gottheiten in das hohle Innere eines Bambusstabs.

In Lateinamerika besagt eine Legende des Pantagoras-Stammes aus dem westlichen Kolumbien, daß nur ein Mann die Sintflut überlebte und jahrelang alleine und traurig lebte, bis Gott sich seiner erbarmte, eine Bambussprosse in eine Frau verwandelte und sie an seine Seite stellte. Seitdem bietet der Bambus dem Menschen Schutz.

Das japanische Fest des Bambusspaltens, bei dem junge Männer unter Anleitung von Shinto-Priestern im Winter unter großem Kraftaufwand die Stäbe spalten, soll auf das 8. Jahrhundert zurückgehen. Beim sogenannten Sagicho-Fest hingegen werden die auf Bambusplattformen stehenden Neujahrsdekorationen zeremoniell verbrannt, gehalten von einer Konstruktion aus Seilen und Bambusstäben.[1]

Von dem chinesischen Weisen Pou Sou Tung ist der Ausspruch überliefert:

«Eine Speise sollte Fleisch, ein Haus sollte Bambus enthalten. Ohne Fleisch magern wir ab; ohne Bambus verlieren wir die heitere Gelassenheit.»

Der chinesische Religionsstifter Konfuzius sagte hingegen:

**«Ohne Fleisch können wir leben,
ohne Bambus müssen wir sterben.»**

From time immemorial bamboo has been an object of reverence for many cultures. In the Vedic tradition, bamboo (in Sanskrit «venu») is used to build the hut in which religious ceremonies are performed. Moreover, a bamboo cane must be used to dig out the earth from which the receptacle is fashioned in which the holy fire is then lit. According to an Indian legend, following a quarrel with the other gods Agni, the god of fire, flees to the safe haven of the hollow interior of a bamboo cane.

In Latin America, a legend of the Pantagoras tribe in western Columbia would have it that a man survived the flood and lived for many years in sadness and solitude until God took pity on him and transformed a bamboo bud into a woman and placed her at his side. Since this time bamboo has offered man protection.

The Japanese bamboo splitting festival, in which under the guidance of Shinto priests young men bring great strength to bear to split open the canes, purportedly goes back to the 8th century. By contrast, in the Sagicho festival, the New Year's decorations on bamboo platforms are ceremonially burned, held by a construction of ropes and bamboo poles.[1]

The Chinese wise man Pou Sou Tung says:

«A meal should contain meat, a house should contain bamboo. Without meat we waste away; without bamboo we lose our cheerful composure.»

Whereas the Chinese philosopher Confucius says:

«We can live without meat,
but without bamboo we must die.»

Rituelle Verbrennung beim Sagicho Fest in Japan / Burning ritual at the Sagicho Festival in Japan

Fest des Bambusspaltens in Japan / Bamboo pole festival in Japan

Nach der Arbeit ein beliebter Zeitvertreib: Schaukeln an Bambusstämmen bei Kathmandu (Nepal).
A beloved pastime when the work is done: swinging on bamboo poles near Katmandu, Nepal

Japanische Soldaten in einem chinesischen Bambuswald während des chinesisch-japanischen Krieges, 1932
Japanese soldiers in a Chinese bamboo forest during the Sino–Japanese war, 1932

	Die Verwendung von Bambus in den verschiedenen Erdteilen wurde nicht nur durch klimatische Verhältnisse beeinflußt. Auch wirtschaftliche und politische Beziehungen führten dazu, daß sich die Bedeutung von Bambus ausdehnte oder regional veränderte.	The use of bamboo in various parts of the world is not only influenced by climatic conditions. Economic and political factors have also led to the spread of bamboo's significance and regional shifts in importance.
- 3 Mio.	**Im Tertiär existierte Bambus auch in Europa, starb aber mit der folgenden Eiszeit aus.**	In the Tertiary period, bamboo also existed in Europe, but became extinct with the onset of the next Ice Age.
- 5550–3500	**Auf diese Epoche wurden Überreste von Bambusbauten geschätzt, die an Stätten der Valdivia-Kultur in Ecuador gefunden wurden.**	This is the age scientific dating gives for the remains of bamboo buildings found at sites of the Valdivia civilization in Ecuador.
- 3300–2800	**In China wurden Überreste von Bambusmatten und -körben aus dieser Zeit gefunden.**	In China, remains of bamboo matting and baskets have been found from this period.
- 100	**In einem Brief von Alexander dem Großen an Aristoteles findet Bambus erstmals in der westlichen Welt Erwähnung. Plinius bezieht sich darauf in seiner «Naturgeschichte».**	Bamboo is first mentioned in the Western world in a letter from Alexander the Great to Aristotle. Pliny refers to this in his «History of Nature».
+ 552	**Europäische Mönche schmuggeln in den Hohlräumen von Bambusstöcken Seidenraupeneier aus China nach Konstantinopel. Sie leiteten damit den Untergang der Seidenstraße ein, die über Jahrhunderte ganz Asien durchzog.**	European monks use the hollow interiors of bamboo canes to smuggle silk worms from China to Constantinople. In doing so they ushered in the demise of the Silk Road which had run right across Asia for centuries.
1534	**Die ersten Chronisten der spanischen Eroberer in Südamerika erwähnen Bambuswohnungen und -flöße, die von den Einheimischen benutzt wurden. Spanische Soldaten auf dem Weg nach Quito stillten ihren Durst nach lokaler Sitte mit Wasser, das sich in den Hohlräumen von Bambusstämmen gesammelt hatte. Um sich gegen die spanischen Eroberer zu schützen, bauten die Indios Bambus-Festungen um ihre Dörfer. Sie spießten die Köpfe ihrer Opfer auf die Bambusstäbe und bohrten Löcher in die Bambuspfähle, die im Wind wie gewaltige Flöten tönten.**	The first chroniclers of the Spanish conquistadors in South America mention bamboo dwellings and rafts used by local inhabitants. Spanish soldiers on the way to Quito quenched their thirst in the native manner – with water which had accumulated in the hollow interiors of bamboo canes. In order to protect themselves against the Spanish invaders, the South American Indians built bamboo defenses around their villages. They speared the heads of their victims on the bamboo canes and drilled holes in the bamboo posts which whistled in the wind like powerful flutes.
1626	**Der deutsche Botaniker G. E. Rumpf veröffentlicht ein siebenbändiges «Herbarium amboinense», in dem bereits 24 Bambus-Arten beschrieben sind.**	German botanist G.E. Rumpf published a seven-volume treatise entitled «Herbarium amboinense», which contains a description of 24 different species of bamboo.
1753	**Carl von Linné führt den Begriff Bambus, in Anlehnung an das indische Wort «Bambu» oder «Mambu», in die botanische Fachsprache ein.**	Linnaeus introduces the term «bamboo» to the vocabulary of botany. It is based on the Indian word «Bambu» or «Mambu».
c. 1850	**Seidenimporteure bringen die exotische Bambus-Pflanze aus China und Japan nach**	Silk importers bring the exotic bamboo plant from China and Japan to Europe, give it as a present to

Europa, schenken sie den Fürsten ihres Landes oder reichen Auftraggebern und pflanzen sie in ihre eigenen Parks.

their princes or rich clients, and plant it in their own parks.

1876 **Alexander Graham Bell zeichnet den ersten Ton eines Phonographen, dem Vorläufer des Plattenspielers, mit Hilfe einer Bambusnadel auf.**

Alexander Graham Bell produces the first sound recording on a phonograph (the predecessor of the record-player) with the aid of a bamboo needle.

1878/80 **Ein Glühfaden aus Bambus führt Thomas Edison und seine Mitarbeiter zum Durchbruch bei der Erfindung der Glühlampe. Man sagt, Edison habe über 6000 verschiedene Materialien getestet, und nachdem er zu dem Schluß gekommen war, daß Bambus das geeignete Material sei, schickte er vier Mitarbeiter nach Lateinamerika und Asien, um geeigneten Bambus zu finden. Auf diesem Wege fand er in Japan eine Art, aus der ein Glühfaden hergestellt wurde, der 2450 Stunden leuchtete – ein Vielfaches von der Glühdauer anderer Lampen. Dies ermöglichte eine kommerzielle Herstellung und Nutzung dieser bahnbrechenden Erfindung. General Electric fertigte daraufhin die nächsten 14 Jahre Glühlampen mit Bambus-Glühfäden.**

A bamboo filament leads Thomas Edison and his team to a breakthrough in the invention of the light bulb. Edison is said to have tested over 6,000 different materials; having reached the conclusion that bamboo was the suitable material, he sent four colleagues to Latin America and Asia to find suitable bamboo. This was how he found a species in Japan from which he fabricated a filament which shone for 2,450 hours – many times longer than other lamps. This enabled the commercial manufacture and use of his revolutionary invention. General Electric subsequently manufactured bulbs with bamboo filaments for the next 14 years.

1880 **Pressenotiz aus «Das neue Universum»: «In der preußischen Armee sind jüngst zwei Ulanenregimenter mit Lanzen aus Bambus versehen worden, die abgesehen von anderen Vorteilen etwa ein Kilogramm leichter sind als die bisher benützten. Dies gibt Veranlassung, hier der Verwendung des Bambus mit wenigen Worten zu gedenken. Vielleicht in höherem Grade als irgendeine andere Pflanzenform ist der Bambus, schreibt Wallace in seinem Buch über die Tropenwelt, für die Bedürfnisse der Halbwilden in den Tropen geschaffen; seine Verwendung ist fast unbeschränkter Art.»**

Press release from «Das neue Universum»: «Recently two Ulan regiments of the Prussian army have been equipped with lances made from bamboo which, quite apart from their other advantages, are two pounds lighter than the lances used hitherto. This gives us occasion to consider the use of bamboo in a few words. Wallace writes in his book on the Tropics that bamboo is perhaps made for the needs of the semi-savages to a higher degree than any other plant; its use and applications are virtually unlimited.»

1902 **Ein Großbrand zerstört Guayaquil, den großen Hafen von Ecuador, der von den spanischen Eroberern aus Bambus gebaut worden war. Mit dem Wiederaufbau traten an Stelle der Kolonialbauten aus Bambus Betongebäude. Auch in anderen Erdteilen begann die Verwendung von industriellen Materialien anstelle von Bambus.**

A large-scale fire destroys Guayaquil, the large harbor in Ecuador, which the Spanish conquistadors had built of bamboo. When it was rebuilt, the colonial buildings of bamboo were replaced by edifices made of concrete. And in other areas of the world, people began to use industrial materials in place of bamboo.

Großbritanniens erstes militärisches Luftschiff «Nulli secundis» von 1907 besaß ein Tragwerk aus Bambusstäben.
Great Britain's first military dirigible «Nulli secundis» in 1907 featured a framework of bamboo strips

Hassan Fathy erklärt die Verwendung von baratsi-Dachelementen aus Bambus oder anderen Stäben in Sohar (Oman), 70er Jahre
Hassan Fathy explains the use of baratsi roof elements made of bamboo or strips of other material in Sohar (Oman), 1970s

von der globalisierung zu regionalen bauformen /
from globalization to regionalization

Schon seit dem 16. Jahrhundert wurden in Kabinetten Gegenstände und Pflanzen aus den europäischen Kolonien in Übersee als Kuriositäten und Raritäten ausgestellt. Im eklektischen 19. Jahrhundert kam in Europa ein Exotismus in Mode, der dazu führte, daß viele chinesische und japanische Kulturgüter importiert wurden. In dieser Zeit wurde auch Bambus in Europa bekannt.

Im 20. Jahrhundert wurde die weltweite Vernetzung und der Austausch von Kulturgütern durch Medien und Fortbewegungsmittel weiter beschleunigt. Die sogenannte Globalisierung ergriff auch die Architektur – hier wurde der Internationale Stil zum Synonym für den Siegeszug der von den westlichen Ländern geprägten Ästhetik in Architektur und Design. Im Zuge dieser Entwicklung sank die Reputation von Bambus als Baumaterial, denn Materialien wie Beton, Stahl und Glas schienen unverzichtbar für ein repräsentatives Haus nach westlichem Vorbild.

Doch schon in den sechziger Jahren entstanden Versuche, das enorme Potential regionaler und lokaler Bauformen aufzuwerten, unter denen das Bauen mit Bambus eine zentrale Rolle spielt. Während Publikationen wie «Architecture without Architects» von Bernard Rudofsky die Intelligenz traditioneller Bauweisen zeigten, belebte der Ägypter Hassan Fathy die Lehmbautradition der arabischen Länder mit modernen Einflüssen. Regionale Traditionen scheinen den sozialen, städtebaulichen und ökologischen Problemen vieler Länder des Südens eher gewachsen zu sein als ein oftmals mit schlechten Materialien und wenig Verständnis kopierter Internationaler Stil.

As early as the 16th century, objects and plants from the European colonies were put on display as curiosities and rarities. In the eclectic 19th century, there was a craze in Europe for such exotic items and this led to many Chinese and Japanese cultural wares being imported. It was during this period that bamboo became known in Europe.

In the 20th century, the media and new means of transport further accelerated global networking and the exchange of cultural goods. So-called globalization has also seized hold of architecture: the International Style became the synonym for the triumphant advance in architecture and design of an aesthetics advanced by the Western world. In the course of this development, the reputation of bamboo as a building material sank, since materials such as concrete, steel, and glass seemed indispensable for a prestigious house after the western model.

Nevertheless, as early as the 1960s there were attempts to underscore the enormous potential of regional and local building techniques, and building with bamboo played a central role in these efforts. Publications such as «Architecture without Architects» by Bernard Rudofsky demonstrated the intelligence of traditional building methods, and Egyptian Hassan Fathy breathed new life into the clay building tradition of the Arabic world by incorporating modern influences. Regional traditions seem more suited to solving the social, urban, and ecological problems engendered by development in many countries in the Southern hemisphere than imitations of the International Style in a manner that not only often did not really grasp the latter's thrust but also often featured poor materials.

Bambusgebäude zur Lagerung der Kaffeernte in Kolumbien. Die Architektur von Simón Vélez ist von der traditionellen Architektur des kolumbianischen Kaffeeanbaugebiets beeinflußt, in der Guadua-Bambus eine zentrale Rolle spielt. Er dient unter anderem zum Bau großer, mehrstöckiger Gebäude.
Bamboo building used for storing coffee in Colombia. Simón Vélez's architecture is influenced by the traditional architecture of the coffee plantation area where Guadua bamboo plays a central role. It is used, amongst other things, to construct multiple-story buildings

Jean-Marie-Tibaou-Kulturzentrum in Nouméa, Neu-Kaledonien, Renzo Piano, 1992
Jean-Marie Tibaou Culture Center in Noumea, New Caledonia, Renzo Piano, 1992

Teehaus, Arata Isozaki / Tea-house, Arata Isozaki

Wohnhaus aus Bambus bei Chiayi (Taiwan) / Bamboo house near Chiayi (Taiwan)

Das unschlagbare Kosten/Nutzen-Verhältnis ist in den Ländern des Südens eines der Hauptargumente dafür, wieder mit Bambus zu bauen. Doch noch immer werden dort die höheren Kosten für Beton und Stahl in Kauf genommen, weil diese Materialien, ebenso wie Auto oder Fernseher, die «moderne» Welt verkörpern. Deshalb hat Bambus als Baustoff nur dann eine Zukunft, wenn zwei Voraussetzungen erfüllt werden: einerseits müssen Häuser aus Bambus den ästhetischen und repräsentativen Anforderungen ihrer Bewohner entsprechen, andererseits muß das Selbstbewußtsein der Bewohner gegenüber fremdem Stilvorgaben gestärkt werden.

Nach diesem Prinzip hat Simón Vélez in den letzten Jahren gezielt Villen aus Bambus für Angehörige der kolumbianischen Oberschicht gebaut und damit das Image von Bambus in der Architektur neu definiert. Außerdem konnte er die Erfahrungen, die er beim Bauen im großen Maßstab sammelte, für Gebäude in Niedrigkostenbauweise nutzen. So entwickelte Vélez parallel zu seinem Pavillon für die Weltausstellung Expo 2000 in Hannover ein Minimalhaus aus Bambus für den sozialen Wohnungsbau. Die Kosten für ein Haus dieses Typs betragen ca. 5.000 US$ oder ca. 10.000 DM, es bietet 65 qm Platz auf zwei Ebenen. Besonderer Wert wurde dabei auf Erdbebensicherheit gelegt.

Die Verwendung von Bambus für die Lösung von Problemen des sozialen Wohnungsbaus wird weltweit in zahlreichen Projekten gefördert. Im Rahmen des ecuadorianischen Projektes «Alandaluz» werden fünf Jahre lang jährlich 200 ha Bambus für den Baubedarf angepflanzt. Einmal im Monat laden die Projektleiter die Bewohner eines Dorfes ein und versuchen, die Bevölkerung wieder an die abgerissenen Traditionen der Bambusarchitektur und ihre Vorteile heranzuführen. Jährlich schließen sich etwa fünf neue Dörfer dem Projekt an.

In den Favelas von Rio de Janeiro versucht ein deutsch-brasilianisches Team, die Wohnverhältnisse durch die Verwendung von Bambus an Stelle teurer Materialien zu verbessern. Dabei kann die Verwendung vorgefertigter Bambus-Elemente für den Häuserbau die Baukosten von ca. 5.500 $ auf ca. 2.200 $ reduzieren. Auch hier war zu beobachten, wie wichtig die Entwicklung von architektonischen Vorbildern auch im sozialen Wohnungsbau ist. Nachdem die ersten Hütten der Zuwanderer noch von der eigenen ländli-

The fact that bamboo provides unbeatable value for money is one of the main reasons for utilizing it again as a building material in the Southern hemisphere. And yet people in these countries still tend to accept the higher costs of concrete and steel because they embody the modern world in much the same way as do cars or TVs. Consequently, bamboo only has a future as a building material if two conditions are fulfilled: first, bamboo houses must meet the requirements of their inhabitants in terms of aesthetics and prestige, and, second, house-dwellers must learn to value their traditional houses over styles based on foreign models.

Simón Vélez has applied these principles in recent years in deliberately selecting bamboo as the building material for villas designed for Colombia's upper classes and thus redefining the image of bamboo in architecture. Moreover, in this context he has brought to bear the experience he has gained designing large-scale buildings in his low-budget housing projects. For example, at the same time as Vélez developed his pavilion for Expo 2000 in Hanover, he also created a basic low-budget, two-story bamboo dwelling. The latter costs around 5,000 US dollars to build. It provides 65 m^2 of living space. He also attaches special emphasis to providing earthquake protection.

Numerous projects worldwide foster the employment of bamboo to solve the problems of low-cost housing. One such project in Ecuador, Alandaluz, has involved planting 200 hectares of bamboo every year over a period of five years to provide building materials. Once a month, project managers talk to village members and try to refamiliarize them with the forsaken traditions of bamboo architecture and its advantages. Every year, some five villages join the project.

In the Favelas of Rio de Janeiro a German–Brazilian team is attempting to improve local living conditions by substituting bamboo for expensive building materials. For example, by utilizing prefabricated bamboo elements for housing, it is possible to lower building costs from around 5,500 US dollars to some 2,200 US dollars. In this context, it becomes equally evident how important it is to develop architectural models for low-cost housing. Though the first huts for immigrants still reflected local traditions, people in the city quickly attempted to emulate the modern houses belonging to the middle and upper classes.

The FUNBAMBU project in Costa Rica enables the construction of up to 1,000 bamboo houses every

▲ **Prototyp eines Hauses für den sozialen Wohnungsbau nach einem Entwurf von Simón Vélez, 1999**
Prototype for low-cost housing designed by Simón Vélez, 1999

▼ **Prototyp für den sozialen Wohnungsbau des CIBAM unter der Leitung von Oscar Hidalgo Lopez in Palmira (Kolumbien)**
Prototype for CIBAM low-cost housing under the direction of Oscar Hidalgo Lopez in Palmira (Colombia)

▲ **Modellhaus des Projekts «FUNBAMBU» in Costa Rica**
Model house for the «Funbambu» project in Costa Rica

▼ **Sozialer Wohnungsbau des Instituto de Credito Territorial in Manizales, (Kolumbien)**
Low-cost housing by Instituto de Credito Territorial in Manizales (Colombia)

[1] Liese, W.: Bamboo: Present, Past, Future, in: ABS Newsletter, Vol. 20 No.1, Februar 1999

[2] Brian Brace Taylor: Bamboo City – A refugee camp, in: Mimar 20, April/Juni 1986, Singapur, S. 44 ff.

[1] W. Liese: Bamboo: Present, Past, Future, in: ABS Newsletter, Vol. 20 No.1, February 1999.

[2] Brian Brace Taylor: Bamboo City – A refugee camp, in: Mimar 20, April/June 1986, Singapore, pp. 44 ff.

chen Tradition geprägt war, versuchte man in der Stadt bald neue Leitbilder nachzuahmen, nämlich die modernen Häuser der Mittel- und Oberschicht.
Das Projekt FUNBAMBU in Costa Rica ermöglicht jährlich bis zu 1000 Bambus-Häuser, deren Material aus Pflanzungen von 60 Hektar Anbaufläche stammt. Für ähnliche Zwecke müsste Holz von 500 Hektar tropischen Regenwalds geschlagen werden![1] Ein anderes Projekt führen das CIBAM (das Bambusforschungszentrum an der Universität Bogotá) und das ICT (Instituto de Credito Territorial) in Manizales, Kolumbien, durch. Bei diesen Bauten werden Bambusmatten als Wände eingesetzt, die anschließend verputzt werden.

Ende der siebziger Jahre wurde in Thailand die Flüchtlingsstadt Khao-I-Dang gebaut. Sie war nach Bangkok zeitweise die zweitgrößte Stadt Thailands und beherbergte bis zu 140.000 Menschen, die vor dem Terror der Roten Khmer aus Kambodscha geflohen waren. Bei dem Bau der Gebäude wurde auf traditionelle Techniken der Flüchtlinge zurückgegriffen, die durch das Wissen von Experten der UNESCO ergänzt wurden. Das Beispiel Khao-I-Dang zeigte, daß Bambus durchaus auch für den Bau einer gesamten Stadt mit allen dazugehörigen Funktionen geeignet ist.[2]

year, built from plants grown on 60 hectares of land. To produce a similar number of wooden dwellings, 500 hectares of tropical rainforest would have to be felled![1] Another project is being conducted by CIBAM (the bamboo research center at the University of Bogotá) and the ICT (Instituto de Credito Territorial) in Manizales, Colombia. The houses in question have walls made of bamboo matting, which is subsequently plastered.

At the end of the 1970s, the Khao-I-Dang refugee camp was built in Thailand. After Bangkok, it was for a time the second-largest city in Thailand and accommodated up to 140,000 people who had fled from the terrors of the Khmer Rouge in Cambodia. Care was taken to apply the building techniques familiar to the refugees, complemented by the know-how of UNESCO experts. Khao-I-Dang is living proof that bamboo is more than suited to constructing an entire city with all its requisite functions.[2]

Wohnhaus im Kaffeeanbaugebiet von Kolumbien / House on coffee plantation in Colombia

Eames-Haus in Pacific Palisades (USA), Charles und Ray Eames, 1952. Charles und Ray Eames machten das preisgünstige Collageprinzip zum ästhetischen Markenzeichen ihres eigenen Wohnhauses.
Eames-House, Pacific Palisades (USA), Charles and Ray Eames, 1952. Charles and Ray Eames made use of the low-cost collage principle to create their own aesthetic style.

tanzende häuser / dancing houses

«bamboo houses dance along the tunes of the earth»

Linda Garland

Bambusstützen nach einem Erdbeben in Armenia (Kolumbien)
Bamboo supports after an earthquake in Armenia (Colombia)

[1] **Adriaan Beukers, Ed van Hinte: Lightness, 010 Publishers, Rotterdam 1998**

[2] **EBF, «Why Bamboo», Website**

[1] Adriaan Beukers, Ed van Hinte: Lightness, 010 Publishers, Rotterdam, 1998.

[2] EBF, «Why Bamboo», website.

Daß Kriege und andere Katastrophen seit jeher Motor für Innovationen sind, gilt auch für die Bambusarchitektur. Ein Beispiel ist der Bau von Flüchtlingsbehausungen in Rekordzeiten, ein anderes die Erdbebensicherheit, die gerade in Ländern wie Japan, Kolumbien oder den Philippinen eine wichtige Rolle spielt. In Japan gilt ein Bambushain als der sicherste Platz, an dem man sich bei einem Erdbeben aufhalten kann. Ein dichter Bambuswuchs wirkt im Boden wie Windbarrieren in der Luft, weil die Wurzeln als Puffer für die Erdstöße wirken.
Als Baumaterial kann Bambus dank seiner Flexibilität und seiner Leichtigkeit schadlos auf den Rhythmus von Erdstößen reagieren, während Bauten aus Stein oder Beton sofort zu reißen oder zu brechen drohen. Die Bauten von Simón Vélez erhalten durch die nach innen geneigten Seitenwände eine Erdbebensicherheit, die sie herkömmlichen Gebäuden weit überlegen macht. Auch sind die Verbindungen der Bambusstäbe so angelegt, daß sie flexibel bleiben. Adriaan Beukers sieht in diesen der Natur entnommenen Strukturen ein großes architektonisches Potential, das mit Elementen der Kybernetik zu mechanisch anpassungsfähigen Gebäuden nach dem «Roboter-Prinzip» führen könne. «Dies wird bereits in relativ einfacher Weise gemacht, um sie gegen Erdbeben abzusichern. (...) Das Wichtigste ist, daß nicht jeder Teil einer Struktur exakt durchgerechnet werden muß, wenn die Struktur intelligent ist und funktional mit dem ihr bestimmten Nutzen übereinstimmt.»[1]
In Limon, Costa Rica, überdauerten nur die Bambusbauten eines nationalen Bambus-Projekts ein starkes Erdbeben im Jahre 1992.[2]
Auch bei einem Erdbeben in Managua 1972, bei dem 30.000 Menschen ums Leben kamen, zeigten sich die Vorteile von Bambus. Viele der damaligen Einwohner, vor allem der älteren Generationen, waren noch selbst als Landflüchtlinge dorthin gezogen und überlieferten nach der Katastrophe die Techniken, aus Bambus Häuser zu bauen. Korbmacher aus dem Handwerkerviertel zeigten den Menschen, wie man Bambus zu Wänden verflechten und wie man ihn selbst anpflanzen kann.
In der kolumbianischen Provinz Armenia wurden nach einem verheerenden Erdbeben in kürzester Zeit über 250.000 neu Häuser aus Bambus gebaut.

It is well known that wars and similar catastrophes have driven innovations forward since time immemorial. Bamboo architecture has also evolved to meet such crises. Refugee housing of bamboo can be built in record time; in countries like Japan, Colombia, or the Philippines, housing must be able to withstand earthquakes. Hardly surprisingly, in Japan a bamboo grove is considered the safest place to seek protection from an earthquake. Dense bamboo canes have a similar effect to wind barriers in the air, because the roots absorb the shockwaves from the tremors.
Thanks to its flexibility and light weight, bamboo used as a building material can survive earth tremors undamaged, while buildings made of stone or concrete immediately threaten to crack or collapse. By designing side walls angled inwards, Simón Vélez ensures that his buildings are earthquake-proof and thus far superior to conventional buildings. In addition, the connecting joints used for bamboo canes are also designed so as to remain flexible. Adriaan Beukers sees great architectural potential in structures based on natural laws, and argues that, if used in conjunction with cybernetic devices, the result could be buildings which can mechanically adjust to conditions. «This is already done at a fairly simple level, in order to protect them against earthquakes. ... The most important thing is that it is not necessary to perform exact calculations for every part of a structure, if the structure is intelligent and functions in line with its intended use.»[1]
In Limon, Costa Rica, only the bamboo buildings of a national bamboo project survived a strong earthquake which struck the city in 1992.[2]
Following an earthquake in Managua in 1972, which claimed 30,000 lives, bamboo took on an important role. Many of the then residents, above all the older generations who had moved to the city from the country in search of work, instructed their fellow citizens how to build bamboo houses. And basket-weavers from the district showed people how to weave bamboo to make walls, as well as how to grow it.
Following a devastating earthquake, over 250,000 houses were built of bamboo in the Colombian province of Armenia.

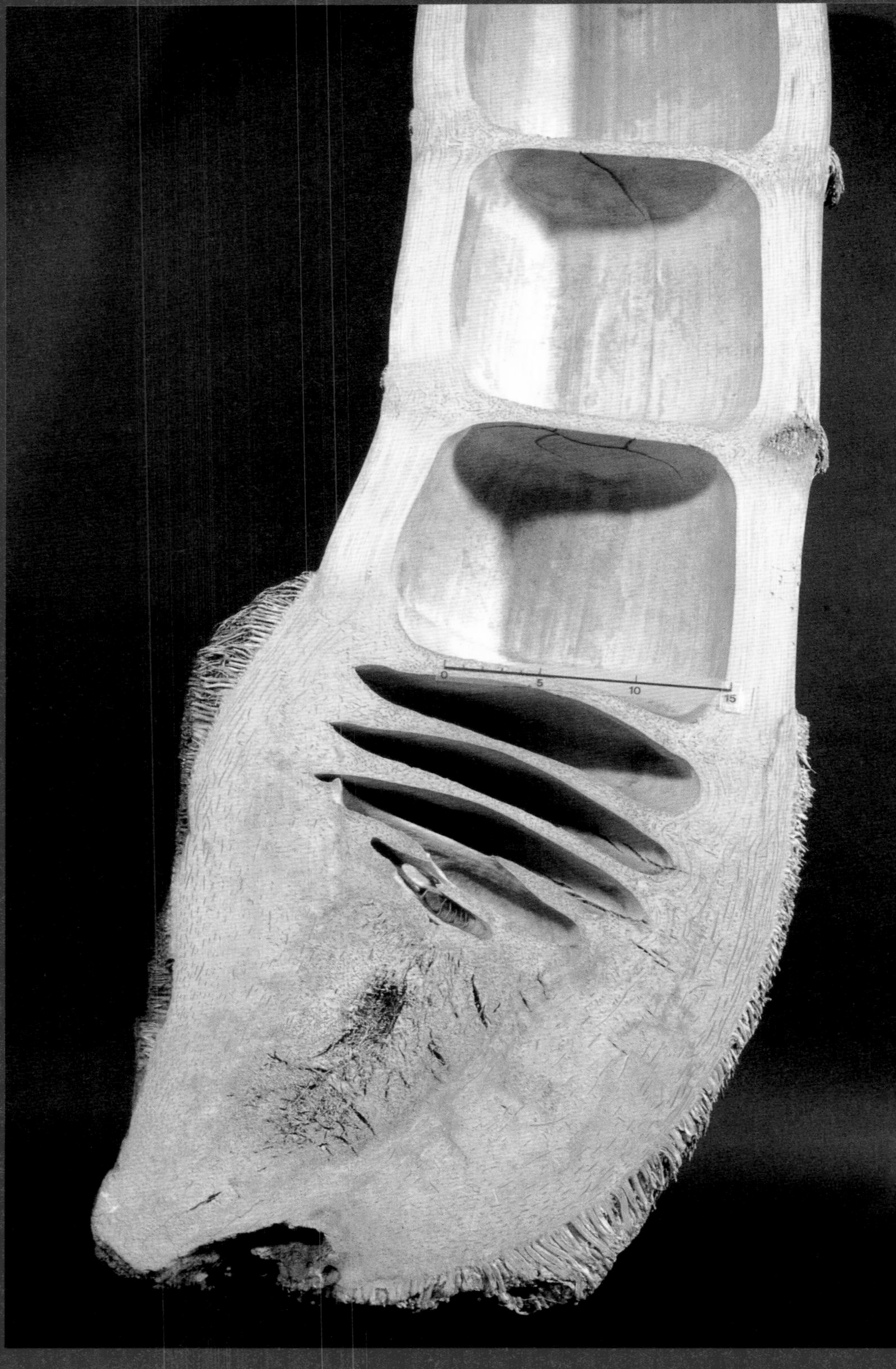

Längsschnitt durch einen Bambusstab und Wurzel
Sectional view of bamboo cane with roots, lengthwise

[1] **Schaur, E.: Die Welt braucht Hütten statt Paläste, im Gespräch mit Eda Schaur, Architektur, Mai 1996**

[2] **für nähere Informationen dazu siehe Otto, F.: Gestalt finden, Stuttgart, oder Portoghesi, P.: Architecture and Nature, Mailand, 1999**

[1] E. Schaur: Die Welt braucht Hütten statt Paläste, im Gespräch mit Eda Schaur, Architektur, May 1996.

[2] For further information, see F. Otto: Gestalt finden, Stuttgart, or P. Portoghesi: Architecture and Nature, Milan, 1999.

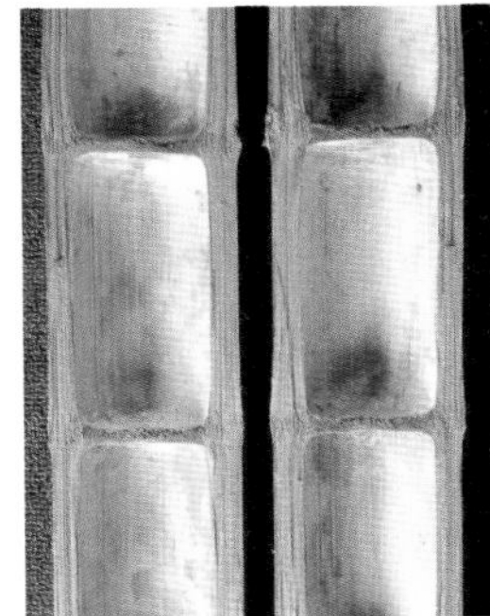

Bambus und seine Verwendung in der Architektur liefern in vielerlei Hinsicht faszinierende Erkenntnisse für eine Bauform, die sich die Anpassungsfähigkeit der Natur zu eigen macht. Bereits der Aufbau eines Bambussprößlings, der sich nach oben verjüngt und im Inneren ausgesteift ist, liefert ein Vorbild für den statisch optimalen Aufbau einer Hochhauskonstruktion. Auch mit dem Bambusstab liefert die Natur dem Menschen ein Material, dessen Aufbau und Eigenschaften denen eines hochmodernen High-Tech-Werkstoffes entsprechen: er ist stabil, aber dank seiner Hohlräume extrem leicht und elastisch, wird durch die Trennwände versteift und hat physikalische Eigenschaften, die denen anderer Baumaterialien wie Holz, Beton oder Stahl teilweise weit überlegen sind. Während Holz einen harten Kern hat und nach außen immer weicher wird, ist Bambus außen hart und innen weich – ein viel stabilerer Aufbau.
Der Entstehung solch effektiver Strukturen liegt das gleiche Prinzip zu Grunde, wie den traditionellen Formen der Bambusarchitektur. In einem Evolutionsprozess findet die Natur Lösungen, wie mit einem Minimum an Energieaufwand die verschiedenen Anforderungen erfüllt werden können. Die Form einer Pflanze nimmt im Wachstum den optimalen Weg, weil die Pflanze ein Informationssystem hat, das die benötigte Masse dorthin leitet, wo Kräfte auftreten. Andere Beispiele für hocheffektive Strukturen sind etwa Luftblasen, Spinnweben oder Vogelflügel. Auch ein bestimmter Gebäudetyp, der über Jahrhunderte der handwerklichen Tradition entstanden ist, stellt die optimale Behausung in einem bestimmten geografischen und kulturellen Umfeld dar. Ein weiteres Beispiel liefern Wachstumsprozesse von Siedlungen und Städten.[1] Die Stärke dieser natürlichen Strukturen liegt in ihrer Anpassungs- und Lernfähigkeit – sie folgen in evolutionären Prozessen den ständig wechselnden Anforderungen.
Auch wenn die Intelligenz und Stabilität natürlicher Formen seit langen in der Architektur nachgeahmt wird, ist eine systematische Erschließung natürlicher Formbildungen für architektonische Zwecke noch im Entstehen. Erste Schritte auf dem Weg dorthin leisteten Architekten wie Buckminster Fuller und Frei Otto oder die Publikation «Architecture and Nature» von Paolo Portoghesi.[2]

It is fitting that such a fascinating plant as bamboo – a prime example of the adaptability of nature – should be used in architecture. Even the form of its sprout – tapering toward the top and with a stiffened interior, serves as an excellent model for the best possible civil engineering for high-rises. And in the form of bamboo canes, nature provides man with a material whose structure and qualities equal those of a highly advanced high-tech material: It is sturdy but, thanks to its hollow interior, extremely light and elastic. It is stiff on account of its dividing walls and has physical properties which in some cases are far superior to those of other building materials such as wood, concrete, or steel. While wood has a hard core, and grows softer toward the outside, bamboo is hard on the outside and soft inside – a far more stable structure.
Such effective structures in nature develop according to the same principle as the traditional forms of bamboo architecture. In an evolutionary process, nature finds solutions whereby with a minimum of energy various demands can be met. The growth of a plant follows an optimal course, because the plant has an information system which directs the requisite mass to where energy occurs. Other examples of highly effective structures are air bubbles, cobwebs, or birds' wings. Equally, a certain type of building which has evolved in the course of hundreds of years of craft traditions, represents the optimal dwelling in a certain geographical and cultural environment. The growth processes of settlements and cities provide a further example.[1] The strength of these natural structures lies in their adaptability and learning capacity – they follow the constantly changing demands in evolutionary processes.
Even though the intelligence and stability of natural forms have long been emulated in architecture, a systematic adaptation of the forms which occur in nature for construction purposes is still in its infancy. First steps in this direction have already been made by architects such as Buckminster Fuller or Frei Otto, and are reflected in the publication «Architecture and Nature» by Paolo Portoghesi.[2]

Petronas Towers in Kuala Lumpur (Malaysia), Cesar Pelli, 1993.
Die 450 m hohen Doppeltürme sind ähnlich wie Bambussproßlinge geformt und aufgebaut.
Petronas Towers in Kuala Lumpur (Malaysia), Cesar Pelli, 1993. The 450m-high twin towers are shaped and constructed like bamboo shoots

Elektronenmikroskopische Aufnahme der Anwachsstelle des Silberwurz
Photograph of the white dryas through an electron microscope

Der Bau des Jenaer Planetarium von Walter Bauersfeld, Dyckerhoff & Widmann, 1924-25
Planetarium construction, by Walter Bauersfeld, Dyckerhoff & Widmann, 1924–5

«Bambus ist als Bauelement und Baumaterial wieder ein Thema. Seit unerfaßbar langer Zeit wird Bambus als Bauelement und Baumaterial verwendet. So waren die fernöstlichen Wohnbauten und Pagoden mit Gras eingedeckt, sie waren «Zelte», die später in Holz imitiert wurden. Man kann sehr wirtschaftlich mit Bambus Häuser und leichte Brücken bauen und diese – wenn nötig – rückstandfrei wieder wegnehmen. Nicht umsonst nennt man Bambus ein ökologisches Baumaterial.

Mit Bambus zu bauen verlangt Erfahrung und Können und bisher immer noch einen hohen Zeitaufwand, der die Verwendung in Hochkostenländern noch behindert. Ich kann mir aber vorstellen, daß auch in diesen Ländern in nächster Zeit Werke einer neuen Bambus-Baukunst von besonderer Qualität entstehen. Ob man mit Bambus eine bezaubernd gute Architektur machen kann, hängt allein von den Menschen ab, die Bambus beim Bauen einsetzen.»

frei otto

«Bamboo is enjoying a renewed popularity as a construction element and material, although it has been used as such since time immemorial. Dwellings and pagodas in the Far East were covered with grass – as «tents» that were later imitated in wood. Bamboo houses and light bridges can be built very economically and – when necessary – removed without trace. And it is with good reason that bamboo is considered an ecological building material.

Building with bamboo requires experience and skill, and to date a large amount of time; this has obstructed its use in countries with high labor costs. I can imagine that in the near future, though, new bamboo constructions of a special quality will also appear in these countries. Whether or not superb architecture can be made from bamboo depends entirely on the brains behind the bamboo building process.»

Die konstruktionsbetonte Ästhetik der Bauten von Simón Vélez ist von der Verwendung ganzer, gerader und teilweise gebündelter Bambusstäbe geprägt. Doch Bambus kann in der Architektur stilistisch und funktional auch ganz anders verwendet werden, etwa in organisch geschwungenen Dachkonstruktionen oder für Tonnengewölbe. Voraussetzung für diese Nutzung ist die Verformung ganzer Bambusstäbe oder einzelner Leisten.

Wegen seiner hohen Elastizität läßt sich Bambus leicht biegen und im gebogenen Zustand vielseitig verwenden. Dünne Rohre können im trockenen Zustand gebogen werden, dickere Rohre biegt man im feuchten Zustand und trocknet sie dann. Manche Konstruktionen aus trocken gebogenen Stäben weisen eine asymmetrische, mit abnehmender Dicke zunehmende Krümmungen auf, weil die Biegbarkeit der ganzen Bambusstange mit wachsender Dicke abnimmt. Diesem Effekt wird zuweilen entgegengewirkt, indem zwei Stäbe gegenläufig miteinander verbunden werden, so daß sich die Stärken ausgleichen. Auch gespaltener Bambus wird für solche gekrümmten Strukturen eingesetzt.

The aesthetics developed by Simón Vélez for his buildings is characterized by the use of whole, straight bamboo canes which are sometimes lashed together. But bamboo can serve quite different stylistic and functional purposes in architecture, for example for organically sweeping roof structures or for vaulted ceilings. Such applications require that the entire bamboo cane or individual strips be bent.

However, given its great elasticity, bamboo is easily bent and once bent serves a wide range of purposes. Thin canes can be bent when dry, whereas thicker canes are bent wet and then dried. Some structures utilizing dry, bent canes have an asymmetric curvature, which increases as the canes' thickness decreases, because the flexibility of whole bamboo canes decreases with mounting thickness. This effect can be counteracted by joining two canes placed against one another top to bottom so that the thickest section of one juxtaposes the thinnest section of the other. Alternatively, split bamboo is used for such curved structures.

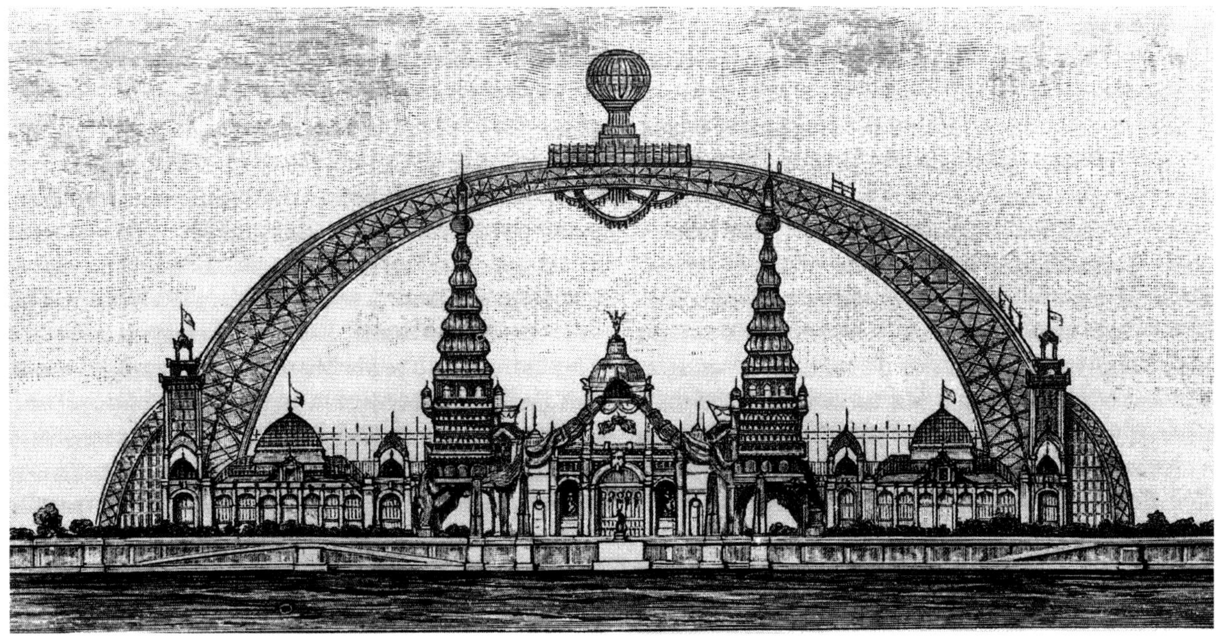

Utopisches Projekt von Charles Alfred Leclerc für die Überbauung des Marsfeldes in Paris (Frankreich) anläßlich der Weltausstellung 1900
An utopian project by Charles Alfred Leclerc designed to be built on top of the Champs de Mars, Paris, France, on the occasion of the World Fair 1900

Bambusbrücke in Taiwan
Bamboo bridge in Taiwan

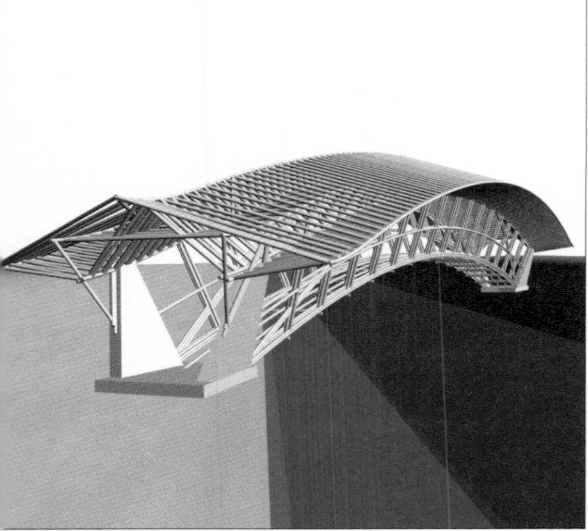

▲ **ING-Bank und NNH-Hauptsitz in Budapest (Ungarn), Erick van Egeraat, 1992-94**
ING Bank and NNH headquarters in Budapest (Hungary), Erick van Egeraat, 1992–4

▶ **Brücke für das Bob-Marley Museum in Jamaica (Projekt), Simón Vélez, 2000**
Bridge for the Bob Marley Museum in Jamaica (project), Simón Vélez, 2000

▼ **Messestand mit Bambusdach der japanischen Firma Ando Electronics**
Stand at trade fair with bamboo roof by the Japanese company, Ando Electronics

▲ **Aufbau einer provisorischen Theaterüberdachung aus Bambus in Ronyoon (Burma)**
Construction of a provisional bamboo theater roof in Ronyoon (Burma)

▶ **Fabrikhalle in Pensilvania (Kolumbien) im Bau, Simón Vélez, 1993**
Factory hall under construction in Pensilvania (Colombia), Simón Vélez, 1993

▼ **Eingang der Metro von Bilbao, Norman Foster, 1990-95**
Bilbao Metro entrance, Norman Foster, 1990–5

▲ **Japanischer Laubengang**
Japanese pergola

▶ **Installation, Hiroshi Teshigahara**
Installation, Hiroshi Teshigahara

▼ **Installation in der Einzelausstellung «Among the Clouds» im Gen'ichiro Inokuma Museum of Contemporary Art in Marugame (Japan), Hiroshi Teshigahara, 1994-95**
Installation in the solo exhibition «Among the Clouds» in the Gen'ichiro Inokuma Museum of Contemporary Art in Marugame (Japan), Hiroshi Teshigahara, 1994–5

nstallation in der Ausstellung «Japan Today» im Lousiana Museum of Modern Art in Kopenhagen (Dänemark), Hiroshi Teshigahara, 1995
nstallation in «Japan Today» exhibition in the Lousiana Museum of Modern Art in Copenhagen (Denmark), Hiroshi Teshigahara, 1995

experimente mit bambuskuppeln / experiments with bamboo domes

Die Zusammenarbeit des Instituts für leichte Flächentragwerke in Stuttgart mit der School of Architecture in Ahmedabad (Indien) unter der Leitung von Eda Schaur und J. R. Vasavada führte ab 1981 zum Bau von Gitterschalenkuppeln aus Bambus.
The joint work of the Institut für leichte Flächentragwerke (Institute for Light Surface Supporting Structures) in Stuttgart and the School of Architecture in Ahmedabad (India), directed by Eda Schaur and J. R. Vasavada, led to the construction of bamboo grid matrices as of 1981

experimente mit bambuskuppeln / experiments with bamboo domes

eda schaur

Warum soll man sich im Zeitalter der zahlreichen ausgezeichneten industriell hergestellten Baumaterialien noch über das Bauen mit Bambus den Kopf zerbrechen? Auf den ersten Blick eine berechtigte Frage. Stellt man aber die ökologischen Probleme unserer Lebensräume und die limitierten Ressourcen dem Bedarf an gebautem Raum der noch immer wachsenden Weltbevölkerung gegenüber, dann gewinnt das Interesse an Bauen mit Bambus seine Berechtigung, zumal Bambus gerade dort reichlich vorkommt, wo der allergrösste Bedarf an Bauten vorliegt.

Die Stärke dieses Materials wird von der Pflanze mit der erstaunlichen Höhe der Bambushalme, die auch zehngeschossige Gebäude übertreffen können, überzeugend demonstriert. Die Schönheit der Halme, ihr schnelles Wachstum und die einfache Bearbeitung machen Bambus zu einem Material, das Beachtung verdient. In den Ländern seines Vorkommens – Afrika, Südamerika und Asien – wird er seit Jahrhunderten zur Herstellung vielfältiger Objekte, von kleinsten Gebrauchsgegenständen bis zu grossen, prachtvollen Bauten eingesetzt.
Beobachtet man Bambushalme im Wind, ihre Bewegung und ihre Formen, dann wird einem aber auch die Flexibilität dieses Materials bewußt. Im Gegensatz zu künstlichen, rohrförmigen Stangen verjüngen sich Bambushalme sowohl in ihrem Durchmesser, wie in ihrer Wandstärke von der Basis zur Spitze, was die typische Krümmungsform mit dem nach oben hin immer kleiner werdenden Krümmungsradius bedingt. Nimmt man diese natürliche Krümmung in die Konstruktionen auf, eröffnet sich die Möglichkeit der Anwendung von deutlich längeren Stäben als in Konstruktionen mit geradlinigen Elementen. Bekanntlich wird ein Element durch die Krümmung tragfähiger, was auch bei Bambus genützt werden kann. Die Krümmungsradien, die sich entlang der Halme entsprechend ihrer Verjüngung verändern, werden so zu einem formbeeinflussenden Faktor, der auch konstruktiv sinnvoll genutzt werden kann. Dies führt zu einer anderen Ästhetik von Bambuskonstruktionen, deren Beispiele vereinzelt in traditionellen Bauten zu finden sind. Die architektonischen und herstellungstechnischen Möglichkeiten derartiger Bambuskonstruktionen sind kaum untersucht und können noch ungeahnte Potentiale beinhalten.

Why should we concern ourselves with building with bamboo in this age where we have so many excellent industrially produced building materials? At face value, a valid question. But if we compare the ecological problems of our world and its limited resources with the need the ever-growing population has for more buildings, then the interest in building with bamboo is evidently justified. And this is all the more the case, as bamboo originates from just those areas where there is the greatest need of building.

The strength of this plant is convincingly demonstrated by the incredible height of bamboo canes – which may exceed the height of ten-story buildings. The beauty of the stem, its rapid growth, and simple processing make bamboo a noteworthy material. In countries where it is found – in Africa, South America, and Asia – it has been used to make a multitude of objects from the smallest utensil to magnificent large buildings.
If you watch bamboo canes in the wind, their movement and form, then you will also realize how flexible they are. Unlike synthetic tubular-shaped rods, bamboo gradually reduces in circumference as well as wall thickness from the base to the tip. This gives it its typical curved form and causes the radius of curvature to taper upward. If you incorporate this natural curve when building, then it becomes possible to use significantly longer poles than in constructions with straight lines. It is well known that an element can bear more load when it is curved, and this principle can also be utilized with bamboo.
The radius of curvature, which changes along the cane according to its circumference, influences the form which can then be put to constructive use. This brings about another aesthetic element in bamboo construction, examples of which can be found here and there in traditional architecture. The architectural potential and the scope for manufacturing technology in such bamboo constructions have not been properly analyzed and could hold unexpected potential.

I have done experiments with split bamboo in cooperation with the School of Architecture in Ahmedabad, India. Our aim was to couple new constructional insights and methods of compressive and tensile structures with this traditional building material. In this way, we hoped to discover new methods for building with bamboo and then test them for modern use.

Ich selbst habe mit gespaltenem Bambus experimentiert. Diese Experimente wurden in Zusammenarbeit mit der School of Architecture in Ahmedabad, Indien durchgeführt.
Unser Bestreben war, die neuen konstruktiven Erkenntnisse und Methoden der druck- und zugbeanspruchten Konstruktionen mit dem traditionellen Baumaterial Bambus zu verknüpfen, um damit neue Möglichkeiten des Bauens mit diesem Material aufzudecken und ihre Eignung für moderne Nutzungen zu prüfen.
Die Untersuchungen zeigten, dass mit gespaltenem Bambus tragfähige Konstruktionen errichtet werden können, die ein sehr geringer Materialverbrauch auszeichnet.
Dafür wurden Bambushalme in 8 Streifen gespalten. Die dünnen Bambusstreifen werden nur durch Krümmung tragfähig. Zusammengefügt zu Gittern mit einer Maschenweite von 35 bis 45 cm wurden sie in Form von Gitterschalen in räumliche Krümmung gebracht. Die freie Spannweite so geschaffener kuppelförmiger Konstruktionen ist durch die geringen Ausmaße einzelner Elemente – Breite von 30 bis 25 mm, Dicke 20 bis 10 mm – auf ca. 10 m beschränkt.
Wegen seiner Zug- und Druckfestigkeit ist Bambus für den Schalenbau gut geeignet.
Die Formwelt der Gitterschalen ist vielfältig, allerdings erfordern solche Konstruktionen noch eine Dacheindeckung, die der räumlichen Krümmung der Tragkonstruktion folgen kann. Der Vorteil dieser Konstruktionen ist, dass sie mit sehr wenig Material, mit wenigen Werkzeugen leicht herzustellen sind und tragfähige, sehr leichte Dächer bilden. Im Rahmen dieser Untersuchungen haben wir auch mit Versuchen begonnen, Bambus für überwiegend zugbeanspruchte Konstruktionen einzusetzen. Hier sind vor allem materialgerechte zugfeste Verbindungen zu entwickeln.
Die Errichtung des Prototyps des Museums für einfache Technologien in Madras, Indien, an dem ich in Zusammenarbeit mit Yona Friedman und lokalen Handwerkern arbeitete, gab mir eine weitere Gelegenheit, die konstruktiven und ästhetischen Potentiale derartiger Bambuskonstruktionen zu studieren.

Die Versuchsbauten, an denen ich beteiligt war, haben deutlich gezeigt, dass man mit Bambus Bauten von besonderer Qualität errichten kann. Seine Stärke voll zu nutzen, seiner Schönheit Ausdruck zu verleihen und seine Schwächen zu

The experiments showed that load-bearing constructions could be built with split bamboo canes, which excelled in their limited use of material.
First of all, we split bamboo canes into eight strips. The thin strips can bear loads only because of their curvature. Woven into grids with a mesh-width of 35–45 cm, they were turned into spatially curved grid matrices. The free span of dome-shaped constructions made in this way is limited by the size of the individual elements – which have a width of 25–30 mm and a thickness of 10–20 mm – to not more than about 10 meters. Bamboo is well suited to dome constructions because of its compressive and tensile strength.
The grid matrices can be made in many forms; however, such constructions still need a roof covering, which can be curved like the supports. The advantage of this sort of construction is that it can be simply assembled with few tools and little material to make load-bearing, but very light roofs. As part of the experiment, we also attempted to use bamboo in constructions predominantly exposed to tensile forces. Strong tensile joints which suit the material are needed more than anything.
In making the prototype for the Museum for Simple Technology in Madras, India, which I worked on together with Yona Friedman and local craftsmen, I had a further chance to study the constructive and aesthetic potential of such bamboo buildings.

The trial buildings I participated in clearly showed that you can make buildings of a special quality from bamboo. But in order to make the most of its strength, to lend expression to its beauty and to overcome its shortcomings, one must be able to work very skillfully with the material. The use of bamboo in combination with other materials may well contribute to promising future solutions. The aim, however, must not be to use bamboo only where other materials are lacking. Rather, bamboo should be used to create architecture which is socially acceptable, otherwise it will become unpopular and lose its meaning, which would be very regrettable.

Eda Schaur is Professor at the Construction Institute at Innsbruck University. She carried out research on the use of bamboo in grid matrices with architect Frei Otto at the Institute for Light Surface Support Structures, and has worked in Asian countries with Yona Friedman on light bamboo construction for social causes.

Lit.: IL 31 Bambus – Bamboo, Mitteilungen des Instituts für Leichte Flächentragwerke, Band 31, Stuttgart 1985 Eda Schaur; Bambus – Baumaterial der Zukunft, in: 4. Internationales Holzbau-Forum, Konstruktionen und Bauwerke, 1998 SH-Holz, CH 2504 Biel

Literature: IL 31 Bambus – Bamboo, Report of Institut für Leichte Flächentragwerke, Vol. 31, Stuttgart, 1985. Eda Schaur: Bambus – Baumaterial der Zukunft, in: 4. Internationales Holzbau-Forum, Konstruktionen und Bauwerke, Biel, 1998 (SH-Holz, CH 2504 Biel).

überwinden erfordert allerdings einen sehr gekonnten Umgang mit diesem Material. Die Verwendung von Bambus in Verbindung mit anderen Materialien mag hier zu zukunftsträchtigen Lösungen beitragen. Das Ziel darf allerdings nicht sein, Bambus nur dort zu verwenden, wo die Mittel für den Einsatz anderer Materialien fehlen. Vielmehr muß Bambus so verwendet werden, daß Architektur entsteht, die gesellschaftliche Anerkennung findet, sonst verliert Bambus an Akzeptanz – und damit an Bedeutung, was meiner Meinung nach eine sehr bedauerliche Entwicklung wäre.

Eda Schaur ist seit 1995 Professorin am Institut für Konstruktion und Gestaltung der Universität Innsbruck. Als wissenschaftliche Mitarbeiterin des Instituts für leichte Flächentragwerke der Universität Stuttgart, Leitung Frei Otto, erforschte sie die Verwendung von Bambus in Gitterschalen und arbeitete in asiatischen Ländern zusammen mit Yona Friedman an Leichtbaukonstruktionen aus Bambus für soziale Zwecke.

Demonstration des Biegeverhaltens von Bambusstäben an der Universität Ahmedabad (Indien)
Demonstration of bending properties of bamboo poles at the Ahmedabad University (India)

Naiju-Wohnzentrum und Kindergarten in Chikuho/Fukuoka (Japan), Shoei Yoh, 1995. Zu dieser spektakulären Verwendung von Bambus als Tragwerk für eine Betondecke wurde der japanische Architekt durch das ortsansässige Bambus-Flechthandwerk inspiriert. Gemeinsam mit den Handwerkern wurde ein flaches Bambusgitter geflochten, das anschließend in die Gebäudeform gebracht wurde.
Naiju Residential Center and Kindergarten in Chikuho, Fukuoka (Japan), Shoei Yoh, 1995. The Japanese architect was inspired in his spectacular use of bamboo to support a concrete roof, by the local methods of bamboo-weaving. Together with the craftsmen, he wove a flat bamboo grid and then included it in the building

Eine große Freiheit bei der Formung von Bambusstrukturen ergibt sich bei der Verwendung von Bambusgittern, wie sie etwa der japanische Architekt Shoei Yoh einsetzt. In seinen Bauten werden regelmäßige Gitter aus gespaltenen Bambusstäben in eine dreidimensionale Form gebracht, die dann als Gitterschale mit einer hohen Traglast dienen kann. Neben seiner enormen Belastbarkeit bildet das sichtbare Bambusgitter auch einen wichtigen Bestandteil der Deckengestaltung des Innenraums.
Ein Pionier in der Konstruktion von Kuppelbauten von beeindruckender Leichtigkeit und Stabilität war der Amerikaner Richard Buckminster Fuller. Mit seinen Geodesic Domes prägte er den Typus eines modernen, geodätischen Kuppelbaus, zu dem er an der Architekturschule in Kalkutta mit Studenten auch Versuche aus Bambus durchführte. Eda Schaur, Mitarbeiterin des deutschen Institut für leichte Flächentragwerke, erforschte kuppelförmige Dachkonstruktionen mit Gitterschalen aus Bambus in den siebziger Jahren bei einem Projekt auf den Philippinen. An die abgehängten Zeltkonstruktionen des deutschen Architekten Frei Otto erinnern die verspannten Bambusgitter der holländischen Gruppe Fleximac. Spektakuläre zugbeanspruchte Konstruktionen aus Bambus sind die Hängebrücken, wie sie auf Java und Borneo, aber auch in den Andenstaaten Kolumbien und Ecuador gebaut werden.

Great flexibility in the forming of bamboo structures can be attained by utilizing bamboo matrices, such as those favored by Japanese architect Shoei Yoh who regularly features such structures in his buildings. To this end, split bamboo canes are shaped into a three-dimensional form, which can then serve as a matrix with a high load-bearing capacity. In addition to providing this enormous tensile strength, the visible bamboo grid also forms an important interior feature of the ceiling.
American Richard Buckminster Fuller pioneered the making of dome structures which were immensely light and stable. His «geodesic domes» represented modern, geodesic structures – and it was in this regard that he conducted experiments in bamboo with students at the Architecture College in Calcutta. Eda Schaur, an employee at the German Institute for Light Surface Support Structures, conducted research into dome-shaped roof structures incorporating bamboo matrices back in the 1970s as part of a project in the Philippines. The suspended tent constructions created by German architect Frei Otto call to mind the covered bamboo grids of Dutch group Fleximac. Spectacular tensile structures in bamboo are the suspended bridges built in Java and Borneo, but also in Colombia and Ecuador.

Uchino-Wohnzentrum in Chikuho/Fukuoka (Japan), Shoei Yoh, 1996 / Uchino Residential Center in Chikuho, Fukuoka (Japan), Shoei Yoh, 1996

Naiju-Wohnzentrum und Kindergarten in Chikuho/Fukuoka (Japan), Shoei Yoh, 1995.
Naiju Residential Center and Kindergarten in Chikuho, Fukuoka (Japan), Shoei Yoh, 1995

Jukai Dome Park in Odate (Japan), Toyo Ito, 1995–97 / Jukai Dome Park in Odate (Japan), Toyo Ito, 1995–7

Geodätische Bambuskuppel in Fukuoka (Japan), Shoei Yoh, 1989
Geodesic bamboo dome in Fukuoka (Japan), Shoei Yoh, 1989

Buckminster Fuller demonstriert Tensegrity-Modelle an der Southern Illinois University, 1958
Buckminster Fuller demonstrates his «Tensegrity» models at the Southern Illinois University, 1958

[1] Adriaan Beukers, Ed van Hinte: Lightness, 010 Publishers, Rotterdam 1998

[1] Adriaan Beukers, Ed van Hinte: Lightness, 010 Publishers, Rotterdam, 1998.

Die Stabilität von synergetischen Strukturen beruht nicht auf der Stärke ihrer Einzelteile, sondern in dem ausgleichenden Zusammenwirken ihrer Elemente. Säugetiere besitzen Muskeln und Sehnen für die Aufnahme von Zugkräften, Knochen für die Druckbelastung. In Atomen wird die Abstoßung der Teilchen untereinander durch die Anziehung des Atomkerns neutralisiert.
Dieses Synergieprinzip wird auch für Architektur und Design erschlossen. Ein synergetisches Gebäude ist mehr als die Summe seiner einzelnen Elemente und Funktionen. Ein Pionier der synergetischen Gestaltung war der Amerikaner Richard Buckminster Fuller. Er beobachtete, daß sich Architekten seit jeher auf die Druckkräfte zu verlassen pflegten, indem sie schweres und massives Material aufeinanderstapelten. Doch die notwendigen Träger und Pfosten neigen unter Last immer dazu, sich zu verbiegen. Fuller entwickelte deshalb seine Tensegrity-Strukturen – in sich stabile Konstruktionen, in denen die auftretenden Kräfte auf das ganze System übertragen und ausgeglichen werden. Wie in Atomen berühren sich ihre Einzelteile nicht (sie werden durch Schnüre verbunden) und bilden doch eine leichte und stabile Struktur. Mit wachsender Größe werden diese Tensegrity-Strukturen im Verhältnis immer leichter und somit immer effizienter.[1] Da die Voraussetzung für synergetische Strukturen in der Architektur leichte und hochfeste Grundelemente sind, eignet sich Bambus dafür ideal. 1976 experimentierte Buckminster Fuller in Kalkutta mit Bambus für Tensegrity-Strukturen, und der Architekt Renzo Piano entwickelte ebenfalls Tensegrity-Modelle und andere innovative Leichtbau-Konstruktionen aus Bambus. Daß Bauten aus Bambus so erdbebensicher sind und als Gerüste bis zu 70 Stockwerke hoch gebaut werden können, basiert ebenfalls auf dem synergetischen Zusammenwirken der Bambusstäbe.
Übrigens muß sich die Nutzung von Synergien nicht nur auf die Statik eines Gebäudes beziehen. Beispiel dafür ist die natürliche Klimatisierung von Lehmbauten: Beim nächtlichen Abkühlen der Lehmbauten nehmen diese Wasser auf, das in den Wänden tagsüber kühlend wirkt.

The stability of synergetic structures does not rest on the strength of their individual sections, but on the balanced interaction of their elements. Mammals possess tendons and muscles to absorb tractive forces, and bones to bear pressure. In atoms, the mutual repulsion of particles is neutralized by the attraction of the atomic nucleus. This synergetic principle is also to be seen in architecture and design. A synergetic building is more than the sum of the individual elements and functions. American Richard Buckminster Fuller led the way in synergetic design. He observed that since time immemorial architects had tended to rely on forces of pressure, by piling heavy and massive materials on top of one another. Yet the necessary supports and posts tend to bend under loads. This led Fuller to develop what he termed tensegrity structures – i.e. structures with inherent stability in which the forces produced are equalized by being transferred to the entire system. As is the case with atoms, there is no contact between individual sections (they are bound by cords). This makes for a light, yet stable structure.[1] As the size of these tensegrity structures increases they become ever lighter in comparative terms and thus ever more efficient. Since synergetic structures in architecture require light, high-tensile basic elements, bamboo is ideally suited to such applications. In 1976, Buckminster Fuller experimented in Calcutta with bamboo for tensegrity structures and architect Renzo Piano likewise developed tensegrity models and other innovative lightweight constructions of bamboo. The fact that buildings of bamboo incur so little damage during earthquakes and can be built up to 70 stories high as skeletal constructions is equally due to the synergetic interplay of bamboo canes.
Incidentally, employing synergies in construction can apply to areas other than the statics of a building. For example, clay buildings have natural temperature-regulating properties: during the night when the temperature drops, clay structures absorb water which then has a cooling effect during the daytime.

Tensegrity-Modelle und andere Leichtbaustrukturen aus Bambus im UNESCO-Laboratorium-Workshop in Punta Nave (Italien), erbaut 1989 von Renzo Piano. Die Einrichtung zur Erforschung der Konstruktionsprinzipien von natürlichem Materialien wird gemeinsam von der UNESCO und dem Renzo Piano Building Workshop genutzt. Während die UNESCO für das kulturelle und edukative Programm aufkommt, wurde die Konstruktion des Gebäudes von Renzo Piano ermöglicht.
«Tensegrity» models and other light constructions from bamboo at the UNESCO Laboratory Workshop in Punta Nave (Italy), built 1989, by Renzo Piano. The facility for exploring the construction principles in natural materials is used jointly by UNESCO and the Renzo Piano Building Workshop. While UNESCO uses it for its cultural and educational program, Renzo Piano has constructed a building there

Tensegrity-Modelle aus Metallstäben von Buckminster Fuller und aus Bambus
«Tensegrity» models made from Buckminster Fuller's metal rods, and bamboo

bambus im test / testing bamboo

[1] William Portefield, Shanghai, 1920–1930

[2] Janssen, J.A.: Bamboo research at the Eindhoven University of Technology, Eindhoven 1990, S. 15

[1] William Portefield, Shanghai, 1920–1930.

[2] J.A. Janssen: Bamboo research at the Eindhoven University of Technology, Eindhoven, 1990, p. 15.

Von der Züchtung von Bambus mit drei- oder viereckigem Querschnitt erhofft man sich eine Standardisierung und weitere Verbesserung der konstruktiven Eigenschaften. Dazu werden über den Sproß Formen des gewünschten Querschnitts gestülpt, in die der Stab hineinwächst.

By cultivating bamboo with a triangular or square cross-section, it is hoped that its constructive properties can be standardized and further improved. To do this, forms with the desired cross-sectional shape would be placed over the sprouts which would then grow up inside them

«Die feine, polierte Oberfläche eines Bambusstabes ist eine bemerkenswerte, fast unnatürliche Eigenschaft. Kein Finish von Menschenhand ist so weich und hart zugleich. Der Grund ist die Sekretion von Wachs und Silikon durch die Epidermis. Die gewachste Oberfläche ist die Basis der Politur, während das Silikon härtet.»[1] So beschrieb in den zwanziger Jahren der britische Wissenschaftler William Portefield in Shanghai die unverwechselbare Oberfläche eines Bambusstabs.
Doch noch in den achtziger Jahren verglich der Holländer Jules A. Janssen den Erkenntnisstand über die mechanischen und technischen Eigenschaften von Bambus mit der Situation des Holzbaus vor ca. 100 Jahren als eine handwerkliche, auf Tradierung basierende Verwendung von Holz zu stabilen, jedoch oft überkomplizierten und verschwenderischen Bauten führte. Der Schritt von einem Low-Tech-Material zu einem innovationsträchtigen Baustoff, den Holz bereits vollzogen hat, stehe Bambus noch bevor. Eine Vertiefung der Forschung könnte dazu führen, den Materialbedarf zu senken und gleichzeitig Standards für eine sinnvolle Verwendung dieses neuen Materials zu entwickeln.[2]
Da jeder Bambusstab unterschiedlich ist und sich auch kaum wie ein Holzbauelement zuschneiden läßt, läßt er nicht standardisieren. Eine Ausnahme bildet einzig der vierkantige Bambus, der entsteht, indem man über den Bambus-Sprößling eine vierkantige Schalung legt, in die der Stab hineinwächst. Der Vierkant-Bambus hat den Vorteil, daß bei Verbindungen grössere Kontaktflächen entstehen. In China wurde im 18. Jahrhundert auch von einem Bambus mit dreieckigem Querschnitt berichtet. Auch Baunormen für Bambus fehlen bislang noch, was die Verwendung in Ländern mit strengen Bauvorschriften erschwert.
Die mechanischen Eigenschaften von Bambus hängen von der botanischen Spezies, dem Alter des Stabes bei der Ernte, dem Feuchtigkeitsgehalt und natürlich von Durchmesser und Wandstärke ab.

«The finely polished surface of a bamboo cane has a remarkable, almost unnatural property. No man-made finish is as soft, yet simultaneously as hard. The reason for this is the wax and silicon secreted by the epidermis. The waxed surface is the basis of the finish, whilst the silicon hardens.»[1]
This is how British scientist William Portefield described the unmistakable surface of a bamboo cane during his travel in Shanghai during the 1920s.Yet as late as the 1980s Dutchman Jules A. Janssen compared man's knowledge on the mechanical and technical properties of bamboo with the situation prevailing in respect to the use of timber roughly 100 years ago. The emphasis then on craftsmen's skills and traditional methods led to constructions which, though sturdy, were often overly complicated and wasteful. Bamboo still has to make the transition (already made by wood) from a low-tech material to a building material with high innovative potential. Intensifying research could lead to lower material requirements whilst at the same time developing standards for using this new material sensibly.[2]
Since every bamboo cane is different and can hardly be cut like an element for a wooden structure, it cannot be standardized. The only exception is square bamboo, which is produced by placing a square sheath over the bamboo sprout into which the cane subsequently grows. One advantage of square bamboo is that larger contact areas are produced for joints. During the 18th century in China there were reports of a bamboo species with a triangular cross-section. Moreover, there are to date no building standards for bamboo, which hampers its use in countries with strict building regulations.
The mechanical properties of bamboo depend on the species, age of the cane at harvesting, moisture content, and, naturally, the diameter and wall thickness.

[3] **Auszug aus: Untersuchungen zur Tragfähigkeit der Bambusart *«Guadua Angustifolia»*, Forschungsbericht vom Otto-Graf-Institut, Dr. Simon Aicher. Die vollständigen und detaillierten Untersuchungsergebnisse und der Testbericht von Dr. Simon Aicher werden im Fachmagazin «Wood, Science and Technology», Springer Verlag, veröffentlicht.**

[3] Excerpt from: Test examinations of the load capacity of *«Guadua Angustifolia»* bamboo, a research report by the Otto-Graf-Institut, Dr. Simon Aicher. The complete and detailed findings of the tests and Dr. Simon Aicher's test report will be published in the journal «Wood, Science and Technology», Springer Verlag

Druckversuche:

Druckfestigkeit $f_{c,0}$	**56 N/mm²**
Drucksteifigkeit $E_{c,0}$	**18.400 N/mm²**

4-Punkt-Biegeversuche (DIN EN 408):

Mittlere Biegefestigkeit f_m	**74 N/mm²**
Mittlere Biegefestigkeit f_m bei idealer Trocknung bzw. idealem Feuchtigkeitsgehalt	**100 N/mm²**
Mittleres Biege-Elastizitätsmodul E_m	**17.900 N/mm²**

Zugsteifigkeitsversuche:

Mittleres Zug-Elastizitätsmodul	**19.000 N/mm²**

Verbindungsversuche:

Mittlere Zugtragfähigkeit der geprüften Verbindung	**140 KN**

Abschließend läßt sich zu den hier auszugsweise skizzierten Prüfergebnissen zur Verwendung der Bambusart *«Guadua Angustifolia»* folgendes festhalten: Bei der untersuchten Bambusart handelt es sich um einen hoch beanspruchbaren, für ingenieurmäßig konzipierte Bauwerke planmäßig verwendbaren Baustoff, dem nach den Testergebnissen eine alternative Verwendung im Vergleich zu Bauholz zuzusprechen sein sollte. Die erzielten Werte bei den wesentlichen, konstruktiv äußerst wichtigen Steifigkeits- und Festigkeitseigenschaften lagen, insbesondere gewichtsnormiert, extrem hoch, im Vergleich zu anderen heute planmäßig verwendeten Ingenieurbaustoffen.

Außerdem ist sowohl bei den Druck- bzw. Biegeversuchen das Nachtragverhalten als äußerst günstig zu beschreiben. Das heißt, auch nach dem Erreichen der maximalen Tragfähigkeit liegt eine Resttragfähigkeit von 1/3–1/2 der maximalen Tragfähigkeit vor.[3]

Voraussetzungen:

- **Bambusart *«Guadua Angustifolia»* mit Querschnittsschlankheiten r/t von $3 \leq r/t \leq 5{,}5$**
- **Nicht klimatisierte Prüfhalle**
- **10–15% Feuchtigkeitsgehalt im Bambus**

Pressure tests:

Resistance to pressure $f_{c,0}$	56 N/mm²
Resistance to pressure $E_{c,0}$	18,400 N/mm²

4-Point bending tests (DIN EN 408):

Mean flectional resistance f_m	74 N/mm²
Mean flectional resistance f_m given ideal drying and / or ideal moisture content	100 N/mm²
Mean flectional/elasticity module E_m	17,900 N/mm²

Tensile strength tests:

Mean tensile/elasticity module	19,000 N/mm²

Connection tests:

Mean tensile bearing load of connectors tested	140 KN

In conclusion, the following can be said on the basis of the above cursory outline of the findings of tests conducted using *«Guadua Angustifolia»* bamboo. The type of bamboo tested can be subjected to a heavy load and can be used for edifices designed and planned by engineers; indeed, our findings show that it be could considered an alternative that bears comparison with timber. The bamboo proved to have extremely high values compared with other building materials commonly used for construction engineering today as regards rigidity and solidity (both of which are of such important parameters for building materials) especially when the figures were normed for the weight of the material.

Moreover, the bamboo's supplementary load-bearing capacity was especially favorable during our bending and pressure tests. In other words, after maximum load-bearing capacity had been reached, the bamboo still exhibited a residual load-bearing capacity of 1/3–1/2 of its maximum capacity.[3]

Conditions:

- Type of bamboo *«Guadua Angustifolia»* with cross-section fineness r/t of $3 \leq r/t \leq 5.5$
- Testing hall without a/c
- 10–15% moisture content in the bamboo

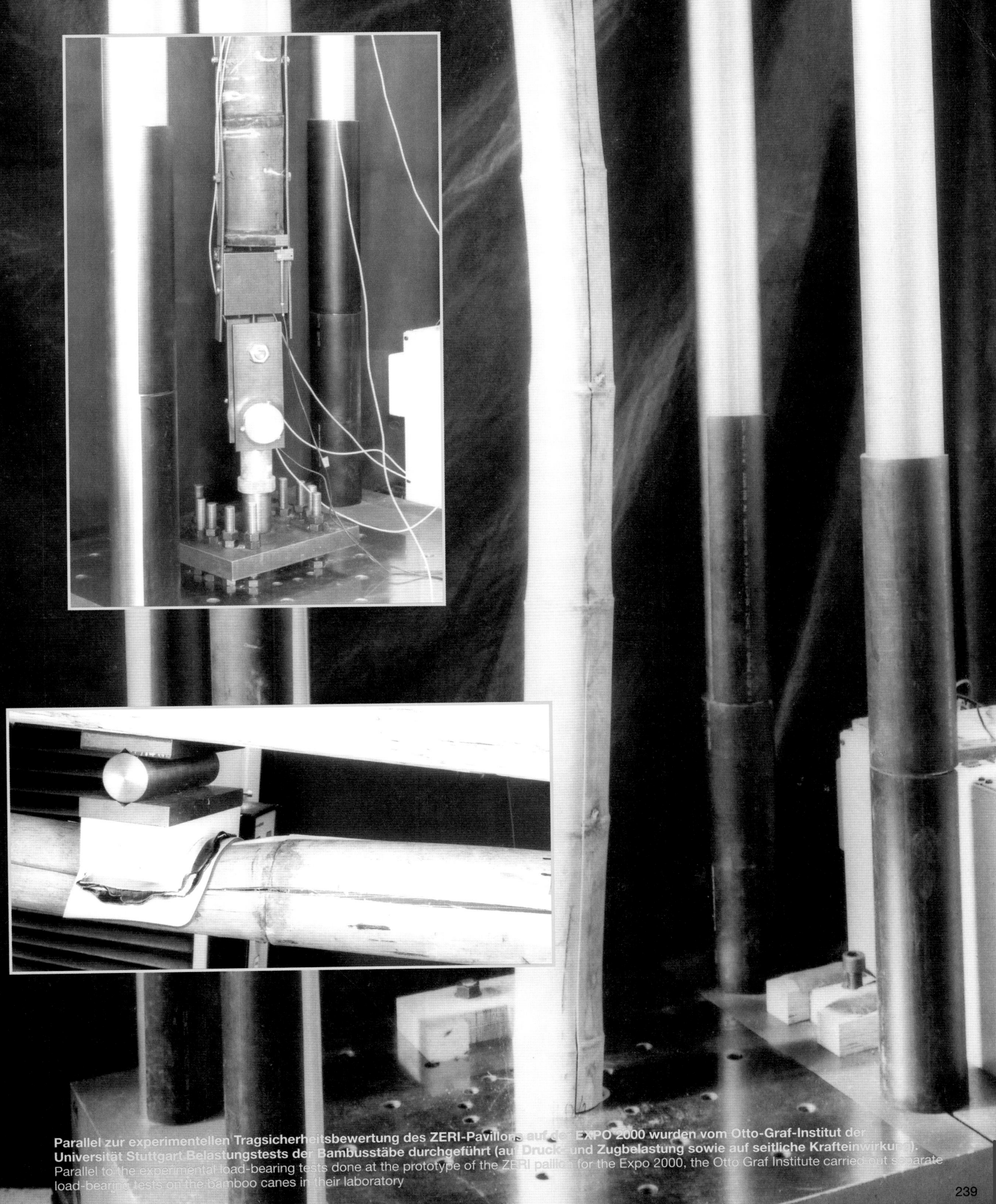

Parallel zur experimentellen Tragsicherheitsbewertung des ZERI-Pavillons auf der EXPO 2000 wurden vom Otto-Graf-Institut der Universität Stuttgart Belastungstests der Bambusstäbe durchgeführt (auf Druck- und Zugbelastung sowie auf seitliche Krafteinwirkung).
Parallel to the experimental load-bearing tests done at the prototype of the ZERI pavilion for the Expo 2000, the Otto Graf Institute carried out separate load-bearing tests on the bamboo canes in their laboratory

Das Ausfachen einer Bambusstruktur mit Lehm in Kolumbien
Inserting clay into a bamboo structure in Colombia

Haus aus Bambus und Lehm in der Provinz Caldas (Kolumbien)
House made of bamboo and clay in the Caldas province (Colombia)

[1] **Auch die ZERI-Stiftung entwickelte zwei Verfahren, die Bambusspäne als Verstärkungsfasern für Beton geignet machen. Eines davon basiert auf der Nutzung eines Pilzes, der in den selben Ökosystemen wie Bambus beheimatet ist und den Zucker abbaut, das andere basiert auf dem Räuchern der Stäbe.**

[2] **Hidalgo, O.: Nuevas técnicas de construcción con bambú, Estudios técnicos colombianos, Bogotá 1978**

[1] The ZERI Foundation has also developed two processes for rendering bamboo shavings suitable for use as reinforcing fiber for concrete. One is based on the use of a fungus which lives in the same eco-systems as bamboo and degrades the sugar; the other is based on smoking the canes.

[2] O. Hidalgo: Nuevas técnicas de construcción con bambú, Estudios técnicos colombianos, Bogotá, 1978.

Besonders in der Luft- und Raumfahrt wird an Verbundwerkstoffen aus zwei Komponenten geforscht, die sich durch höchste Festigkeit bei minimalem Gewicht auszeichnen. Dabei werden Kunststoffe wie etwa Epoxidharze oder Polyester durch Fasermatten oder -gewebe verstärkt, die meist aus Glasfaser oder Carbonfaser bestehen. Auch Bambus kann für solche High-Tech-Werkstoffe verwendet werden: 1997 wurde ein Surfbrett entwickelt, das aus einer hochfesten Mischung aus Epoxidharz und Bambusspänen besteht.
Auch Simón Vélez kombiniert in seinen Bauten die Bambusstäbe mit anderen Werkstoffen, z. B. mit Beton. Er facht Skelettkonstruktionen aus Bambus mit Beton aus oder füllt die Enden der Bambusstäbe mit diesem Material, um die entstehenden massiven Bauteile leichter miteinander verbinden zu können.
Bambus kann als Ersatz für die krebserregenden Asbestfasern verwendet werden. Um Bambusspäne als Betonverstärkung zu verwenden, muß ihnen allerdings der Zucker entzogen werden, was einen hohen Wasserverbrauch mit sich bringt. Die japanische Firma ASK Board hat für diesen Prozeß erstmals ein ökonomisches Verfahren entwickelt und eine Fabrik in Indonesien gegründet, in der auch die Dachplatten für den ZERI-Pavillion gefertigt wurden.[1]

Als Basis für Verbundwerkstoffe wird Bambus übrigens seit langem genutzt. So werden Lehmbauten dadurch noch stabiler gemacht, daß dem Lehm Bambusspäne oder Stroh zugesetzt werden. In Valdivia, Ecuador, wurden Mauerreste aus Bambus und Lehm ausgegraben, die 7.550 bis 5.500 Jahre alt sind. Als Wandelemente dienen auch verputzte Bambusmatten. Mit der Verwendung von Bambus als Betonbewehrung wurden 1914 am Massachusetts Institut of Technology (MIT) die ersten Versuche gemacht.[2] In den siebziger und achtziger Jahren wurde in Ländern des Südens verstärkt versucht, Armierungsmatten aus Stahl durch Bambusgitter zu ersetzen.
Bambus-Parkett, Bambus-Schichtholz (engl. «laminated bamboo lumber») und Sperrholz oder Spanplatten aus Bambus sind weitere Beispiele dafür, wie Bambus mit modernster Technologie zu hochwertiger Halbware verarbeitet werden kann.

Particularly in aeronautics and astronautics, much research is being performed on combining two substances to form composites which are characterized by a higher degree of tensile strength than their individual parts – and minimal weight. To this end, plastics such as epoxy resins or polyesters are reinforced using fiber mats or fibrous tissue typically consisting of fiberglass or carbon fiber. Bamboo can also be used for such high-tech materials: in 1997 a surfboard was developed comprising a high-strength mixture of epoxy resin and bamboo shavings.
Simón Vélez also combines bamboo canes with other materials, e.g. with concrete. He fills skeletal bamboo structures with concrete, or fills the ends of the canes with this material. This produces solid building elements which are easier to connect to one another.
Bamboo is also suitable as a substitute for carcinogenic asbestos fibers in concrete panels. However, the bamboo shavings used to reinforce the panels must first be de-sugared, and this entails high water inputs. In this context, ASK Board, a Japanese company, has developed the first effective process and has opened a factory in Indonesia which has also manufactured the roof panels for Simón Vélez's ZERI Pavilion.[1]

Incidentally, bamboo has long been used as a basis for composites. Clay buildings, for instance, are lent a sturdier structure by adding bamboo shavings or straw to the clay. In Valdivia, Ecuador, remains of walls containing bamboo and clay were excavated which were between 7,550 and 5,500 years old. Plastered bamboo mats also serve as wall elements. Experiments were first conducted to use bamboo as concrete reinforcement in 1914 at the Massachusetts Institute of Technology (MIT).[2] In the 1960s and 1970s, efforts were stepped up to replace reinforced steel mats by bamboo grids in the Southern world.
Bamboo parquet, laminated bamboo lumber, and plywood or chipboard of bamboo are further examples of how it is possible to combine advanced technology with bamboo to produce high-quality semi-finished goods.

Aussichtsturm im Parque de la Cultura Cafetera in Montenegro/Quindío (Kolumbien), Simón Vélez/Marcelo Villegas, 1993. Dieser 19 m hohe Turm widerstand 1999 einem Erdbeben, dem in Armenia zahlreiche Bauten aus Beton zum Opfer fielen.
Observation tower in Parque de la Cultura Cafetera in Montenegro, Quindío (Colombia), Simón Vélez/Marcelo Villegas, 1993. These 19 m-high towers withstood an earthquake in 1999 in which numerous concrete buildings were destroyed

[1] Ambasz, E., in: Joan Kron, Suzanne Slesin; in: High-Tech, The Industrial Style and Sourcebook for the Home, Crown Publishers, New York 1978

[1] E. Ambasz in: Joan Kron, Suzanne Slesin: High-Tech, The Industrial Style and Sourcebook for the Home, Crown Publishers, New York, 1978.

... auf diese stilistische Formel könnte man die Architektur von Simón Vélez bringen. Vélez beweist, daß man mit Bambus High-Tech-Architektur bauen kann – ebenso wie Renzo Piano es 1999 mit seinem Kulturzentrum in Neu-Kaledonien für den Baustoff Holz bewiesen hat. Vélez setzt gezielt neue Technologien und Materialkombinationen ein, und seine Gebäude leugnen ihren Assemblage-Charakter nicht, den Emilio Ambasz als Ausgangspunkt des High-Tech bezeichnet hat.[1]
Doch ebenso wie Renzo Pianos spektakulärer Bau adaptieren die Gebäude von Vélez lokale Bauformen. Und Bambus bleibt ein Naturmaterial, dem man seine Urwüchsigkeit ansieht. So ergeben die einfachen Lösungen der Natur, kombiniert mit hochentwickelter Technologie – eine Architektur der Zukunft.

... is an apt description of the style of architecture practiced by Simón Vélez. Vélez's work testifies to the fact that it is possible to build high-tech architecture using bamboo. In 1999, Renzo Piano had proved the same for wood by building his cultural center in New Caledonia. Vélez consciously makes use of new technologies and material combinations and his buildings do not deny their assemblage character – which Emilio Ambasz described as the starting point of high-tech.[1]
Yet, in common with Renzo Piano's spectacular building, Vélez's buildings are inspired by local building styles. And bamboo remains a natural material whose natural origin is evident. In this manner, combining the simple solutions of nature with highly advanced technology results in an architecture of the future.

Riesen-Raumtragwerk für die Weltausstellung in Osaka (Japan), Kenzo Tange, 1970
Gigantic supporting structure for the World Fair in Osaka (Japan), Kenzo Tange, 1970

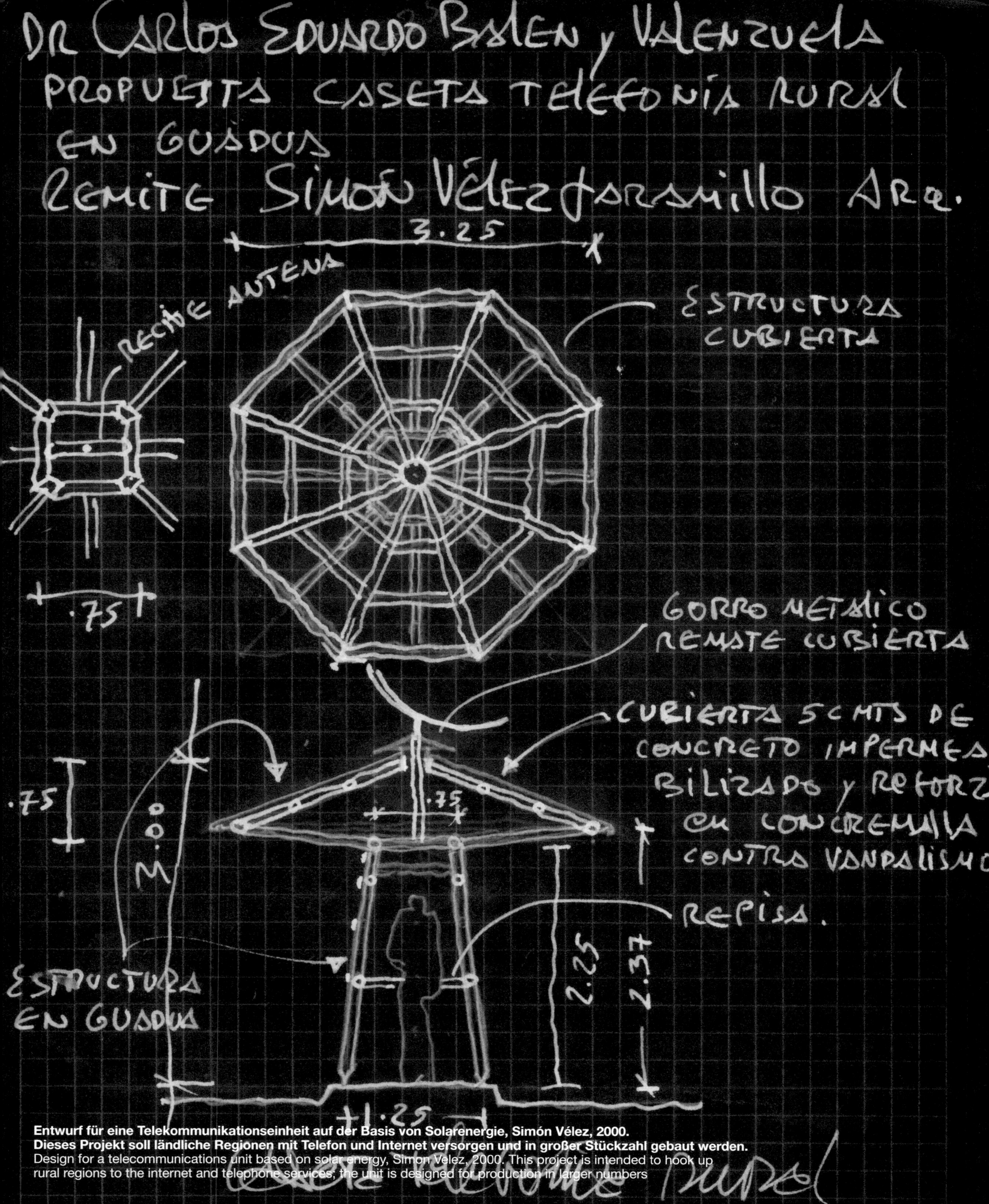

Entwurf für eine Telekommunikationseinheit auf der Basis von Solarenergie, Simón Vélez, 2000.
Dieses Projekt soll ländliche Regionen mit Telefon und Internet versorgen und in großer Stückzahl gebaut werden.
Design for a telecommunications unit based on solar energy, Simon Velez, 2000. This project is intended to hook up rural regions to the internet and telephone services; the unit is designed for production in larger numbers

Projekt für einen Aussichtsturm aus Bambus im Parque Guadua von Pereira, Risaralda (Kolumbien), Simón Vélez, 2000. Modell
Project for a bamboo belvedere in Parque Guadua von Pereira, Risaralda (Colombia), Simón Vélez, 2000. Model

Entwurf für ein Tropenhaus, Jean Prouvé, 1949 / Design for a tropical house, Jean Prouvé, 1949

Haus und Studio, Erick van Egeraat, Rotterdam, 1992
House and Studio, Erick van Egeraat, Rotterdam, 1992

Bambusbauten von Linda Garland in Ubud (Bali)
Bamboo huts by Linda Garland in Ubud (Bali)

Künstler wie die Japaner Hiroshi Teshigahara oder Akio Hizume bilden aus Bambus Skulpturen von beeindruckender Feinheit, und die Bambusbauten von Simón Vélez, Yoh oder Arata Isozaki können ästhetisch mühelos neben Beispielen konventioneller Architektur bestehen. Eine Vorreiterin für die Ästhetisierung von Bambus ist die Designerin Linda Garland, die auf Bali lebt. 1995 stellte sie den 4. Internationalen Bambuskongress unter das Motto: «Laßt uns den Bambus schön, lukrativ und sexy machen!» Nach einem Besuch in ihrem Bambus-Idyll propagierte 1999 auch die Zeitschrift «Marie Claire Maison»: «Er ist in Mode, man pflanzt ihn überall: auf Balkons, Terassen, Gärten.»
Schon vor fast 60 Jahre schuf die Französin Charlotte Perriand, eine der bekanntesten Designerinnen des 20. Jahrhunderts, in Japan Möbelentwürfe aus Bambus, die unverdientermaßen kaum bekannt geworden sind. Perriand kam 1940 nach Japan und sollte, im Rahmen eines Programms zur Wiederbelebung des Handwerks und zur Entwicklung hochwertiger Designartikel, die Erfahrung europäischer Designer an einheimische Handwerker, Hochschulen und Studenten weitergeben. Da Bambus in der japanischen Kultur eine lange handwerkliche Tradition hat, griff Perriand auf dieses Material zurück. Sie paßte es jedoch modernen Erfordernissen an, indem sie unter anderem Bambusstreifen einsetzte, die federn und doch stabil sind. Daraus fertigte sie Möbel, die eine erfolgreiche Synthese aus dem Repertoire der europäischen Avantgarde und der japanischen Ästhetik darstellen. Unter ihren Entwürfen war unter anderem eine Bambus-Version der berühmten Chaiselongue, die Perriand 1928/29 zusammen mit Le Corbusier und Pierre Jeanneret in Paris entworfen hatte, und heute ein Klassiker des modernen Designs ist. Außerdem entstanden mehrere Freischwinger und andere Sitzmöbel. Perriand stellte diese Möbel 1941 in der Ausstellung «Tradition, Sélection, Création» in Tokyo und Osaka vor.

Artists such as Hiroshi Teshigahara or Akio Hizume (both from Japan) have created amazingly refined bamboo sculptures, and the bamboo buildings of Simón Vélez, Yoh, or Arata Isozaki can easily hold their own alongside examples of conventional architecture. Designer Linda Garland, who lives on Bali, has done pioneering work enhancing bamboo aesthetically. In 1995, she promoted the 4th International Bamboo Congress under the motto: «Let us make bamboo attractive, lucrative, and sexy!» After visiting her in her bamboo paradise, the magazine «Marie Claire Maison» declared in 1999: «It is in fashion; people plant it everywhere: on balconies, terraces, in gardens.»
And almost 60 years ago Frenchwoman Charlotte Perriand, one of the most famous designers of the 20th century, created bamboo furniture designs in Japan which undeservedly received scant attention. Perriand went to Japan in 1940 assigned with the task of imparting the knowledge of European designers to local craftsmen, universities, and students, as part of a program aimed at reviving traditional crafts and developing high-quality design articles. Perriand specifically chose bamboo because it has a long history of use in Japanese handicrafts. Yet she took care to adapt it to modern requirements by using, amongst other things, bamboo strips since they are flexible yet sturdy. She designed furniture which was a successful synthesis of European avant-garde and Japanese aestheticism. Her designs included a bamboo version of the famous chaise longue, which Perriand had created in 1928/29 in conjunction with Le Corbusier and Pierre Jeanneret in Paris, and which is today a classic example of modern design. She also produced several cantilever chairs and other chairs and sofas. Perriand presented this furniture in 1941 in an exhibition entitled: «Tradition, Sélection, Création» in Tokyo and Osaka.

Bambusskulptur «Star Cage», Akio Hizume
Bamboo structure «Star Cage», Akio Hizume

Bühnenbild für das Noh-Theaterstück «Susano» in Avignon, Hiroshi Teshigahara, 1994
Stage setting for the Noh theater play «Susano» in Avignon (France), Hiroshi Teshigahara, 1994

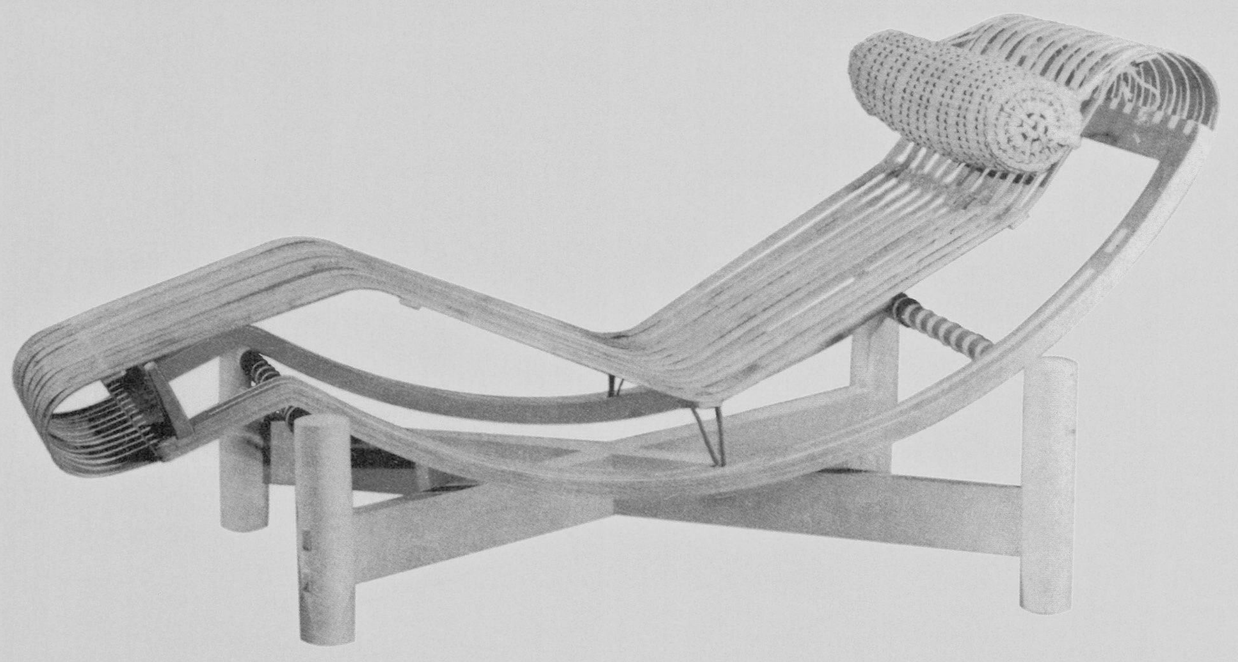

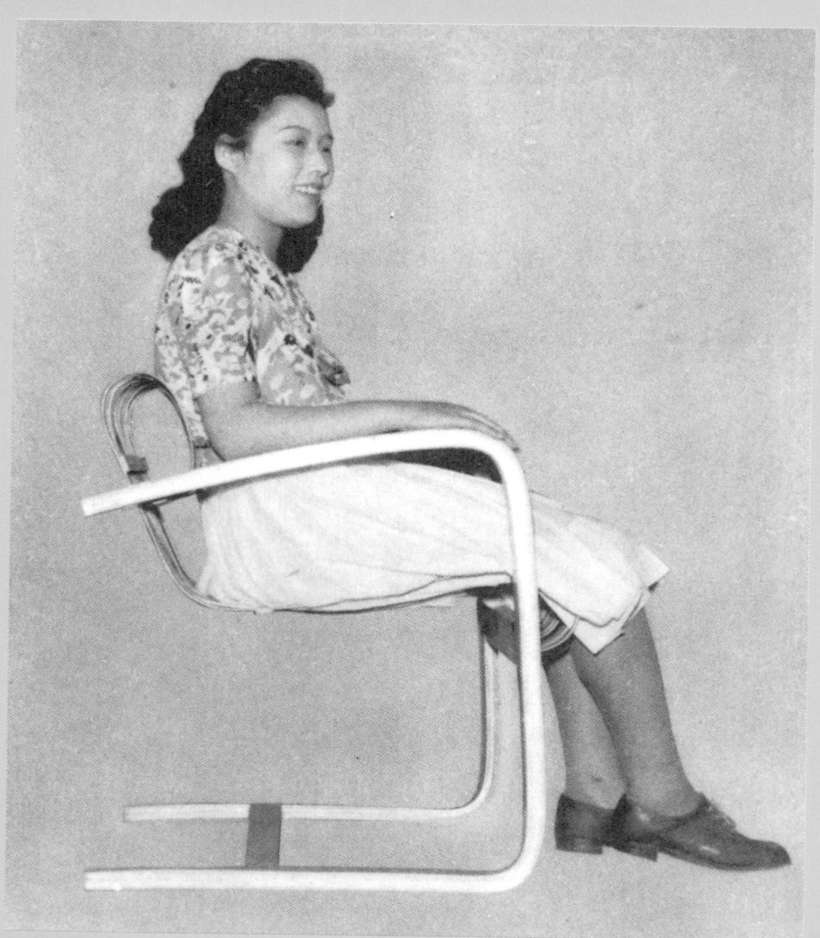

▲ **Chaiselongue aus Bambusstreifen mit Untergestell aus Holz, Charlotte Perriand, 1940/41**
Chaise longue made from bamboo slats with wooden base, Charlotte Perriand, 1940–1

◀ **Freischwinger aus Bambusstreifen mit Holzgestell, Charlotte Perriand, 1940/41**
Cantilever chair made of bamboo slats with wooden base, Charlotte Perriand, 1940–1

▶ **Faltsessel, Charlotte Perriand, 1940/41**
Folding chair, Charlotte Perriand, 1940–1

Teehaus für die UNESCO-Zentrale in Paris, Charlotte Perriand, 1993
Tea-house at the UNESCO Head Office in Paris, Charlotte Perriand, 1993

Simon Aicher, Stuttgart: 239
AKG Photo, Berlin: 141, 155, 167 l., r., 171 l. o.
Perigot Antoine/Marie Claire Maison, Paris: 248, 249
Shigeo Anzai/Sogetsu Art Museum, Tokyo: 218 r. u., 251
Jorge Eduardo Arango, Kolumbien: 74, 75 r. o., l. u., 72/73, 94 o., 96, 97 o., 114 r. m.,126, 175, 190, 205, 208 l. u., 240 r. o.
Shigeru Ban: 114 r.o.
Bruno Barbey/Magnum, Hamburg: 183
Olf Bergmann/Sogetsu Art Museum, Tokyo: 219
Werner Blaser, Basel: 79, 91, 134 m. o., l. m., 145 r. o.
Jim Brandenburg/Minden Pictures, Aptos: 172
Bundesarchiv, Koblenz: 243
Richard Davies, London: 218 m. u.
Gert van Delft, Drunen: 60 l. u., 63, 132, 240 l.
DPA, Frankfurt: 207
Dyckerhoff & Widmann, München: 210
Wolfgang Eberts, Baden-Baden: 127, 129, 156, 158, 165 r. m., 235, 250
Edition Leipzig: 215
Freya Eisenbrandt, Lebach: 140
Elephant Parkett, Sottrum: 171 m. m.
FlexiMac/Horst Grütering, Amsterdam: 114 r. u.
Fregoso & Balsalto/Renzo Piano Building Workshop, Genua: 116/117, 234 u.
Yukio Futagawa, Tokyo: 247 o.
Berengo Gardin/Renzo Piano Building Workshop, Genua: 107
Gettyone Stone, München: 104 r. u., 112, 121, 128, 134 m. m., 145 l. u., 152, 163, 175 l., 177, 178, 184, 187
J. Gollings/Renzo Piano Building Workshop, Genua: 191
Nicholas Grimshaw & Partners Ltd., London: 83
Hiroyuki Hirai, Japan: 99
Institut für Auslandsbeziehungen, Stuttgart: 146 l.
Institut für Leichte Flächentragwerke, Stuttgart: 8, 86 u., 95, 98, 104 l. o., l. u., 114 l. o., 120, 123, 134 l. o., l. u., 138, 139, 142 r. o., l. u., r. u., 145 r. u., 147, 150, 166 l. o., r. u., 170 r. u., 196 l. u., r. u., 208 l. o., m. u., 209, 211, 218 m. o., 220, 223 l., 234 o., 236, 237
Mikio Kamaya/Toyo Ito & Associates, Tokyo: 228/229
Stanislaus Kandula, Witten: 194
Osamu Kumasegawa/Sogetsu Art Museum, Tokyo: 218 r. m.
Walter Liese, Reinbek: 90, 94 u., 100/101, 114 m. m., 136, 137, 146 r., 148/149, 161, 162, 165 l. m., l. u., 166 r. o., l. u., 170 l. o., l. m., m. m., r. m., l. u., m. u., 171 m. o., r. o., l. m., 174, 176, 193, 196 r. o., 204, 216/217, 258/259
Ximena Londoño, Kolumbien: 71 l. o.
Jose Fernando Machado, Kolumbien: 78, 102, 114 l. u.
P.+G. Morisson, Den Haag: 247 u.
Trish Morrissey, London: 15,
Archives Charlotte Perriand: 253
Paolo Portoghesi: 86 o.
Prestel Archiv, München: 76 l., 80
Bodo Rasch, Leinfelden: 208 r. o.
Christian Richters, Münster: 218 l. o.
Rudolf/Archivo Villegas Editores: 142 l. o.
Henning von Schultzendorff, Lörrach: 6
Julius Shulman, Los Angeles: 200/201
Toshihiro Sobajima, Japan: 25, 114 m. o.
Paul Starosta, Saumane: 113
Shinzi Takama, Gifu: 105, 124/125, 180/181, 182, 206, 214
The Estate of Buckminster Fuller, Sebastopol: 230, 232, 235 u.
Cerstin Thiemann Takvorian, Lörrach: 56, 60 l. o., 60 r. o., 60 r. u.
Simón Vélez, Bogota: 20/21, 44, 135, 218 m. m., 244
Antoon Versteegde, Uden: 97 u., 111, 143, 144
VG Bild-Kunst, Bonn: 246, 252

Marcelo Villegas, Manizales: 169 l.
Max F. Wetterwald, Basel: 114 l. m., 170 m. o., r. o.
Ishimoto Yasuhiro, Japan: 122
Shoei Yoh + Architects, Fukuoka-Shi: 108, 132/133, 224, 225, 226/227, 231
ZERI Foundation, Genf: 4/5, 12/13, 14, 23, 26/27, 33, 34, 37, 38, 40 l., 45, 51, 52, 55, 66, 74/75, 77 o., 81, 82, 84, 85, 87, 88, 89, 92, 104 r. o., 106, 114 m. u., 115, 119, 130 u., 134 r. o., 145 l. o., 154, 165 o., 168, 169 r., 196 l. o., 197, 198/199, 202, 208 m. o., 218 l. m., 223 r., 240 r. u., 242, 245, 261

l.o. = left top / m.o. = middle top / r.o. = right top
l.m.= left middle / m.m.= middle middle / r.m. = right middle
l.u. = left bottom / m.u. = middle bottom / r.u. = right bottom

Baier, B.: Gräser als konstruktive Baustoffe, in: Gesundes Bauen und Wohnen Nr. 2, 1996
Benton, C.: From Tubular Steel to Bamboo – Charlotte Perriand, the Migrating Chaise longue and Japan, in.: Journal of Design History, No.1, Vol. 11, Oxford, 1998
Beukers, A., Hinte, E.v.: Lightness – The inevitable renaissance of minimum energy structure, Rotterdam, 1998
Blaser, W.: Bauen mit Bambus – Vorbild China und Japan, in: Anthos 28, 1989
Brandenburg, J.: Bamboo, the giant grass, in: National Geographic No. 4, Vol. 158, Washington, 1980
Crouzet, Y., Starosta, P.: Bamboos, Köln, 1998
Cusack, V.: Bamboo Rediscovered, Trentham, 1997
Dujarric, C., Martinez, H., Merlet, J.D.: Le développement des constructions en plâtre au Sénégal et en Mauritanie, C.S.T.B. Magazine Nr. 36, 1985
Dunkelberg, K. u.a.: Bauen mit pflanzlichen Stäben, Stuttgart, 1985
Farelly, D.: The Book of Bamboo, San Francisco, 1984
Friebe, W.: Die Architektur der Weltausstellungen, Leipzig, 1983
Friedman, Y.: Appropriate Technology for Self-Reliance, in: Open House International 13, 1988
Garber, J., Schneider, R.: Bauen mit Stäbchen. Bambus – Baustoff der Zukunft?, in: Deutsche Bauzeitung Nr. 9, 131, 1997
Goldberg, G.: Iron Grass, Vegetable Steel – The Architecture of Simón Vélez and Marcelo Villegas in Colombia, Santa Barbara, 1999
Graefe, R.: Zur Geschichte des Konstruierens, Wiesbaden, 1989
Hidalgo, O.L.: Manual de construcción con bambú, Bogotá, 1974
Janssen, J.A.: Building with Bamboo, London, 1995
Janssen, J.A.: Bamboo Research at the Eindhoven University of Technology, Eindhoven, 1983
Jencks, C.: Die Sprache der postmodernen Architektur, Stuttgart, 1988
Judziewicz, E.J. et al.: American Bamboos, Washington, 1999
Harada, J.: The Lesson of Japanese Architecture, Boston, 1936
Haeckel, E.: Kunstformen der Natur, München, 1998
Hilscher, G.: Bambus wird technisches Konstruktionselement – Bambu Tech erschließt dem Naturprodukt ungeahnte Einsatzmöglichkeiten, in: Wohnung und Gesundheit 17, Nr. 75, 1995
International Association for Bridge and Structural Engineering (Hrsg.): Mixed Structures including New Materials, Zürich, 1990
Kaltenbach, F.: Dach mit Symbolgehalt – Torajahäuser in Sulawesi, Indonesien, in: Detail 39, 1999
Krausse, J., Lichtenstein, C.: Your Private Sky. Richard Buckminster Fuller – Design als Kunst einer Wissenschaft, Baden, 1999
Lauber, W.: Das Konstanzer Favela-Haus – Versuch einer bautechnischen Innovation, in: Trialog Nr. 4, 1996
Lorenz, P.: Traditionelles bauen in Südchina – Die Wohnbauten der Dai, ein Beispiel für klimaangepaßtes Bauen im tropischen
Naturraum, in: Architektur, Innenarchitektur, Technischer Innenausbau Nr. 1/2, 1987
Marks, R.W.: The Dymaxion World of Buckminster Fuller, 1960
Meissner, M.: Die Malocas-Langhäuser imm brasilianischen Urwald – Wohnstätten der Amazonas-Indianer, in: Bauen mit Holz 89, Nr. 4, 1987
Minke, G.: Earthquake-resistant low-cost houses utilizing indigenous building materials and intermediate technology, in: Earthquake relief in less industrialized areas, Zürich, 1984
Papanek, V.: Design for the Real World – Human Ecology and Social Change, London, 1984
Otto, F.: Ein Vorschlag zur Ordnung und Beschreibung von Konstruktionen, hrsg. Vom Institut für leichte Flächentragwerke, Stuttgart, 1992
Otto, F., Rasch, B.: Gestalt finden, München, 1995
Pauli, G.: Upsizing: The Road to Zero Emission. More Jobs, More Income and No Pollution, Sheffield, 1998.
Pollock, N.R.: Shigeru Ban – Mad Scientist or a Magician, in: Korean Architects No.1, Seoul, 1994
Portoghesi, P.: Natura e architettura, Milano, 1999
Rasch, H.: West-Östliche Mischung im Goldenen Dreieck, in: Häuser Nr. 6, 1997
Rasch, H.: Bambus – Das stärkste Gras der Welt, in: Häuser Nr. 6, 1995
Recht, C., Wetterwald, M.F., Simon, W.: Bambus, Stuttgart, 1988
Revelli, P.: Ecuador – Bambus in der Stadt und auf dem Land, in: Wohnung und Gesundheit Nr. 83, 1997
Riley, T.: Light Construction, New York, 1995
Rudofsky, B.: Architecture Without Architects, New York, 1964
Schaur, E., Nuber, K.H.: Die Welt braucht Hütten statt Paläste! Im Gespräch mit Eda Schaur, in: Architektur Nr. 3, 1996
Schnittich, C.: Verbinden durch Binden, in: Detail 37, 1998
Steele, J.: An Architecture for People, London, 1997
Tular, R.B., Sutidjan: Bamboo as a building material and its processing methods, Bangkok, 1986
Subrahmanyam, B.V.: Bamboo reinforcements for cement matrices, Glasgow, 1984
Takama, S.: Die wunderbare Welt des Bambus, Köln, 1996
Tamolang, F.B.: State of the art of bamboo as a housing material in the Phillipines, Bandun, 1986
Teshigahara, H.: The Art of Ikebana, Tokyo, 1996
Villegas, L.: Arte factos – Elementos de la vida cotidiana del Viejo Caldas, Bogotá, 1988
Villegas, M.: Tropical Bamboo, Bogotá, 1993
Waterson, R.: The Living House – The Anthropology of Architecture in South-East Asia, London, 1990

Impressum / Imprint

«Grow your own house – Simón Vélez und die Bambusarchitektur»
ist eine Publikation des Vitra Design Museums in Kooperation mit der ZERI-Stiftung und C.I.R.E.C.A.
«Grow your own house – Simón Vélez and bamboo architecture»
is published by the Vitra Design Museum in cooperation with the ZERI Foundation and C.I.R.E.C.A..

Herausgeber / Editors: Alexander von Vegesack, Mateo Kries
Konzept, Texte und Koordination / Concept, texts and coordination: Mateo Kries
Bildrecherchen / Picture research: Nicolai Rünzi
Mitarbeit für die ZERI-Stiftung / ZERI Foundation team: Gunter Pauli, Carolina Salazar, Pamela Salazar, Liliana Villegas
Autoren / Authors: Jean Dethier, Walter Liese, Frei Otto, Eda Schaur, Klaus Steffens
Grafik / Graphics: Thorsten Romanus (Büro für Gestaltung)
Koordination der Produktion / Production coordination: Elke Henecka
Übersetzungen / Translations: Uschi Bachmann, Jeremy Gaines, Mateo Kries, Claire Norton, Anja Peschel, Angela Tschorsnig
Lektorat / Editorial staff: Jane Havell, Eva Tauber
Satz / Lithos: Fotosatz Strütt & Rünzi
Druck / Printer: HD Grafischer Betrieb, Balingen

ISBN 3-931936-25-2

Buchhandelsvertrieb / Bookstore distribution: Vitra Design Museum

Vitra Design Museum
Charles-Eames-Str. 1, D-79576 Weil am Rhein
Tel: +49 (0)7621/702 3514, Fax: +49 (0)7621/702 3146
info@design-museum.de

Fondation ZERI
11 chemin des Anémones, CH-1219 Chatelaine–Genève
Fax: +41 (0)22/979 90 83 oder 917 80 83
e-mail: pauli@zeri.org

C.I.R.E.C.A.
Domaine de Boisbuchet, F-16500 Lessac

Für die tatkräftige Unterstützung dieser Publikation möchten
wir uns bei folgenden Personen bedanken:
We would like to thank the following persons for their
lively support for this publication:

Jorge Eduardo Arango
Mario Calderon Rivera
Luis Guillermo Camargo
Jean Dethier
Gerd van Delft
Wolfgang Eberts
Gabriele Heim
Walter Liese
Frei Otto
Gunter Pauli
Carolina Salazar
Pamela Salazar
Klaus Steffens
Shinzi Takama
Liliana Villegas
Marcelo Villegas
Shoei Yoh

安全生产
人人有责